PRAISE FOR
MY LIFE ACCORDING TO ROCK BAND

"Cade Wiberg's debut deserves a spot next to Rob Sheffield and Nick Hornby—a life-affirming, coming-of-age story that celebrates a generation's shared love of music and popular culture. It's not often that you come across a memoir that's as big-hearted as it is laugh-out-loud funny. Inventive, witty, and true blue, this book is a genuine treat."

—Jay Varner, lecturer in writing, rhetoric,
and technical communication at
James Madison University and
author of *Nothing Left to Burn*

"*My Life According to Rock Band* is the tale of a hopeless romantic who wishes dating came with difficulty settings. I laughed, I cried, I regretted selling my *Rock Band* set a decade ago."

—R.J. Haynes, writer/producer of
This is My Year and *Kidney Beans*

"A nostalgic look-back filled with friends, laughs, and music. A must-read for any rock music or video game loving millennial. This book will take you through the personal growth of a young man finding himself within the things he loves."

—Tarik Begic, filmmaker, writer/director
of *Inhalation* and *The End of the Circle*

MORE PRAISE FOR
MY LIFE ACCORDING TO ROCK BAND

"Within an endless setlist of the moments that shaped our adolescence, *My Life According to Rock Band* feels like a perfectly nostalgic and brutally honest memoir that easily earns five gold stars."

—Kyle Johnson, camera operator and assistant editor
of the Emmy-winning show *Made in Virginia*

"*My Life According to Rock Band* is an intimate look at the familiar struggles of growing up, making friends, losing girls, and everything in between. With humor and heart, Cade Wiberg shows us that sometimes life is a 100% expert solo, and other times it's being stuck playing the piano controller no one wants."

—Kelsey Sullivan, English professor
at the Taylor Institute

My Life According to

ROCK BAND

Or Fifty-Eight Short Stories About Life, Love, and the Greatest Video Game Ever Made

Cade Wiberg

BELLE ISLE BOOKS
www.belleislebooks.com

This book is a work of non-fiction told from my point of view. Most people's names have been changed to avoid reminding them of embarrassing stories. I do not agree with some views and statements expressed during certain stories, but I felt it necessary to edit specific entries as little as possible to be true to the person I was when I lived them.

ISBN: 978-1-953021-69-4
LCCN: 2022900044

Printed in the United States of America

Published by
Belle Isle Books (an imprint of Brandylane Publishers, Inc.)
5 S. 1st Street
Richmond, Virginia 23219

BELLE ISLE BOOKS
www.belleislebooks.com

belleislebooks.com | brandylanepublishers.com

For Joan, Carl, Emma, and Keith;
for the 2014-2015 James Madison University
Program Board Exec Team;
and for the Krazy Unikerns

TABLE OF CONTENTS

"There are two basic motivating forces: fear and love. When we are afraid, we pull back from life. When we are in love, we open to all that life has to offer with passion, excitement, and acceptance. We need to learn to love ourselves first, in all our glory and our imperfections. If we cannot love ourselves, we cannot fully open to our ability to love others or our potential to create. Evolution and all hopes for a better world rest in the fearlessness and open-hearted vision of people who embrace life."

— John Lennon

29 FINGERS
By the Konks

December 2007

"Cheap guitars and only two lousy drums"

I remember every part of it.

I remember how it sat underneath the Christmas tree for three weeks in a multi-colored bag just big enough to conceal the whole box. I remember watching, in the weeks leading up to Christmas, countless YouTube videos of people unpackaging the new game and playing it for the first time. I remember running down to my parents' bland living room that morning, the room that we rarely used because it contained only a small TV, antique furniture, and the woodstove that heated the whole house. It sat below what my sister and I referred to as "the fun living room" upstairs, which housed our large TV (a massive thirty-two inches), a video game console, and hundreds of DVDs. But this morning, we raced past all that and straight to the Christmas tree in the "boring living room."

I remember unwrapping my final present on that Christmas morning with unparalleled enthusiasm and a 101-degree fever. I had saved the best present for last, and there it was: *Rock Band: Special Edition*. I gazed in awe at the big blue box for a solid minute, unable to speak. That could have been because of the fever.

My little sister, Emma, sat down next to me. "Can I see it, Cade?" she asked.

"I'm not done looking at it," I whispered, still entranced.

"You've been looking at it for hooooouuuuurs! Mom!"

"Cade, share with your sister!" Mom said from the sofa behind us. "Emma, be nice to your brother. He's not feeling well."

My parents sat on the couch drinking their coffee, probably hoping that some year soon, their fifteen-year-old son and thirteen-year-old daughter would stop waking them up at a ridiculous hour every Christmas morning. But they had woken *me* up early nearly every day for school or church, so it only seemed fair that I should be permitted to wake *them* up early once a year, to shower me with gifts.

"Can I go play?" I begged them. "Can I please!?" I could feel my sickness start to wear off.

"Fine," my father sighed, "but include your sister. And thank your grandfather for the gift. It doesn't look cheap."

I ran upstairs into the living room with the large box, thinking of how I would thank my new favorite relative (*Nay!* My new favorite *human*) for buying me *Rock Band*: my Grand Old Gramps, my Awesome Amazing Abuelo, my Prudent Prophetic Patriarch. He could have gone by many names, but we called him G-dad.

I carefully laid the box down on the living room floor and slowly removed its contents. I pulled out one plastic guitar, one game disc in its case, one microphone with a ten-foot cord, one plastic drumkit that required some assembly, and two drumsticks. I had waited for this day for an entire month; longer if you counted from the day I found out about the game's existence instead of from the day I knew my grandfather was going to buy it for me.

I studied the fifty-eight-song setlist. Once you mastered each song separately, there was a final task called "The Endless Setlist," in which you had to play through every song in order of difficulty. It started with "29 Fingers" by the Konks and ended with "Won't Get Fooled Again" by the Who; I couldn't wait to learn every single one. Looking back, it is truly crazy to realize how much each one of these songs crafted my opinion of music, and more importantly, how each one helped shape my *life*.

I don't even remember why I was so interested in the game—truth be told I only knew about four songs in the whole game when I first opened it. I didn't really listen to or enjoy music at all until four years prior to that Christmas. My mother would occasionally play a few select pop albums like *The Essential Billy Joel*, Fountains of Wayne's *Welcome Interstate Managers*, or *Sugar Ray* by Sugar Ray when she drove us to school every day, but I never went out of my way to find new songs or bands.

Then, in the spring of 2004, my father had taken my sister and me on a road trip. He brought the Beatles' *One* album, twenty-seven of the best songs ever written. All of a sudden, my whole body had been infected with this *need* for music, and I couldn't get over it. I listened to all twenty-seven songs over and over again, each one taking a special place in my heart. I bought another Beatles record, and another, and another, until I had every single one. It took me about four years to acquire all of them (like most middle schoolers, I was unemployed), but I still have every one of those albums to this day.

By that Christmas morning, I knew only four songs on the *Rock Band* disc that weren't by the Beatles:

"WANTED DEAD OR ALIVE" by Bon Jovi

My uncle had bought me Bon Jovi's greatest hits for my birthday the day before I started high school. Those hits had become my school bus anthems every morning at the ungodly hour of 6 a.m.

"(DON'T FEAR) THE REAPER" by Blue Oyster Cult

My friend, Gordon, and I would sing this nearly every day in middle school after we had seen the "More

Cowbell" sketch on *Saturday Night Live* for the first time. To this day, we have yet to get enough of both the song and the sketch.

"NEXT TO YOU" by the Police

Outlandos d'Amour was the first non-Beatles record I bought. Though "Roxanne" will always be my favorite Police song, "Next to You" has a special place in my heart for kicking off one of the greatest rock albums of all time.

"FOREPLAY/LONG TIME" by Boston

My love for the band Boston can be traced back to the air-banding episode of the show *Scrubs.* Some of the hospital staff formed an "air band" and performed "More Than a Feeling" in the hospital parking lot. I was blown away by Donald Faison's ability to lip sync, but even more impressed by Boston. I borrowed their self-titled album from my friend, Bruce, and, presumably like most people who have heard the album, immediately fell in love with every harmony, guitar solo, and rich pop hook.

"What song do you want to play?" I asked Emma.

"Oooooh I really like 'Here it Goes Again' by OK Go! That's the song with the cool music video!" she replied.

My sister's taste in music at the time was one of passionless imitation. If her friends liked it, she thought it was cool; if they hated it, it sucked. Every kid in the goddamn school knew about the treadmill-dance music video for "Here It Goes Again," but none of them seemed to care about the Beatles.

"All right, that's fine," I said, ready to play anything.

I took the guitar, and she took the drums. I've played the real guitar for over a decade now, and I remember the feeling of holding that plastic guitar for the first time much more vividly than the first time I held my father's nylon-stringed acoustic.

We finished that first song despite quite a few mess-ups.

Emma furrowed her brow and looked at her feet. "I kept screwing up because of that orange bar at the bottom. What is that?"

"That's the foot pedal. You have to stomp on it with your foot at the same time you hit the drums with the sticks," I said, not knowing the proper name for a bass drum.

"It makes the game way harder. Can we do a song without it?" she asked.

"I think I read there was one song that didn't have it." I scrolled through the slim list of starter songs. "Here it is: '29 Fingers.'"

"29 Fingers" is by no means my favorite song on the disc, but I do admire its simplicity. It says that *anybody* can play music; you don't have to be good, you don't have to study it for years, and you don't even need more than two lousy drums. *Rock Band* was made for those who wanted to feel like rock stars with the push of a few plastic buttons on a plastic fretboard. No matter where I'd be in my life, during any high or low, *Rock Band* would always be there letting me know I could be *whoever* the hell I wanted to be, *whenever* I wanted to be it.

Emma wanted to be someone who didn't play the foot pedal, and thanks to *Rock Band*, she was.

SAY IT AIN'T SO
By Weezer

December 2007

"Things are good or so I hear"

"Dude, you're not going to believe it! I got *Rock Band* for Christmas!" I shouted over the phone to my best friend.

"No way! That's awesome!" Keith shouted back. "Did you get all the instruments?"

"It came with all of the instruments, dude. I've been playing all day for the past couple of days."

"You *have* to bring that over here when you visit tomorrow. Chris and Delynn are here for the whole week; they'll probably play with us!"

I had met Keith in preschool. The story (as I remember) is that my mother dropped me off for my first day, and Keith soon approached me to ask if I wanted to play with him. I don't remember any other details from that day, but ever since then, Keith and I have been best friends. Like, actual *best* friends—not just the friend you are most fond of, but your *family*. Some believe you can have more than one best friend, or that you can just hand out the honor to whomever you are texting most frequently that month. Those people are wrong. Keith and I were like brothers, which made his sister, Delynn, my sister. She was four years older than us, and she often looked out for us and gave us sage, older-sibling advice.

I had not met her boyfriend, Chris, yet, but I hoped he liked *Rock Band*.

For those of you who have never played *Rock Band*, it's quite simple: You have three plastic instruments and one microphone (you can have up to three microphones in order to do vocal harmonies, but that technology didn't come about until 2010). After you pick a song, notes will be visually streamed at you on the screen. If you hit a note on your instrument at the same time it comes up on the screen, it explodes, and you get points. If you miss a note, the game makes a discordant noise to indicate you are ruining the song.

There are four levels of difficulty you can play: easy, medium, hard, and expert. The lower the difficulty, the slower the notes appear in front of you, and the fewer there are, and by the time you are ready for expert, it should feel like you are playing the song in full. When you finish the song, you're told the percentage of total notes you hit, along with a rating of one to five stars. If you're playing on expert level, you can receive gold stars when you do exceptionally well. If you miss too many notes, you will be kicked out of the song until you are saved by a bandmate who has accumulated enough points (or "overdrive") to save you. If one or more members of the band are out of the song for too long, the song will end, the simulated audience will boo you, and your band will be asked to restart the song or pick another.

There's a "no fail" mode, for drunk people and newbies of the game; I always have it turned on whenever I throw a *Rock Band* party. Nothing kills your buzz faster than "You Give Love a Bad Name" stopping halfway through because some asshole stopped playing bass when he spilled his beer on the girl he's been flirting with all night.

"Dude, this game is amazing!" Keith said as we finished playing through "Wanted Dead or Alive" by Bon Jovi. Keith was on drums, and I had taken the guitar. My family moved away from Keith's when I was in the first grade. Because we were so fond of each other, our mothers made a point to make sure we could visit each other at least twice a year. During the summer, Keith would come to my house for a couple of weeks, and during the winter, I would go to his. Once we got older, we were able to plan visits ourselves. We went on each other's family vacations so often that we were each considered an honorary family member by not only the other's parents, but by their extended family as well. When we weren't spending time with our families, we were playing video games. The basement in which we now played *Rock Band* had already housed us for over a decade and entertained us for countless hours.

"Let's name our band Static-X!" Keith exclaimed.

"How'd you think of that?" I asked, tightening my guitar strap.

"It's one of my favorite bands; I listen to them on the way to school like every day."

Keith clearly did not understand the whole "Be your own unique musician" aspect of the game yet. At the time, he was still a young teenage kid with a passion for skateboarding and Wayne Static. We had just finished playing our first song when a stranger entered the room.

"Was that Bon Jovi?" the stranger asked, wide-eyed.

"You know it." I nodded.

"Fucking right!" he said, grabbing the mic. "I'm singing the next one!"

"This is Chris, Delynn's boyfriend," Keith said.

You know those moments when you meet someone, and you immediately know you're gonna get along?

Before Chris, Delynn had dated a guy named James. He seemed like a cool guy at first, but then last summer he had suggested we see Adam Sandler's *Click* in theaters, so he clearly wasn't *the one*.

"Hi," I said shyly.

"Whoa, they have Weezer on here? That's what we're playing next." Chris said, scrolling through the song menu.

After the three of us had spent a few minutes scrolling through the song library and talking about killer tunes, Delynn found her way downstairs.

Her eyes lit up when she saw the screen. "No way! You guys got *Rock Band*?"

"Delynn, we need you. I can't do both the foot pedal and play the drums," Keith said, holding his shin in pain.

And just like that, the rest was history. The four of us played *Rock Band* for nearly five days straight, pausing only for food, sleep, and bathroom breaks. We even peed with the door open so we could sing along with the songs (well, everyone but Delynn did). At the time, we only had around fifty songs and no downloadable content, so the few songs in our catalogue became a bit redundant, especially at the beginning when we hadn't unlocked a majority of them. We must have played the game's starting song, "Say It Ain't So," over forty times. I had liked *Rock Band* before, but now I *loved* it. I held down guitar, Keith took drums, Chris sang, and Delynn switched between vocals and drums. We named our band The Krazy Unikerns, and we were taking off. We would start nearly every virtual show with Weezer's amazing nineties guitar riff, and every time the chorus hit, Keith and I would bang our heads and shout the titular line, "SAY IT AIN'T SOOOOOOOO!" I had never heard anything quite like that chorus in my four years of actively listening to music.

By the end of the week, the four of us were inseparable. Like every band at the beginning of their career, we had dreams of playing music with each other for the rest of our lives. In a basement full of empty Mountain Dew cans, bean bags we frequently slept on, and four music-loving teenagers, The Krazy Unikerns were born.

THE HAND THAT FEEDS
By Nine Inch Nails

July 2008

"So naive, I keep holding on to what I wanna believe"

"Dad, how did you meet Mom?"

On a hot summer night so picture-perfect it could have come straight out of Meat Loaf's "You Took the Words Right Out of My Mouth," my father and I found ourselves sitting around a fire built for aesthetic purposes only. There was a smell in the air composed of smoke, nature, and dust from the old shed we kept the camping gear in for three quarters of the year.

"When I was in a band, remember? My drummer set us up on a blind date," he said over the light crackle of the fire.

I poked the fire with a stick and looked up at him. "I know that part. But how did you actually meet? What happened on the date?"

My father smiled into his tin cup full of bourbon. "Well, my drummer, Tom, and I drove over to G-dad's house to pick up your mom and her friend. When we pulled up to her house, your grandma opened the door, and Tom thought she was your mother, so he shouted, 'You ready to go out for a date?' from the car."

I laughed. "He said that to G-mom?"

"Yes, she was very flattered. She went back in the house and told your mother to come outside."

"What did Mom look like?"

He paused. "She was the most beautiful girl I had ever seen."

"What did you guys do?"

"Well, the four of us all had a picnic by the river—nothing too crazy for a first date. We had a couples' piggy-back race, and your mother and I won."

"What was she like?"

"Very shy. She didn't eat in front of me for several dates. Later on, she told me she was constantly anxious whenever we made plans, but she smoked pot to feel better."

"Mom smoked pot?!" My adolescent brain couldn't process this new information. What other life-changing revelations was he going to drop on me? Was I really adopted? Did my parents fight crime in secret? Was Jesus not real?

He took another sip from his cup. "Yeah, those were different times," he said. "You'll find out all about it when you start high school next month."

This was turning into one revelatory camping trip. It was a shame my sister had fallen asleep early and missed out on all of this illuminating new info. It was just my father and I spending quality time together around a crackling fire.

I paused. "Can you please send me to private school with Martin, Julian, and Jimmy? None of my friends are going to public school."

"Bruce and Gordon are."

"They're districted to different schools! The only way I get to hang out with my old friends is if I go to private school." At this point, a majority of my stick had burned up, so I threw the rest of it into the fire with the last sentence.

"Those parents are spending an insane amount of money on private high school. Money that could be spent on college tuition. Plus, their private school is an hour away, so they're spending ten hours minimum in a car *per week*. Is that what you want?"

"I want to be with my friends."

"You'll make new friends in high school before you know it."

My father has always been a very truthful man. He has only lied to me three times over the course of my life:

1. If you don't get straight A's in high school, you will never get into college.
2. *Harold & Maude* is a better film than *X2: X-Men United*.
3. You'll make new friends in high school before you know it.

"Who knows," he continued, "you could even meet your future wife in high school, just like I did." He sipped the last of his bourbon. I thought about that; if my father found his soulmate in high school, why couldn't I? Maybe his luck was genetic.

Dad stood up from his seat and walked toward the tent. "All right, I'm going to bed. I love you, son."

"I love you too, Dad."

MISSISSIPPI QUEEN
By Mountain

July 2008

"I'd do what I can"

"Now this is real music," I said, playing The Police's "Next to You" through the car speakers.

"It's not bad. They're not quite Buddy Holly or The Big Bopper but it's better than most music these days," G-dad said, driving us to the beach. "Your mother used to constantly play this kind of music on her record player late at night. It drove your uncles and your grandmother nuts. She really loved the song 'Mississippi Queen.' Do you know that one?"

My grandfather never remembered any song titles other than "Chantilly Lace," so the fact that this one stuck must have meant it was important. Unfortunately for him, at fifteen years old I didn't have anything other than the Police or the Beatles on my mp3 player.

"Sorry G-dad, I don't have that one," I said, hoping he would settle for listening to "So Lonely" next.

"Eh, we don't need music anyway." He turned off the car stereo. "How about a riddle?"

"Bring it on!" I turned to him in my seat. "I watch so many mystery shows I'll probably figure it out immediately."

"Okay, there are three blanks and they are all filled in with different variations of the same word. The BLANK doctor was

BLANK to operate because he had BLANK."

I paused to think. "I don't get it, is this like an anagram?"

"No, it's one word, and then the same word gets used twice more but it is broken up into multiple words. For example, if the word was morbid, the first blank would be morbid, followed by mor bid and or morb id."

"But those aren't words, G-dad."

"That's why you have to find the right word. The word that can be broken up into multiple words."

I sat for a moment, frowning. "I don't get it. Can't you just tell me?"

"Where would the fun be in that? You're a smart kid, you'll figure it out if you put your mind to it," he said, turning the radio back on.

I didn't want to put my mind to it. I wanted to know the answer. I spent the entire vacation begging him to tell me, but he never budged. Whenever I asked, he would either remind me I was smart enough to figure it out or he'd change the subject.

The first time I actually heard "Mississippi Queen" outside of *Rock Band* was July of 2008 at the Fauquier County Fair. The girl I was interested in was named Kayleigh. She had shiny brown hair and liked Bon Jovi. There had never been a more perfect match in the history of relationships.

"Just go talk to her," my friend Erin said.

"What?! Like with words?!"

She laughed. "Yes, girls like it when you go out of their way to talk to them."

"I want to believe that, but my brain is telling me nothing could be less true."

"Stop being a wuss," she said as she pushed me forward.

Erin went to elementary school with me for eight years. We still hung out on occasion even though we went to different high schools, like I did with the rest of the Saint John's Boys. One night, we made a pact that I would help her win over the love of my friend Bruce if she helped me win over whatever girl I was interested in at the time. That girl was now Kayleigh, and she was conveniently running the soundboard at the concert currently going on at the fair. I normally hated going to the fair; the air smelt like manure, and the wardrobe of most attendees brandished either camouflage or a confederate flag. I almost always felt as if I didn't fit in, but that night the band was playing "Mississippi Queen," I was in good company, and I was quickly falling in love with the sound girl.

Erin and I were standing about ninety feet behind Kayleigh. She was looking at her soundboard and watching a loud band, so I couldn't just wave at her from afar; I would have to approach her and initiate the conversation. My worst nightmare. I felt like I was in a Stephen King book. I thought about bailing, but then out of nowhere she turned around, and I froze. I would say I looked like a deer in headlights, but even a startled deer looks a bit more majestic. I must have looked like a coma patient who had just woken up to find a tube in his urethra—equal amounts anxious and terrified. She saw me and waved. *Fuck, now I have to talk to her.* I slowly approached, my hands in my pockets and my eyes darting in every direction except hers, trying to keep my cool.

"Kayleigh?" I said, pretending to be surprised. "I didn't see you there!" Like I hadn't been standing behind her for an hour.

"Hey! How have you been?" She sat on a stool and looked up at me with a twenty-four-tooth smile and a gleam in her eyes. She had curled her hair, which I had only seen her do twice before. Her hair was so shiny that it reflected the red and white lights of the soundboard, which was now to her back, the band playing southern rock hundreds of feet behind her. She was the prettiest girl I had ever talked to up to that moment.

And the dialogue that followed reflected that.

"I've been good." I looked away from her brown eyes and pointed to the soundboard. "This is so cool you're doing this. How long have you been the sound girl?"

"It's a hobby. I've been doing it for a couple of years. I like it a lot."

"Well you're really good at it, the band sounds great." I gestured at the four guys on stage right as the guitar solo started.

"Thanks."

"And your hair looks awesome curly." I swallowed, trying to think of something clever to say. "Glad I'm not the only one with curly hair!" I immediately wanted to punch myself in the face.

"Thanks," she said. She seemed unphased by what was surely the weirdest sentence she had ever heard.

I wanted to talk to her all night, but all I could think to say was, "Well . . . I have to meet some people," I quickly turned away.

"Okay, it was great seeing you!" she called from behind me.

I waved goodbye and walked over to the ferris wheel to reconnect with Erin. She was waiting for me with her hands interlocked in front of her chest as though she was praying. She watched me approach, her eyes wide and her mouth open in an excited grin.

"Did you talk to her?" she asked.

"Yeah," I mumbled.

When I got home, I couldn't stop thinking about Kayleigh. I sat down and wrote a song called "I'm Gonna Spend the Night with the Sound Girl." It was terrible. I turned on *Rock Band* and dreamed that she was in the audience, hearing me play for her.

TRAIN KEPT A ROLLIN'
By Aerosmith

March 2009

"Train kept a rollin' all night long"

Keith spent almost every pre-college spring break at my house, and for years, we spent those five perfect days the same way: we would wake up at noon, grill burgers for lunch, play video games all day, go outside for thirty minutes because my mom made us, eat dinner, watch either *Digimon: The Movie*, *Home Alone*, *Galaxy Quest*, or *Die Hard*, go to sleep, and repeat.

For our tenth-grade spring break, we decided to shake up the routine a bit and do the impossible: the Endless Setlist. Every *Rock Band* game has an Endless Setlist challenge at the end. This entails playing every song on the disc from start to finish, consecutively; as the setlist progresses, the songs get more and more difficult. We had yet to attempt *Rock Band*'s Endless Setlist, but nearly eighteen months after we began playing the game that would definitively change our lives, we felt we were ready.

We had each received *Rock Band 2* a few months prior; Keith found his copy a week before Christmas while snooping around his parents' bedroom closet. He had called me after school one day so he could open the box discreetly and tell me what the new instruments looked like. I had waited until Christmas day like a good Catholic boy, despite knowing my mother had hidden my copy under a blanket in my father's toolshed.

By the time spring break rolled around, we'd had three months of practice. We had mastered every song on the disc and were ready to take on *Rock Band 2*'s eighty-four-song Endless Setlist. We buckled down for what we calculated would be a minimum eight consecutive hours of *Rock Band*. The time would increase if we took bathroom breaks or food breaks. If one of us missed too many notes in a song, he would be dropped out of the song until the other person earned enough points to bring him back. If a player was out of the song for longer than thirty seconds, the song would end, and we would be asked to replay the song.

We had practiced the entire day before and reviewed all of the difficult songs earlier that morning. Keith played bass while I played guitar, just like we did whenever we played with Chris and Delynn. We chose to play expert difficulty, and we agreed not to stop at any point for any reason, because we would lose our flow, and because, well . . . we were professionals.

"Okay, I'm gonna hit start," I said, clutching my plastic guitar. "Are you sure you don't need to pee?"

"No, stop asking. You're the one who pees every thirty minutes."

"I do not."

"You're like a goddamn woman. I bet we don't get through five songs before you have to pee."

"I'm starting." I tightened my guitar strap.

"Cool. Let's do this."

About twenty minutes later, I realized we weren't even five percent through the setlist, and it started to set in for both of us just how long this would actually take, but we kept playing. By the time we got to track six, Duran Duran's "Hungry Like the Wolf," I had to pee. Songs like Cheap Trick's "Hello There" were short enough to give us the confidence we needed to press on with our task, but songs like Bad Company's "Shooting Star" really dragged on and made us question our decision to do the list in the first place.

When we got to The Go Go's "We Got the Beat," Bruce called. I wasn't able to pick up the phone and call him back until the drum solo toward the end of the song. I held the phone between my ear and shoulder as I played the remainder of the song; I could barely hear him ask if we wanted to hang out over the loud eighties distortion of Jane Wiedlin's flawless pop rock power chords.

When I told him what we were doing, he lost all interest in spending time with us.

One of the worst stretches of songs we had was "Teenage Riot" by Sonic Youth (arguably the most boring song to play in the *Rock Band 2* catalogue) immediately followed by "Shackler's Revenge" by Guns N' Roses (Keith couldn't seem to complete a bass part in that song without failing out). After about seventeen tries, we finally got to the songs that were always fun to play no matter how cramped your hands got; "Spoonman" by Soundgarden, "Everlong" by Foo Fighters, and "Battery" by Metallica gave us the energy we needed to play the final stretch of the setlist.

After more than eight hours, only three songs remained: "Panic Attack" by Dream Theater, "Painkiller" by Judas Priest . . . and a third song we had unfortunately not accounted for. We hadn't thought to practice it because we had not unlocked it yet. We hadn't unlocked it yet because neither of us had ever heard of the fucking song, and therefore never had a desire to play it during our virtual world tour—which is how we unlocked every other song on this list. That was our biggest mistake. Out of nowhere, the third-to-last track was some awful grindcore/black metal/deathcore bullshit called "Visions." The guitar and bass played nonsensical noise alongside intense deep screams. The crazy riffs sent Keith and I back in time to when we had first started playing the game. Despite years of practice and countless hours of playing the game, we were instantly novices again.

We both failed out immediately. We tried again and again, and eventually made it past the song's first bridge. But the non-melodic riffs, the sporadic drum beat that sounded like Animal from The Muppets was having a stroke, and a vocal melody comparable to that of a blender made the song unplayable. After an hour, we decided to quit. Ten hours of our lives went down the drain; a full day wasted. We still consider it our greatest defeat to this day.

Right after that, we did what any pissed-off sixteen-year-olds would do; we left a hateful comment on the song's YouTube video. The admin of the page responded to the comment the next day saying, "Nobody cares."

We have not attempted an endless setlist since.

I'M SO SICK
By Flyleaf

May 2011

"Worthless, hopeless, sick"

"One more?" I asked, sweating through my black Foo Fighters' t-shirt and cargo shorts in the front seat of Penny's car. We had spent thirty minutes of the hot, sunny afternoon attempting to fix her air conditioning but failed. At the moment, neither of us really cared.

"No, we just kissed," Penny said in her fashionably torn-up Monster energy drink t-shirt, sweating just as much as me.

"I know, I just want to do it again."

High school was over. I would never have to set foot in that horrible building ever again. It was just me, Penny, and infinite possibilities as we drove home from a spontaneous trip to our local music store.

"We can kiss when I get back," she responded with a gleam in her eye.

"That's like a week from now." I leaned over the armrest between us. "Are you sure you still want to go?" I asked again, already knowing the answer.

Penny grinned from the driver's seat and pushed me back into the passenger seat. "You know how hard it was to convince my mom to let me go on this trip with Brett and his friends," she said. "I still can't believe she said yes."

I leaned back in my seat. "Yeah, who would have thought she'd be cool with her seventeen-year-old daughter going to a beach house with her boss and his friends?"

"We graduated high school. We're adults now. It's totally not weird. You're not weirded out by it, are you?"

"Of course not," I lied. "You're just going to the beach with some friends. I do it all the time."

"Probably never with just you and four other girls."

"That's true, but I'd trade that trip for one with just you."

Penny smiled. "The Girl with Golden Eyes" by Sixx:A.M. came on her car radio. We listened as the lead singer wailed, "I wish I'd never kissed her, 'cause I just can't resist her."

"Kind of ironic lyrics, don't you think?" she asked.

"Actually, Nikki Sixx wrote this song about his heroin addiction. He's talking about drugs." I didn't realize it at the time, but Penny was trying to be cute and flirty with this statement; she was not, in fact, looking for that bit of music trivia . . . nor for the several pieces of Mötley Crüe lore that I followed it up with.

"Okay, I really got to go," she said.

"Oh, come on, can't we just hang out for five more minutes?" I begged.

She rolled her eyes. "We've been sitting in your driveway for an hour. Keith will be here in like thirty minutes. He'll entertain you."

"You're right," I said, and opened the passenger door. "Date number seven when you get back?"

"You know it's weird when you count them, right?"

"Oh, sorry."

"It's fine," she said. "I'll be back before you know it."

She drove away, and I stood in the driveway thinking. *Why didn't it work out with Kayleigh? Because I was too scared to talk to her. It's so easy to talk to Penny: mission accomplished. I have feelings for a girl and I'm doing everything right this time!*

Day 1

I went inside to eat a late lunch. I made myself a hot dog and mac and cheese and took it upstairs into the living room. I turned on an episode of *Scrubs* and sat down. I was about to begin eating when, out of nowhere, I heard a voice in my head say, *She's definitely sleeping with him.*

I nearly dropped my plate. I felt queasy. *Why would I think that? We've been on six whole dates and made out a few times. She was my first kiss! There's no way she'd kiss someone else, let alone have sex with another guy while she was seeing me. I mean, I wouldn't, so why would she?* I dismissed the thought and went back to eating my food, attempting to get my mind off Penny.

After one episode of *Scrubs*, I had finished my meal. I stood up to grab more food when I suddenly had a second, unexpected thought: *I'm gonna throw up.* I ran into the bathroom, but before I could even get to the toilet, I covered the sink with my bile. I threw up my entire meal; I looked down at my lunch. I couldn't remember the last time I had thrown up. Why the hell was I doing it now?

I cleaned up the sink until it was spotless. I went back to watch TV until Keith showed up.

Day 2

Martin was throwing a graduation pool party for his high school friends. Fortunately, like most parties any of us threw, my close childhood friends whom I had met years ago at Saint John's Elementary School were all there, despite not having attended the same high school. The party was a much-needed distraction from missing Penny, so I was thrilled to be there.

It was a standard party for us: we were all hanging out by the pool, laughing together and avoiding the girls there out of fear (also because I was in an exclusive relationship), and Bruce and I were seeing how long we could lock Martin out of his iPhone by entering the incorrect passcode several times. We had achieved a thirty-minute lockout by the time Martin got out of the pool. Bruce attempted to put the phone back in Martin's pants that were lying on the table, but he was caught in the act.

"What the hell, guys!" Martin said as he approached us.

"It was Cade's idea!" Bruce shouted and stepped back. Martin pushed me in the pool fully clothed. I landed square on a peaceful Keith floating in a raft.

"What the shit, man!" Keith yelled. "You made me spill my soda!"

I spat out some pool water. "Goddammit Martin," I coughed out, "my wallet's in my pocket." Keith and I crawled out of the soda-infested shallow end. I took my wallet out of my pocket and threw it on the table to dry.

"This wasn't gonna end any other way than you and your belongings getting wet," Martin said, attempting to keep a straight face.

I looked up from my wallet to Martin. "Goddammit. Can you get on your phone real quick and Google a way to quickly dry wallets?" He looked at his phone for a split second before he realized he was locked out. Bruce and I looked at each other and laughed.

Keith was examining my wet wallet and its contents. "At least you don't carry around any cash." He pulled out my driver's license, my GameStop membership, and a card that had been ripped into four pieces. "What the hell is this?" he asked, holding up the shreds of paper.

"Oh, you guys are gonna love this," I said. "So, you know in health class how they make you sign an abstinence card that says you won't have sex before marriage? Penny was going through my wallet, she found it, and she tore it up in front of me! How hot is that?"

Bruce lifted an eyebrow and looked at me. "Why did you keep a torn-up card in your wallet?" he asked.

"Why the *fuck* did you sign an abstinence card?" Keith said, still staring at the pieces in his hands.

I grabbed them from him. "Did you not take health? They show you fucking genital warts the size of tennis balls for two weeks straight. I didn't jerk off for a month after that class," I said, shuddering.

"I have no words." Keith said. Martin and Bruce laughed.

"Hey guys, pizza's here!" Jimmy called from the front yard. He was forever the responsible one, helping Martin's parents bring pizza inside while his friends played childish pranks on each other and talked about STDs. Everyone dried off and went inside.

All of this talking about the card made me realize I hadn't texted Penny since she left. I followed my friends inside and grabbed my phone off the kitchen table where I had left it, right before the entire room was swarmed with starving teenagers. I walked into the bathroom and closed the door. After several minutes of pondering the right message to send, I settled on, "Hey, how's your trip?" Not too clingy or eager, but it got the point across.

I stood in the bathroom for ten minutes waiting for a response. *I'm sure she'll respond right away,* I thought. *It's a text from me.* I waited twenty minutes, then thirty, before I realized it was time to get out of the bathroom. Most of the party had finished eating and had gone back to the pool, but Bruce and Martin had moved to the living room with the remainder of the pizza.

"Must have been quite a shit," Bruce said, handing me a slice.

"Just dicking around on my phone," I replied.

"A *penny* for your thoughts about who you were texting." Martin winked at me. "Ha ha! See what I did there?" Bruce punched him in the arm.

"She didn't respond." I offered casually. "She went to the beach. She'll probably be swimming for most of the day."

"Gotcha." Martin winked again. "Well, let's head back to the pool."

Day 3

The following day, Keith and I made a trek to Wal-Mart to get burger patties to grill for lunch. Despite my consistent anxiety, there was still a part of me that could enjoy the smell of impending summer. It was a sunny day with the perfect amount of breeze, I was driving the family's '96 Honda Odyssey, and my best friend and I were in the front seat blasting Saliva's "Badass" over the speakers. The best part of finally being able to drive was that Keith and I could finally listen to whatever the fuck we wanted without our parents complaining about the songs being "too loud" or how "Limp-Bizkit-heavy" our playlists were.

After a few minutes, I interrupted our silent admiration of shitty hard rock. "Did you get the new Avenged Sevenfold songs they added on *Rock Band*?" I asked.

"Nah, I didn't recognize either of them." Keith replied, adjusting his sunglasses on his face.

"'Unholy Confessions' is off their second album, and 'Welcome to the Family' is off *Nightmare*."

"The song 'Nightmare' is cool. I just bought the single though, so I haven't really listened to the rest of the album."

We drove past a murder of crows picking apart a deer carcass. It seemed to be an edgy and appropriate reflection of nature contributing to our conversation about metal bands. "I got *Nightmare* for my birthday," I said. "It might be my second-favorite Avenged Sevenfold album next to their self-titled, even though the Rev is dead."

Keith shook his head. "Gone too soon. He was a good goddamn drummer."

"Amen. As for *Rock Band* songs, I've been buying whatever comes out every so often even if I haven't heard of it. I often end up surprised about how much I end up liking the songs I buy. Like when I randomly bought 'Saints of Los Angeles.'"

Keith grinned. "And it ended up being our fucking theme song."

I laughed. "Exactly. I'm glad Mötley Crüe had a proper comeback."

"Those drums were fucking hard at first," Keith recalled, shaking his head.

"No joke. Penny and I broke out *Rock Band* the other day and played 'Through the Fire and Flames.' Shit was impossible." I shook my head and let out a very tiny laugh that turned into silence.

My best friend immediately picked up on my nonverbal cue. "Has she texted you back yet?" he asked.

"Nope."

"You okay?"

"No. Why do you think you're here? You're the only person I care about as much as her." Keith hid his reaction like any male teenager would, but I knew he appreciated my sentiment. I have a great family and several other great friends, but I truly meant what I said: the only person who could distract me from Penny's absence at this particular moment was Keith.

"Happy to be here, brother."

Day 4

Four days. She'd been gone for four days. Keith had left the day before, and I hadn't been able to keep a meal down since. I'd woken up every morning that week at seven, which was five hours before my usual wakeup time. Plus, a weird rash was starting to spread on my back. *Maybe this is growing up?* I thought. *You graduate high school and out of nowhere you start waking up early, struggling to eat, and sprouting weird rashes.* It had nothing to do with Penny, I was sure of it. It was just growing up. Blink-182 definitely should have mentioned these physical inconveniences in "Dammit."

But then why hasn't Penny texted me yet? I had texted her over forty-eight hours ago. *What if I was dying? I would like to think she would care to know if I was on my deathbed.* I thought back to our first kiss, in the library parking lot right next door to my friend Dan's house. We had been on a few dates by then, and had talked about kissing, but we hadn't actually kissed before that night. On our walk back to my car, the moment just struck me. I pulled her close to me underneath a streetlight, looked her in the eyes, and said, "Kiss me." It was the perfect moment. After spending four years in high school, in a dearth of moments like this, it was a thrilling change of pace. I was sure there'd be nothing but good things from there on out.

So why wouldn't she respond to me?

It was a miserable day. I had done nothing for most of it except be awake. I was exhausted, but I couldn't sleep. I was hungry, but I couldn't eat. After seventeen hours of that, I eventually fell asleep waiting for my phone to vibrate.

Day 5

I once again woke up way too early. The hunger had gotten worse. The exhaustion had gotten worse. The rash had gotten worse. Before she had left, Penny had taken a rubber band and lovingly snapped it against my arm so hard it left a mark. I put a rubber band on my wrist and snapped it against my skin to simulate the feeling.

Fortunately for my sanity, I received a Netflix DVD in the mail that morning. I mustered enough energy to open it: *The Dilemma.*

I don't remember why I had added this movie to my Net-flix queue weeks before. If you've never seen this movie, it's shit. Vince Vaughn and Kevin James star as a pair of genuinely un-funny friends. At the start of the film, Vince Vaughn sees Kevin James's wife making out with another man, and spends the whole movie struggling with how to tell him. So aside from being subjected to a veritably terrible film, this movie sent my anxiety off the goddamn charts. *Penny is fucking him, I know she is,* I kept telling myself. *I'm Kevin James in his worst possible role before* Zookeeper.

I didn't sleep at all that night. I just lay in my bed, snapping my rubber band against my wrist until it was raw and covered with welts.

Day 6

By around 6:50 the next morning, I had finally conceded that my current sleep habits were the new normal. After yet another night of tossing and turning, I heard a buzz on my nightstand.

On the sixth day of our separation, I finally received a text from Penny.

"Hey, sorry I'm just now reading your text. My phone died as soon as I got here, and I didn't have a charger. I'm on my way home. Do you wanna get pizza when I get back?"

I felt immediate, uncontrolled joy. You know the feeling I'm talking about: it's the same kind of giddiness you get when you receive a text from a girl you like, or when you do a line of cocaine. *Oh, glorious day! She finally responded! And she has a good reason for not responding! She wasn't sleeping with her manager! She really wanted to talk to me, but her phone died, and she had no way to reach me for six days!*

"I'd love to get pizza! Missed you!"

"Missed you too."

A few hours later, we met at a small pizza shop equidistant from both of our houses. We ate outside and enjoyed the sunset together. I'd missed the taste of pizza those few days. I'd missed food in general, but eating a fresh, homemade pizza after involuntarily fasting is a special kind of delight the whole world deserves to experience.

"So, it wasn't boring hanging out with a whole bunch of college dudes?" I asked Penny, accidentally dropping a piece of sausage on the picnic bench we shared.

"No, we had a really good time," she said, wiping her mouth. "Mostly just went to the beach and drank beers. What did you do?"

Nearly died came to mind. "Nothing really. Keith came to visit, we went to a party, played some *Rock Band*. . . . The usual stuff."

After we finished our pizza, we got back in Penny's car so she could drive me home. As I sat down and buckled in, she leaned over to kiss me. It was definitely one of our better kisses, and it was intoxicating after my six days of detox.

"What was that for?" I asked.

"I really missed you," she said, smiling.

"I really missed you too."

We drove home. She told me all about the fun parts of her trip. She told me it was the first time she had seen a beach in seven years. She told me they had found a cool hobby store where she bought a katana replica from her favorite anime. She told me she got to drink and do other fun adult stuff all high schoolers dream of doing before they become boring adults who wish they were in high school again. I smiled as I listened to all of her stories; I had strong feelings for Penny, and I could see that all of my anxiety and insanity over the past six days had been in vain. She truly cared for me . . . right?

PARANOID
By Black Sabbath

May 2011

"The things in life that I can't find"

I was raised Catholic. Both my mother's and father's sides of the family are practicing theists. Though I don't really follow any of the rules behind Catholicism anymore, I haven't necessarily given up faith in a higher power of some kind; I just have trouble worshipping something I don't understand. My questioning of religion took my parents some getting used to. In fact, at the time that I'm writing this book, they still haven't gotten over it completely.

There are three events in my life to which I can trace the origin of my doubts, the first being a camping trip I went on with my father and sister back in 2001.

"Cade, come out of the tent. I have to talk to you about something."

I put down my Harry Potter book and unzipped my tent. I looked out at the campsite; it was still bright outside, but cold enough to warrant making a fire before sundown. My father was on the other side of the campsite, sitting with my sister next to the campfire. He was wearing the Stetson hat he usually brought on camping trips; he always looked like Indiana Jones in a flannel shirt whenever we were in nature. Emma wore a pink sweatshirt and a look of eagerness in her eyes, as if she was about to bust the lid off an age-old conspiracy. I approached them.

"Your sister asked me a question," my father said, "and I figured you should both be here for the answer."

A sense of nervousness washed over me. "What is it?"

"Emma, ask the question for your brother to hear."

Emma cleared her throat, sat up straight, and asked, "Is the tooth fairy real?"

"Why would you ask that?!" I exclaimed, placing my hands on my head in disbelief.

"Because I want to know," Emma said, as serious as any seven-year-old could be.

I threw my hands in the air. "Why question it? What if he says there's not?! Then we don't get free money anymore!"

My father laughed at our exchange. "Okay, do you really want to know?"

We both said opposite answers simultaneously, and he laughed again. "Okay, Emma, come over here and I'll whisper the answer in your ear."

Emma jumped over to my father with a giggle. As he whispered the answer into her ear, her face lit up.

"Cade! The tooth fairy isn't real!" she shouted.

I covered my ears too late. "Why did you tell me that? I didn't want to know!"

"Emma, you didn't need to do that," Dad said.

"Wait," Emma said, her smile dropping, "does this mean the Easter Bunny isn't real?" she asked.

I gave my sister a death stare. *First, she ruins free money, next she's gonna ruin Easter baskets and plastic eggs with candy in them?*

My dad sighed. "Well . . . I guess now is as good a time as any. No, the Easter Bunny isn't real."

"I knew it!" Emma exclaimed. I stood there, devastated, learning that half of my childhood had been lies.

"Santa isn't real either, is he?" I moped, looking at my shoes.

"Sorry, son, he's not. Parents just tell their children these things because it's a lot more fun to believe when you're younger.

Now you're getting older and you don't need to believe in magical characters on special holidays."

I looked up at him. "So, Jesus isn't real either, right?" I asked.

My father frowned. "What? No, no, no, no. He's definitely real. Jesus is real."

Five years later, during the height of my fascination with the Fab Four, my father rented us the Beatles Anthology documentary series: a ten-hour, in-depth television spectacle going through the history of the world's most iconic band. I started to look forward to coming home every Friday night just so I could watch the next part, to find out what happened to the four co-creators of music.

We had finally reached the mid-sixties, otherwise known as the peak of the band's touring fame. There were several reasons why the Beatles stopped touring, but one of the big reasons was the hostility they got from a small percentage of fans after John claimed in an interview that the Beatles were "more popular than Jesus." The documentary showed men and women of all ages taking to the streets and burning their Beatles merchandise. They burned posters, albums, and every other piece of memorabilia that you could possibly fathom. A girl on screen said she no longer liked the band because her religion was more important. She also said her new favorite band was Herman's Hermits. Herman's. Fucking. Hermits. I can't imagine being invested enough in *any* religion to trade listening to musical perfection for complete mediocrity. That's like saying, "I really like Radiohead, but Thom Yorke said something I thought was silly so I'm gonna go listen to Smash Mouth forever."

My father and I sat on different couches in the "fun living room." The room was dark aside from the glow of the TV and its reflection on the coffee table in front of us. The smell of pizza filled the air.

"Dad?" I asked.

He looked at me. "Yeah?"

"Why are they burning all of the records?"

"You've been watching. It's because John said they were bigger than Jesus." He finished his last slice of peperoni and placed his plate on the coffee table.

"But why are they burning all of these things that they paid a lot of money for?"

"Because religion is very important. It's more important than almost anything; definitely more important than any music or band."

At this point in my life, I had been to church every week (twice a week when Catholic school was in session) for fourteen years. But I had never felt closer to God than when I had heard "I Should Have Known Better" or "Ticket to Ride" for the first time. Attending a lecture that I rarely understood, dozens of times a year, didn't make me feel close to God—it made me feel like I was having to go to school on a Sunday.

"I guess I just don't understand," I told my dad while shaking my head. "I'd never burn any of my Beatles albums."

My father smiled. "You'll understand when you're older one day."

I still don't.

I had prayed every night before bed until the end of high school, because it's what I was raised to do. My father told me at a young age that if I prayed for anything hard enough, I would eventually get it, one way or another. He then added the stipulation it had to be important; it couldn't be toys or anything "fun." Once I got to middle school and started to notice girls, I started saying three prayers per night: the first one was for my family and Keith, the second one was for poor people or some other Miss America bullshit, and the third was for girls to notice me. I spent all of middle and high school falling in love with so many different girls, and the end result was always the same: nothing happened, and nobody cared. All I wanted was to have a girl over to my house to watch a movie, then maybe have a friend walk in and see me with my arm around her, like in every TV sitcom where the attractive girl somehow falls for the completely average guy. I prayed every night for seven years.

With Penny, I was certain my prayer had been answered.

In May 2011, I took Penny to D.C. to see the D.C.101 Chili Cook Off music festival. The lineup consisted of Middle Class Rut, Paper Tongues, Neon Trees, Panic at the Disco, Papa Roach, Seether, and Weezer. We had both been excited for weeks, so naturally I expected it to be a day we would remember for a long time. But as soon as we arrived, Penny acted really distant. She watched the first few bands with me, but then she went off to the side of the fairgrounds to sit under a tree and look at her phone. I went to check on her during Papa Roach (that was the time I was certain I wouldn't miss anything important). She told me everything was fine, and that I should just enjoy the show. I had paid a lot of money for the tickets, so I took her words at face-value and went back into the large crowd of people. It was hard to enjoy the show without Penny, especially when Seether played our song, "Broken," and a forty-five-year-old man wearing a jean jacket was standing next to me in her place. I had no idea what was going on. Like I said, we had both been looking forward to this show for months.

After a couple more hours of music, she found me and asked if we could leave before Weezer's encore. The drive home was quiet at first. I didn't want to reveal that I was upset at the fact she had asked me to leave before I even heard the song "Buddy Holly."

After nearly half an hour, she broke the silence.

"I made out with Matt."

"Oh," I said, completely caught off guard. "Isn't that your co-worker?"

"Yeah."

"Should we talk about it?"

"I had sex with Brett."

"Your manager?"

"Yeah."

I felt sick to my stomach, but at no point on this entire drive did I react in a non-robotic demeanor. I didn't know how. "When?"

"Before the beach trip. During the beach trip. After the beach trip."

I sat in silence for a while, completely paralyzed, staring at the houses we passed on the side of the road.

"I just . . . I thought we . . . I told my parents I didn't want to go to JMU. I told them I wanted to stay here with you."

"You shouldn't. You should go to school."

"I just thought . . . I mean we hang out alone a lot, we've made out a few times, I thought . . . I thought we were . . ."

She looked over at me and realized what I was struggling to say. "You thought wrong."

I spent the rest of the car ride sitting in silence. I knew I felt sad, but I had never been more uncertain of how to show it. I felt like a little kid who had just been told a relative had died; you know you're supposed to be sad, but your brain can't really grasp the permanence of the situation.

When I dropped Penny off at her house, that was the last I ever saw of her. As soon as I got home, I stormed past the living room where my parents were watching TV and locked my bedroom door. I crawled into bed and I cried. I cried a lot. I cried all night long and didn't sleep for a second. I looked at the crucifix my mother had suspended above my door after my first communion and I wondered how a higher power I had been praying to for years—a higher power I *worshipped*—could let me feel such absolute misery. I thought about that for hours, until around eight the next morning, when my father knocked on my door and told me it was time to get ready for church.

I THINK I'M PARANOID
By Garbage

August 2011

"Maim me, tame me, you can never change me"

I was eighteen and about to enter my first year of college. Though Keith and the rest of the Krazy Unikerns had been an hour away from me throughout my high school years, there was another group of guys who had always been there for me. We had met in first grade at Saint John the Evangelist Catholic School and had been inseparable ever since. We called ourselves the "Saint John's Boys."

First, there was Bruce, the attractive jock; all the guys wanted to be his pal, all the girls wanted to be his gal. But don't let the stereotype fool you—Bruce is still one of the nicest people I know.

Julian was the music buff. He listened to anything and everything, and he could play most of it on the drums. Although he's always been fascinated with all kinds of music, we bonded over classic rock and Blink-182.

Jimmy was the brains of the group. While the rest of us spent most of grade school and high school dicking around, Jimmy spent more time studying than sleeping. His interests included hiking, cooking, saving money, and being responsible.

Martin was the artist. He spent every class doodling cartoon strips or various sketches, hoping to one day do it on a professional level. Martin also shared my love of film and the Beatles from a young age.

Finally, there was Gordon, the actor. I have never and will never meet anyone as genuinely nice as Gordon. He would entertain us by reenacting scenes from our favorite movies and *Family Guy* episodes, and he was very good at it. We swore he would be on *Saturday Night Live* one day. He's not today, but there's still time.

Every year before the new high school year started, we would take a trip to my family's cabin in King George, Virginia, and spend a weekend reminiscing about grade school and enjoying each other's company. Once we had graduated from our private school in eighth grade, we didn't get to spend every day together anymore, so we relished any and all the time we had with each other.

It was the last cabin trip before we all went to college; Julian, Bruce, and I were going to be roommates at JMU, while everyone else went their separate ways. To honor such a special occasion, I had invited Keith (who had become an honorary SJS Boy over the years) to join us.

We were all taking a walk in the woods around the cabin. I had my old video camera with me, because we always made a few short movies on every trip.

"What do you think college is gonna be like?" I asked.

"Probably like the *American Pie* movies," Bruce responded.

I looked at him. "Really?"

He nodded. "Either that or *Blue Mountain State*," he said.

"Did you guys buy condoms yet?" Julian asked.

"Yep," Bruce said quickly.

I stopped walking. "Shit, were we supposed to? I didn't."

"Dude, you've gotta be ready. You don't want a girl to walk into your room at night and you not have a condom," Julian said.

"Don't we need to be in relationships before we worry about condoms?" I asked.

"That's not what college is about, man," Julian said. "Everyone has sex with everyone. Nobody gets in relationships their freshman year."

"Holy shit, you guys! Get over here!" Keith yelled from ahead of us.

The seven of us gathered in front of an old, dying tree. The inside was hollow. It had a huge hole on the side, and hornets were flying all around it.

"Shit, what do we do?" I asked.

"Let's just walk around it," Jimmy said, forever being the voice of reason.

"Fuck that, we can't pass up this opportunity," Keith said, rallying the troops. In his defense, to an eighteen-year-old boy, a tree full of hornets is the coolest thing you could find in the woods—other than a girl willing to have sex with you.

Before anyone could respond, Keith jammed a large stick into the tree and ran away. The hornets *poured* out of the tree; there had to be well over a hundred of them. We all took off and retreated to a safe distance to watch and plan our next move.

"I don't think they're mad enough," Bruce said, picking up a rock.

"Dude, no. They're plenty mad." Keith turned to look at the group. "We have to get someone to run past them while Cade films it."

It was the most amazing idea any of us had ever heard.

"But who's gonna do it?" I asked.

"Gor-don, Gor-don, Gor-don," Keith started chanting. Before we knew it, we were all chanting with him.

"Ah, what the hell," Gordon sighed. "Let's do it, guys." Not only would Gordon put up with our shit, but he did it with a smile. He could see the mischievous light in our eyes as we sent our friend off to fight nature and possibly die, and all he did was grin.

I hit record on the camera. He stood up and poised himself to run. "Okay, okay, here we go," he said, and then he bolted. He ran faster than anyone I've ever seen, right by the nest, and I got it all on tape.

We ran to catch up with him on the other side, keeping a safe distance from both the tree and Gordon. He seemed to be doing fine . . . until he slowed down. Then out of nowhere he bolted again and started screaming.

"FUCK FUCK FUCKFUCKFUCK! Ahhhhhh!!!" he shouted as a group of three or four hornets swarmed around his head, taking turns assaulting his scalp.

We've all watched this tape over a dozen times since then, and to this day I have never heard Keith laugh as loud or as hard as he does on that tape. It was like we were the stars of our own *Jackass* film. We finally met up with Gordon a quarter mile away from the tree.

"Hoooooly shit, dude, that was amazing!" Julian shouted. "Did you get stung?"

"Ugh, yeah I think so."

"That was awesome," I said, grinning ear to ear.

"I did that for you," Gordon said, pointing at me while returning my grin.

"Alright, Bruce is next," Keith said.

"Fuck it. I'll go," Bruce responded.

We walked back over to the tree. The hornet swarm was smaller once again. Bruce tied his shirt around his head for optimal protection and got into position.

"All right, I'm ready. Someone count down, and I'll go."

"Not yet," Keith said, and he threw a large rock into the hornet hole. In a matter of seconds, the swarm was twice as large as it had been the first time.

"Holy fuck!" Bruce shouted.

"Okay, now you can go," Keith said, grinning. We were all giddy.

"Three! Two! One! Go!" we shouted together.

Bruce ran as fast as he could, and the camera followed every move he made. After the initial dash, he slowed down to look behind him and make sure he wasn't being chased.

"Ouch! Fuck!" he yelled as he picked up speed again. He ran out of the view of the camera, and we lost track of him in the woods.

We ran after him, trying not to pass out from all of the hysterical laughing we were doing while running. We finally found Bruce right where we ended up with Gordon the first time.

"What happened?" Gordon asked.

"A hornet got into my pants and kept stinging me until it found its way out," Bruce panted. He pulled down his pants to show us a large welt on his ass. We all lost our shit.

"Oh my god, this is the best cabin trip ever!" Julian exclaimed.

Everyone ran past the tree at least once; we kind of owed it to Bruce and Gordon. People never believe the details when we tell the story—not only the amount of hornets, but also the fact that we were stupid enough to do it in the first place.

All we have to do is show them the tape.

BLOOD DOLL
By Anarchy Club

September 2011

"No turning back"

The company that makes *Rock Band*, Harmonix, is located in Boston. Along with the many popular anthems on *Rock Band*'s setlist, Harmonix chose nine local bands (lucky bastards) to be immortalized in one of the greatest collections of songs ever pieced together. I would often fantasize about moving to Boston and writing a song that got added to the ever-expanding *Rock Band* library.

Unfortunately, as a freshman at James Madison University, all I had was my guitar, a relatively empty dorm room in Harrisonburg, VA, and Gavin.

Gavin was the worst. He lived in our dorm freshman year. He would often come over to our room to start controversial arguments or have excessive PDA sessions with his girlfriend. On the plus side, he was pretty funny, but mostly we put up with him because we were all new at making friends in college, and we didn't know anybody else.

"Dude, you're never gonna believe what I read," Gavin said as he barged into my room one day.

"What?" I put down my guitar, conceding the fact I wouldn't write my *Rock Band* hit that day.

"Dude, it's really gross. I'm not sure if you can handle it," he bragged. If you've ever seen *South Park*, Gavin is a brawnier, college-age version of Eric Cartman.

"Well, you walked into my room, so I get the feeling you're gonna tell me anyway."

"Check your Facebook messages. I sent it to you." He grinned.

I picked up my phone. "Dude, this is like fifteen pages."

"Okay, I'll just tell you. Basically, this kid was swimming one day and he sank to the bottom of the pool. He put his ass too close to the vent at the bottom, and when he swam up really fast, all of his intestines got ripped out through his asshole!"

"That's gross, dude."

"Knew you couldn't handle it."

"Hey Gavin, can we go to Target?" Quinn said as she walked into the room.

Quinn was Gavin's girlfriend. She had short red hair, pale white skin, and a body reminiscent of Scarlett Johansson in *The Avengers*. I had spent all of high school completely unable to talk to most girls, and not much had changed for me in college. But within the first week of freshman year, Gavin was dating one of the prettiest girls in the dorm. I tolerated Gavin so much because I felt like I could learn something about relationships from him.

"What do you need at Target?" I asked.

"Lady shit. Hop off my dick!" Quinn replied. I laughed. Bruce and Julian walked into the room.

"All right guys, what are we doing tonight?" Julian asked.

"I don't know, but can we *not* go out looking for parties again?" I asked. "My self-esteem is still recovering from last week."

Julian pointed at me. "You were the one who wore your free "Class of 2015" t-shirt! That's how everyone knew we were freshmen," he said.

"Bruce was wearing cargo shorts!" I pointed at Bruce, defending myself. "Anyway, they're having karaoke at TDU tonight. We could go do that." TDU was the campus hangout spot and venue, Taylor Down Under. It had a small stage and a ton of chairs and tables, so the school often hosted karaoke, open mic nights, etc.

"We can't get drunk there," Gavin whined.

"We didn't get drunk last weekend. The only cups we could find at the party were sticky," I retorted.

Gavin glared at me. "You don't even drink, you don't get a say," he snapped. He had a point; I *didn't* drink. I didn't really have a major reason not to, aside from breaking the law. I just didn't want to give in to peer pressure, and plus my mom would have *murdered* me.

After several more minutes of arguing, Gavin and Quinn agreed to postpone their Target trip and go to karaoke with us. Gavin went to change and came back in ten minutes dressed in what we liked to call "douchebag casual" attire: white shorts, a tank top, and sunglasses. It was 9 p.m.

When we arrived at TDU, there were already people singing. I went to the stage and added my name to the list of performers. I looked around the room for a minute and recognized someone sitting in the back; her name was Emily. I had sworn off girls forever after Penny, but then I had met Emily. She lived in our dorm and she was one of the most beautiful girls I had ever seen. She had straight brown hair, tan skin, a timid smile, and a great laugh, and she dressed like a *Smallville* character whom you were bringing home to meet your parents for the first time. Every time we talked, I could feel my heart try to leap out of my chest, and my brain fantasized about a life together: holding her hand on the beach, feeling her head on my shoulder when she falls asleep during a movie, and waking up early to surprise her with chocolate chip pancakes.

She was sitting next to her roommate, Katie, who went by the name "Moon Eyes" for some reason (we never found out why).

"Hey, what's up?" I said as my friends and I approached Emily and Moon Eyes.

"Hey!" Emily responded. Quinn greeted them with a big group hug while Bruce, Julian, and Gavin threw a casual head nod and "Hey" in their direction.

"Are you singing?" I asked Emily.

She shook her head. "No, there's no way I ever could in a million years," she said. "Are you?"

"Absolutely. I love karaoke."

I love karaoke was a much less frightening way of saying, *I mostly just play a lot of* Rock Band *and sing in my underpants when nobody is around.*

Emily's jaw dropped. "That's awesome! What song are you doing?"

"I'm leaning toward 'Hey Jude.' It's my favorite song." I offered.

Emily smiled, but before she could respond, Moon Eyes interjected. "So what's your guys' major?" she asked my friends and me.

"I'm undeclared," I responded.

"You should be an art major," she said and leaned back in her chair. "Smoking weed is what it's all about."

"I'm pretty sure making money is what it's all about," Gavin disagreed.

"Nah." Moon Eyes shook her head. "It's all about smoking weed and making money on the side."

"I'm pretty sure that's called being poor," Gavin said dryly. We all laughed.

After a few more minutes, I was called to the stage. As I got up, my friends cheered. Julian said, "Good luck," Bruce gave an enthusiastic "Wooo!" and Gavin smacked my ass really hard and shouted, "Yeah!"

What better way to start off my college career? I was singing the best song ever written in front of an audience gathered together for a fresh start, a new stage in life. After being ignored by hundreds of people for an entire four years in high school, all eyes were on me. College was going to be different. *Better.* I had the crowd's undivided attention; they cheered, they sang along, they shouted, "My boy is getting laid tonight!" (Well, that last part was just Gavin). At the end, everyone stood up and cheered. I had never felt more confident in my life. I was sure that, before I knew it, I would be in Boston, writing songs that would end up on everyone's favorite music game.

The woman running karaoke that night ran up to me afterwards and said, "That was amazing. Here, take this." She handed me a coupon for a free sub at Jimmy John's. I still have it in my wallet to this day.

BRAINPOWER
By Freezepop

January 2012

"And we'll learn"

"What about this?" Emily asked.

"It's good, it's just very similar to the last page. You're using the word 'that' too much. You can almost always cut it out and the sentences sound much more like they're written instead of spoken."

I sat next to Emily on her bed. She was freshly showered, wearing a sweatpants and t-shirt combo similar to the one she had worn the past three nights.

She looked up from her laptop toward me. "How'd you get so good at writing?"

I shrugged. "You know, I practiced a lot."

That was a lie. I hadn't practiced a lot. Truth be told, I'd never fancied myself a good writer. But I was starting to have strong feelings for Emily, so when she came to our dorm room and asked if any of us were willing to help her with her essay for history class, I didn't think twice. Every night around 7 p.m., I went up to her room, disregarded my own schoolwork, and helped Emily with hers. We would sit on her bed, huddle around her laptop for a few hours, and occasionally get sidetracked and talk about life. I savored every second of it.

"Would you mind helping me with another paper I have coming up? I have to write about a culture on campus."

My brain raced to think of an idea. I wanted to spend every second being around Emily. I would do anything to keep up this tutoring arrangement. "Hmmmm . . . well, I play open mic every Tuesday at TDU. That's sort of a culture of musicians." My voice was shaky, but Emily's widening smile told me she liked it.

"Oh, is that the place you did karaoke that one time?"

"The very same. Every Tuesday they have open mic nights, and a lot of the same people show up, so I think that's a pretty defined culture at this point in the school year."

Her face lit up. "That's perfect! Can I come with you next week?"

I did everything in my power to stop myself from hopping off the bed and actually jumping for joy. If Emily watched me sing *and* play guitar . . . well, let's just say we all know how *The Wedding Singer* ends.

I kept my voice calm. "Next week works great. I'll just need to find a good song to play."

"We can look through my iTunes," Emily said. She minimized her word document on her Mac and pulled up her music library. I started scrolling through the songs.

"'1985' is a classic," I said. "Nothing like some middle school pop punk to get the room singing."

"I do like that one. I've always wanted to learn it on guitar."

"Wait, for real?" I turned to face her, seizing my moment. "I could totally teach you. It's really easy."

"Really? I would love that! Maybe we could have my first lesson after you play the open mic show?"

"It's a date," I said, hoping she would interpret the expression as a fun and whimsical way of saying, "We have plans," instead of the much more embarrassing, "I love you."

Fortunately, she took it as the former and smiled. "Great! Well, I really appreciate your help. I'm probably gonna finish up my math and go to bed. I'll see you later this week?" she asked as I got up off the bed.

"Definitely." I got up and walked to the door. "Goodnight, Emily."

"Goodnight!" she said, smiling at me.

I closed her door and walked back to my room. They say your sense of smell is the sense most closely linked to memory; I remember distinctly that Emily's room and the entire girls' fifth-floor hallway smelled like a tropical breeze air freshener, with just the right amount of floral perfume. I've randomly smelled it a few times since then, and every time I do, I'm transported back to 2012, when I was so happily infatuated with Emily.

I floated through the building until I entered my dorm room, which reeked of three-day-old Sbarro's Calzones, farts, and deodorant (in all fairness, I was equally as responsible as my roommates for all three of those smells). Gavin, Julian, and Bruce were playing *Super Smash Bros* on the GameCube.

Julian was reading something off of his phone. "Okay," he said, "marry, fuck, kill: Patrick Bateman, Dexter, or Hannibal Lecter." Bruce and Gavin put down their controllers just as the match ended and thought for a moment.

"I'd marry Dexter," Bruce said.

Gavin nodded. "Yeah, I'd also marry Dexter because he's the only one who wouldn't actually kill you," he agreed.

"I'd probably kill Hannibal Lecter out of principle," Bruce responded.

"I don't know, I feel like getting eaten is at least intimate," Gavin replied.

They all looked over to me. I sighed. "Marry Dexter because I genuinely love him, kill Hannibal Lecter because both of the other options would scar me for life, and fuck Patrick Bateman because we could probably listen to good music while we do it." I sat down at my computer and turned on my music. "Your Arms Feel Like Home" came on my shuffle.

"I agree with Cade," Gavin said, looking at his phone. "It sure as hell beats Julian's answer for the Jessica question."

"I wouldn't fuck Jessica Biel; she looks like a dude!"

Bruce threw his hands in the air. "Do you not like women?" he asked.

"If you put a dick on her, she'd be a man!" Julian exclaimed.

None of us really knew how to respond to Julian's claim. After a few seconds, Gavin just said, "Yep," and we all laughed.

Gavin turned his attention back to me. "Cade, why the fuck are we listening to country music?"

"It's not country, it's 3 Doors Down!"

"If this was *The Voice*, Blake Shelton would turn his chair around!" He had a valid point regarding everyone's favorite vocal reality competition from 2011.

They started another game of *Super Smash Bros*, and I got on Facebook to message the wisest Krazy Unikerns band member for advice.

Delynn had recently graduated college, and she was living back at home while she waited for Chris to finish his final semester at West Point Military Academy. She had a part-time job at the preschool where Keith and I had met, but she spent most of her time preparing for her wedding in June. The advantage to this was she was almost always near her phone or laptop.

"Hey, can you talk?" I asked.

She responded a few minutes later: "Hey, what's up?"

"So, I've been spending more time with Emily recently. I think it's going really well, but I need some pointers."

"That's great! Give me the details."

"Well, I've been helping her with her history paper like I told you about, but recently, every time I go up to her room she's showered beforehand, she constantly plays with her hair, and we sit on her bed together whenever we write."

"Hmmm, it does seem like there's something there. What do you need help with?"

"What's my next step? I don't want to end up in the friend-zone."

"Lol, the friendzone is made up. Girls like getting to know someone before they are in a relationship with them."

"Really? My roommates have been talking to me about the friendzone an awful lot."

"I'm a girl. I'm planning a wedding as we speak. There's no such thing as the friendzone."

"So, what should I do?"

"Just take it slow. It's not a race. Don't get anxious and rush things. Her opinion of you won't change in a day."

"She did ask if I could teach her guitar."

"That's perfect! Have a couple lessons and then maybe ask her if she wants to see a movie. Just take it slow."

"Okay. Slow. I can do that. Thanks, sis. I'll keep you posted."

"Anytime!"

I closed my laptop, pulled out my guitar, and started learning "1985."

MAIN OFFENDER
By the Hives

January 2012

"Why me?"

I hadn't eaten in four days. That night was the night I would play at the open mic in front of Emily; I had no idea what was going to happen next. Would she find it endearing and want to spend more time with me? Or was she really just using this karaoke event as research for her paper? I had no way of knowing, and it kept me up every night.

I had spent two weeks crafting and practicing the *perfect* set-list. I was allotted fifteen minutes, which translated to about four songs. I was going to open with "When It's Time" by Green Day, lead into "There Is" by Box Car Racer, change it up and play an original I wrote called "Kayleigh," and then close with "Only One" by Yellowcard. I had pumped the brakes on playing video games, watching TV, and even doing homework for several days. This was for true love and therefore it took precedent; all I had time to do was make sure every chord was perfect.

It was two hours before the event when I saw Emily had posted something on Facebook. It was a link to the song "Chasing Cars" by Snow Patrol with a cliché teenager post about feelings that said something along the lines of "these lyrics are my heart." At the time, I was so naïve and blinded by love I found this sentiment to be unique and endearing. *That catchy, palatable, pop chorus says all of the things I think too! Emily is so smart and pretty and smart.* And then I panicked. *Shit, does she like that song more than any of the ones I'm gonna play? Should I play that song tonight? Have I been practicing the wrong songs for two goddamn weeks???*

My frantic thought process was interrupted by the door opening. Gavin plowed through the dorm room door with the intensity of Cosmo Kramer and the grace of the Kool-Aid man.

"Where are Julian and Bruce?" he asked, sporting his douche-bag-casual attire.

"They have class," I said, picking up my guitar from its stand next to my desk so I could squeeze in another hour or so of practice.

He looked at his watch. "Shit. Wanna get dinner then?"

I began to tune my guitar. "I'm not really hungry, dude."

"Come on, you were sitting in the same spot when I stopped by this morning. Get out of your fucking dorm room and get dinner with me." He gestured toward the door.

"Fine," I said. He may have bullied me, but is it really bullying if nachos are the end result?

I sat across the table from Gavin in the student cafeteria, Dukes. I picked at my nachos while he ate chicken strips with fries.

He broke the silence. "It's Emily, isn't it?" he asked.

I looked up and dropped my nacho. "What?"

"You haven't been coming to dinner, and all you've been doing is playing guitar for two weeks. Plus, Bruce told me you were going to open mic with her tonight."

"Well, yeah."

"Listen. I've got a lot of anxiety myself, so I know what you're going through."

"Wait, what? Really?"

"Absolutely. Remember when I started dating Quinn four months ago?"

"Yeah, so what?"

"Remember how we met? How you, me, Bruce, and Julian all

went upstairs to play board games with her and her roommates?"

"Yeah. You commented on the t-shirt she was wearing. You said she had good taste in music." Truth be told, I was jealous of that story. I had fantasized for four years of shitty, shitty high school that I would meet my future wife in a story like that. But it didn't happen to me. It happened to Gavin.

"I didn't even like the band," Gavin laughed. "I just thought she was cute, and I wanted to get to know her. Then after we hung out for a week, she told me she wasn't looking to be in a relation-ship—"

"How did that *not* prevent you from pursuing her?"

"Girls at this age can change their mind about anything in a heartbeat," Gavin said confidently. "All I knew is I liked her, so I was persistent. I realized I could either mope around in my room or I could do something about it. I did homework with her, watched movies with her, hung out with her stupid roommates, and after a couple of weeks she randomly asked me to shower with her."

"Really?" I asked.

"Yeah, you wanna see the texts she sent me?" He grabbed his phone.

"No, that's okay. You don't need to show me."

He showed me anyway.

"All I'm saying," Gavin continued, "is girls love persistence and big gestures. I'm sure of that. You've been hanging out with her regularly, doing homework with her and stuff, so you've got the persistence covered. All you need now is a big gesture, or else you'll end up in the friendzone."

At the time, this sounded like flawless logic. All I knew was Gavin had the most perfect "How did you meet?" story, and there-fore he was an expert on the subject at hand. I thought about how I hadn't eaten or slept for most of this week and realized I'd do whatever it took to make that feeling go away. Besides, it was better than any plan that I had.

"Umm, I'll think about it, dude. I do appreciate the advice though," I said, looking back down at my half-eaten nachos.

When we returned to the dorm, Gavin went back to his room to watch TV, and I formed a last-minute, anxiety-ridden, non-sensical plan. I'd switch out one of the songs I had practiced for "Chasing Cars," and right before I played it, I'd say something to her—whatever came into my head—on the stage. It was a huge gesture, and it showed that I knew her because I saw she showed interest in a song on Facebook. *Foolproof.*

Though I saw no flaws with this plan, I figured I should get a second opinion from my relationship advisor. I grabbed my phone and called Delynn.

"Hello?" she answered.

"Hey, it's me, do you have a second?"

"Yeah, I'm just picking out flowers for the wed—"

"That's great. I have an Emily plan I need to run by you."

"Oh, all right. What's up?"

"I'm going to make a move tonight. It's been over a month. If I don't make a move, I'm gonna be in the friendzone."

"There's no such thing as the friendzo—"

"Delynn, you don't understand! I need to make a bold gesture. She's coming to open mic night tonight to watch me play. I'm going to say something romantic and endearing on stage in front of everyone."

She was quiet for a moment. ". . . Cade, don't—"

"Delynn, I have to. You don't know what it's like to feel this way about someone."

"I'm planning a wedding right now. . . ."

"Okay, fine. What do you suggest I do?"

"I'd say avoid the big gesture, see how tonight goes, then wait a few days and ask her to go to a movie. Then keep making casual plans until something happens."

"Wait until something happens?! I'll tell you what happens! I don't do anything, a Ryan Gosling-type swoops in and makes a move, and then she tells me all about their sex life on our way to our *casual* movie theater trip!"

"You're overthinking this. Like, a lot."

I took a breath. "Duly noted. But I still have to try."

Delynn sighed. "I guess I can't stop you. Good luck."

"I'll let you know how it goes," I said and hung up the phone.

Moments later, there was a knock on my door. It was Emily, all dressed up in a skirt I had never seen and expensive-looking cowboy boots.

"Hey!" she said.

"Hey! Wow, you look . . . really great."

"Aww thanks," she said, smiling.

I grabbed my guitar and amp. "Ready to do this?" I asked.

"Lead the way," she said, letting me walk past her into the hallway with my heavy equipment. I don't lift weights frequently, and both the guitar case and amp had to be at least thirty pounds each; my arms felt like spaghetti carrying two suitcases full of bricks. This was coupled with the fact I hadn't eaten or slept well in a lengthy period of time, not to mention I was trying to entertain Emily with hilarious banter.

Despite these obstacles, we made it to the venue and found a place to sit. The front of TDU was filled with couches and sofa chairs, while the back had several tables designed for eating and studying. We selected a high-top table next to the soundboard in the back of the venue and sat across from each other.

"Are you enjoying your week so far?" I asked.

"Yeah, I'm just ready to be done with this TDU paper," she admitted, frowning as she pulled her laptop from her backpack and set it on the table. "Thanks again for doing this; it was very nice of you to offer." Her frown turned to a smile.

"Don't mention it. Still on for our guitar lesson tomorrow?" I inquired casually, trying to avoid seeming too eager.

"Yes! It will be a nice break from work."

"Perfect." I exhaled a small sigh of relief.

"Did you decide what songs you were going to play when you get up there?" she asked, playing with her hair. My hope that she was here more for me and not homework was slowly turning into a belief.

"Yeah—a Green Day song, a Yellowcard song, a Box Car Racer song, and one I wrote."

"Ooo, I love Yellowcard!" she exclaimed. "And that's really cool you wrote a song. I can't wait to hear it."

I shrugged. "Don't get your hopes up, it's really not that great," I said, though I secretly hoped she'd think it was a track Oasis could have left off their album *(What's the Story) Morning Glory.*

The current performer wrapped up his mediocre rendition of "Yoshimi Battles the Pink Robots Pt. 1," which was a song I recognized from the *Rock Band 3* catalogue, and the MC approached the microphone. "Is there a Cade in the house?" he asked.

I took a breath and turned to Emily. "Here I go, I guess."

"Good luck!" Emily whispered. She grinned and clapped along with the crowd.

Little did I know, this would be the last enthusiastic, excited, or even happy expression I would ever see on Emily's face. I also didn't know that, within less than half an hour, I'd be committing—hands down—the most embarrassing act of my entire life.

"Thanks," I said, and carried my guitar and amp to the stage. I looked out on the dozens of people in the audience, people sitting on the couches, eating dinner at the tables, and doing homework in the back. They all looked up at me as I took the stage. I plugged everything in, and the sound guy gave me the thumbs up to start playing.

Okay, before I start, let me think this through: Why didn't it work with Kayleigh? Because I was too scared to talk to her. I can talk to Emily. Check. Why didn't it work out with Penny? Because I never made a big enough romantic gesture to win her over. Okay. I'm going with Gavin's advice.

I had performed in front of several audiences before, and I'd never had a problem with stage fright. But I had also never played in front of anyone as pretty as Emily. I looked around the room; it was a good-sized audience of about twenty to thirty people. Most of them had turned back to their laptops to do homework or were drinking coffee to prepare themselves for a long night of studying, but Emily was focused solely on me.

"Hey everybody, thanks for coming out tonight. This first song is a Green Day song," I said as I began to sweat.

I started playing "When It's Time." I lost most people's interest in the song about halfway through. *Why the hell would I pick this song? This is a shit choice. The few people in the audience who actually want to hear Green Day right now don't want to hear a fucking deep cut from their goddamn Broadway musical.*

I finished the song. There was an uproar of applause from the fifty percent of the room who were there for the music, and a very lackluster collection of apathetic *woos* from people who were there solely for scholarly purposes. I pressed on anyway. "Thanks everyone, this next one is a song by Box Car Racer," I said.

I started to play "There Is." Once again, people's interest died off pretty quickly. *This is another shit choice. Who the fuck even knows who Box Car Racer is? They want Blink-182. They want anything off* Enema of the State *or* Take Off Your Pants and Jacket. *They* don't *want any of Tom's goddamn side-projects.*

I reached the end of the song and heard an even smaller clamor of applause. The sweat began to seep through the t-shirt underneath my quarter-zip pullover. The stage lights raised the temperature by a few degrees, but I knew the sweat was mostly from playing in front of Emily. Only about fifteen percent of the audience remained focused on me, and even Emily's face began to display a little boredom. I was only halfway through my set, and Emily was seconds away from opening her laptop and writing her paper.

I had to soldier on. "So, this is a song I wrote about a girl I had a crush on in high school. I never really had the courage to talk to her, and oddly enough, the second I got to college I wrote a song about her. I think it was because, at that point, I knew it was never gonna happen. . . ." I heard a few claps from the audience, and one (probably lonely) guy gave a spirited *woo*. "Anyway, this song is called 'Kayleigh.'"

I began playing, and something great happened: this time, the audience was paying me their undivided attention. The several people who had zoned out were pulled back in by my poorly constructed narrative about high school romance. Nearly all of the eyes in the room were on me. *You're doing it,* I told myself. *You're a fucking star. Emily is eating this up! She's bound to say yes when you ask her out! I wonder what our wedding will be like.*

The entire audience burst into applause as soon as I finished. Over my four years at JMU, I would play on that stage countless times, but aside from singing "Hey Jude" for karaoke night, this was the most applause I got for a show. It made me a little too confident for my final song.

Unfortunately, I'll never forget what I said next.

"Thanks a lot, guys. This next song is a middle school anthem, you all know it. I want to dedicate this one to the girl in the back. Emily, you mean a great deal to me."

I jumped right into "Chasing Cars" without fully knowing the impact of the verbal cancer that had just left my mouth. Since the song was a last-minute addition to my setlist, I hadn't practiced it at all, and it sounded pretty bad. But that's the thing about middle school anthems: nobody cares if they sound good, they just care about whether or not they can sing along. Nearly the entire room was singing every word. Everyone, that is, but Emily.

Emily was in the back with a mortified frown on her face. It was as if she'd called her teacher "Mom" on the first day of school, and then the teacher fired back by telling the class every one of Emily's most personal fears. She looked like she wanted to be anywhere else in the world but also didn't want anyone to know she wanted to be anywhere else in the world.

I played through the entire song without stopping, even though Emily looked upset and I was butchering every third chord. As soon as I finished, the crowd broke into applause. I said, "Thanks, guys," unplugged my guitar and amp, and approached Emily immediately.

"So, what did you think?"

Emily's mortified expression had been replaced with a calm smile; she didn't seem upset, but she wasn't acting like her cheery self. "It was good," she said. "Can we head back now?" She was already putting her backpack on.

"Oh . . . yeah. Do you not want to stay and watch the rest of the performers? Or maybe grab some food?"

"Nah, I've got to finish this paper and get to bed. You know, busy week."

"Oh, yeah, definitely."

I grabbed my guitar and amp, which felt twice as heavy as they had on the walk over. Emily walked toward the exit, and I followed her. She kept the same pace as me, but at the same time she felt miles away.

"Thanks again for helping me with my paper," she said. "It was really nice of you."

"Oh, yeah. No problem at all." *Why aren't we talking about my grand gesture? Did she not even notice it? Was it not grand enough? Shit. I totally blew it. Gavin told me to make a grand gesture and it was too small to even register on Emily's radar.*

I thought that if I said nothing for the rest of the evening, Emily would go back to her dorm and tell her roommate, "Something weird happened tonight. Cade said I meant a great deal to him during his set," and her roommate would respond, "Hmmm, that's weird. Guys are weird. Wanna eat ice cream and watch *Intervention*?" Then they would completely forget I made a tiny faux pas on stage, and that would be the end of it. Everything would return to normal the following day. My big gesture would have been for nothing.

"Are we not going to talk about it?" I asked.

She continued to look forward. "What?"

"Back there . . . what I just did."

"We don't have to—"

"Emily, I have feelings for you," I said, going all-in on this horrible romantic poker game. Emily was silent. The embarrassed expression on her face said she didn't want to talk about it, but I continued to talk about it. "So . . . do you feel the same way?"

"I'm really flattered," she said, looking down at her shoes, "but I really don't see you that way. I just got out of a long relationship, and getting into another is the last thing on my mind."

"Oh."

"It's not you, I'm really flattered. . . ."

I didn't pay attention to anything she said after that. I was devastated, but more surprised than anything. It didn't make any sense to me: she showered before I would go up to her room to help her with her homework, she played with her hair constantly while talking to me, and we sat on her bed together when we hung out. I'd never do any of those things for a girl I didn't have feelings for. You think I'd ever go out of my way to shower if I was just gonna hang out with Barb from *Stranger Things*? Guess again.

"Do you get what I'm saying?" she said, breaking me out of my stupor.

I had nothing left to lose. "Yeah. I get it. I've just been thinking about you a lot. I haven't been able to eat or sleep for days. I just thought we really . . . *clicked*. I didn't mean to freak you out," I said, almost certainly continuing to freak her out.

We got back to the dorm, and Emily opened the door for me. We walked inside and stood still in the hallway.

"Well . . . goodnight," she said as she turned to walk toward the elevator and away from this moment forever.

"Hey, still want to have that guitar lesson tomorrow?" I asked, standing as still as a tree, my amp and guitar in my hands. I already knew the answer, but I reluctantly gave it one final shot.

She pressed the elevator button. "Oh, no thanks," she said to the elevator doors. "I'm really busy this semester. Probably not the best time to start learning guitar." She tapped her foot.

"Oh, gotcha. Yeah. No worries." I lugged my equipment up the stairs to prevent any more awkward moments.

When I was eleven years old, I overheard a conversation my father had with an older gentleman; they were talking about girls they had dated in high school and missed opportunities. The older guy had said he was once in love with a girl who went to high school with him; they were close friends, nearly inseparable. But no matter how many opportunities came up for him to tell her how he felt, and no matter how badly he wanted to tell her, he never made a move. He then said something that I'll never forget: "I don't regret asking girls out or making stupid mistakes with money or jobs. I regret not acting on opportunities when they came up. There's no way anything that girl could have told me would make me feel worse than not knowing what could have been."

If that guy was still alive, I would tell him one thing: *YOU'RE FUCKING WRONG! HOLY FUCK DID YOU BLOW THE LIFE ADVICE PORTION OF YOUR FINAL YEARS!* I once had a kid in college tell me mac and cheese tasted better on a burger than Kraft Singles. That advice was *infinitely* better than the old guy's, and I've used it *way* more throughout the course of my life.

I've done a lot of stupid things under the influence of alcohol and woken up full of immense regret the next morning. That specific following morning, after a completely sober night of following my heart, was still worse than any hangover or drunk regret I've ever had.

I texted Delynn about what happened, and she sent me a package of homemade cookies the following week.

A month later, Emily went on a date with the man who would eventually be her husband.

On the plus side, Delynn makes really good cookies.

MAPS
By the Yeah Yeah Yeahs

June 2012

"They don't love you like I love you"

After several years, the day had finally come. On June 3, 2012, Chris and Delynn got married in the Charleston Aquarium in front of their friends, family, and the two best ushers a bride could ask for—or so Keith and I thought. We had front row seats to the love event of the century; two members of The Krazy Unikerns were getting married.

Keith, Chris, and I stood at the front of the venue's outdoor balcony, waiting for Delynn to take her walk down the aisle. The ocean was to our backs, but the saltwater air was all around us. Keith, Chris, and I exchanged glances as "Pachelbel's Canon in D" began. We all grinned. Then everyone in attendance looked toward the door to the aquarium as Delynn emerged in her wedding dress.

But I'm getting ahead of myself.

1 Day Earlier

Chris and Delynn had their rehearsal dinner at an Italian restaurant in downtown Charleston. The food was delicious, the tables were littered with pictures of younger versions of the couple, and everyone was enjoying the atmosphere. Chris and Delynn sat toward the front of the room at a large table with the best man, the maid of honor, and a few other members of the wedding party. Keith and I sat in the back corner next to the door, surrounded by Chris's groomsmen. Chris had just graduated from West Point Military Academy in New York; as a result, nearly all of his groomsmen were in the army. They were all very nice, but needless to say, there was a good amount of testosterone at our table.

One of Chris's groomsmen ordered rum and cokes for Keith and I, since we were underage. The waiter casually brought three drinks to the groomsman, as if he was going to drink them all himself. Then he gave two of them to us after the waiter walked away.

Keith grabbed my drink. "Don't worry, bud. I got you covered," he said, drinking from my glass.

The groomsman noticed our interaction. "Oh, I'm sorry man. I didn't know you don't drink. I didn't mean to make you feel uncomfortable."

"It's no problem," I said.

A slightly more intoxicated groomsman with a crew cut and a green army jacket joined the conversation. "Wait, why the hell don't you drink?" he slurred, sipping his gin and tonic.

I looked at Keith. He just shrugged. I turned back to the groomsman. "I just don't," I offered.

"Good thing he's got me," my best friend said, putting his arm around my shoulder and finishing off my rum and coke. It was true—between the two of us, we made one functioning adult.

After we ate our food, the guests were asked to give speeches regarding their favorite things about the happy couple. "I love how Chris and Delynn bicker in the most adorable way," Chris's friend from his high school said. "They argue a lot, but it's always so endearing."

Another groomsman approached Chris from behind and surprised him with a shot of vodka. "Okay, Chris, I'm gonna tell the Irish car bomb story, and then you are gonna take this shot!"

"Fuck," the groom-to-be said, burying his face in his hands.

The groomsman laughed and continued. "So, anyway, Chris loves to brag about how he doesn't vomit or get hangovers when he drinks, right? Well, there was one night when we all went out to the bar and had waaaaay too much to drink. Then Chris went and ordered an Irish car bomb to top it all off. The guys and I had to carry him to the parking lot; he couldn't even walk. Then right when we get to the car, he throws up everywhere! All over the car, our shoes . . . *everywhere*. And ever since, the Irish car bomb has become a drink Chris loathes. So I tried to get him one, but they were all out of stuff to make them . . . and any other bomb drink for that matter, so we got you a shot of vodka! Drink up, buddy!" He raised his own shot in the air and grinned ear to ear. Chris reluctantly raised his shot, took it, shook his head, and frowned when it was over. Delynn patted his arm with pride.

There was silence for a bit. I wanted to give a speech, but the moment had to be right. After a few seconds of thought, I realized following the Irish car bomb story would probably be my best chance to wow people. I stood up and asked for everyone's attention.

"When I first met Delynn, I was at a sleepover with her sister, Keith."

"You mean brother?" I heard someone shout.

"Oh, wow, I already messed up my speech . . . which really sucks because I'm a communications major."

Several people chuckled. *Saved it.*

"Anyway, I was at Keith's house when we were five, and he got put in time out."

"Ah shit! Calling your boy out!" the man in the green army jacket said, nudging Keith. Keith just sipped his rum and coke and shrugged again.

"Keith was sent to his room, and Delynn came to play a Thomas the Tank Engine board game with me. Ever since, she has always been super nice to me, like the big sister I never had. In ninth grade, I met Chris. Keith and I had just gotten *Rock Band* for the PS3, and we were playing guitar and drums, when Chris walks in and says, 'Is that Bon Jovi?' to which I responded 'Yes.' He then told me, 'I'm singing the next song.'"

Everyone laughed.

"And ever since then, I started to like Chris as much as Delynn. Maybe even more than Delynn."

That one got a lot of gasps from people who didn't understand how great that bit was, but the groomsmen loved it. Chris nodded in my direction and gave me a thumbs up. Delynn just laughed.

"Delynn, you know I'm kidding. And seriously, the four of us have been on so many adventures together. At no point were Chris and Delynn snobby adults who didn't want to hang out with two lame high schoolers. They always treated us like equals, and I'm very grateful for that. So if we could . . ." I lifted my water glass into the air. "Let's raise our glasses to Chris and Delynn. You guys are the couple I look up to the most, and an example of the relationship I hope to have someday. I hope the next several decades you guys spend together are at least half as good as the past four years you guys have spent with Keith and me. Cheers."

The rest of the night was quite pleasant; we got to hear more stories from old friends and enjoy a lovely Italian meal. At the end of the night, everyone went home to prepare for the big day. Delynn had vows to write, Chris and his groomsmen had bars to conquer and bottles to empty, and Keith and I had a lot of *Chappelle's Show* to watch. Keith's parents had rented a beachfront house we stayed in for the week; everyone but the male half of the bridal party returned there. Keith and I played pool across from the glow of the TV and wit of Dave Chappelle, while Delynn was a few feet away, writing her vows.

"Do you need any help, Delynn?" I asked as I shot the cue ball into the corner pocket, earning my third scratch of the evening. "I watched *50 First Dates* earlier this week if you want your vows to have flair."

Delynn smiled. "That offer is hard to refuse, but absolutely not."

"The nerve," I said, knocking the eight-ball in.

Keith laughed. "How are you this bad at pool?"

I ignored him. "Do you need any non-Sandler advice? I like to think I know what Chris likes."

"That makes two of us," Delynn sighed, crumpling a piece of paper.

"Maybe you should have written them last week like Chris did," Keith interjected. "Then you could be out at the bars like he is."

"Thank you for your input, both of you," Delynn said, so calmly you wouldn't know that two teenagers were badgering her mere hours before the biggest day of her life. "I'm gonna go finish these in my room," she said, already retreating down the hallway.

We returned to billiards and *Chappelle's Show*. After about an hour, Keith got a text.

"Chris is ready for us to pick him up," he said, looking up from his phone. He grabbed his keys and walked toward the door.

"Shotgun!" I shouted, already right behind him.

"I like Chevelle, I really do. I'm just saying I don't think any song can compare to 'Face to the Floor.' Nothing in their discography comes close."

"It's all great, dude. I'll play more. You'll get it," Keith promised, fidgeting with his iPod Nano.

I groaned. "We listened to them the entire eight-hour drive to Charleston. I like Chevelle, I just don't think of them as highly as you do."

We pulled up to the bar as "Black Boys on Mopeds" came on. We spotted the groomsmen standing in a group on the sidewalk out front. Chris was in front of them, sitting on the curb. A few of the groomsmen were playfully pushing each other and trying to start an impromptu game of leapfrog. One of them stood away from the group looking as pale as a ghost. I assumed he didn't want to join them out of fear of throwing up his Italian meal from earlier.

"Does it *feel* good when you drink?" I asked Keith.

"Every time," he said with a smile.

"You lose complete control of common sense, get sick, and act like fourth graders . . . and for what? It must feel fucking great."

"Don't knock it until you try."

"Fair enough," I said.

Chris saw us and walked toward the car.

"What's up, boys?" he said when he opened the car door to get in. He didn't appear as drunk as the groomsmen; he was able to form complete sentences and spoke at a reasonable volume. Everyone else was so loud they were attracting glances from families in the Applebee's parking lot next door.

"Are they gonna be okay?" I asked.

Chris smiled. "They might be hungover in the morning, but they've seen worse nights," he said.

The ride home was quiet. Chris kept requesting Keith play some Black Keys, but Keith remained adamant we hit our goal of three entire play-throughs of Chevelle's discography before the week was over. I thought about how far we had all come; it seemed like only yesterday we were all in Keith's basement playing *Rock Band* together. I remembered hearing the chorus to "In Bloom" for the first time in that basement. I remembered Chris choking on his drink while singing "Timmy and the Lords of the Underworld," and how he kept singing anyway. He was in tears by the end because he was laughing so hard. I remembered that any time one of us asked the question, "What is it?" the other three of us would respond with, "It's it," referencing "Epic" by Faith No More. I remembered hating metal of all kinds until Keith played me Avenged Sevenfold's "Afterlife." It was as if the Beatles had come back together and written an extremely catchy, harmonious hook for twenty-first century music.

It occurred to me on the ride home that, after the wedding,

everything would change. No longer would Chris and Delynn be waiting for me in the basement, plastic instruments in hand. They would most likely move away, play *Rock Band* much less, and eventually focus more on actual offspring than singing songs by the Offspring. I was happy for them but devastated for the future.

When we got back to the beach house, Keith turned off the car, and we all got out and walked toward the front door. It looked like the alcohol was finally starting to hit Chris, as he stumbled through his first few steps up the porch staircase.

Keith went inside ahead of us. I was walking behind Chris when he turned around and pulled me in for a hug. "Great speech today, man," he said.

"Your bride is especially beautiful today, Chris," one of Delynn's bridesmaids said with a smile.

"She looks like that every day," Chris assured her.

It was a beautiful, sunny, seventy-degree day at the South Carolina Aquarium in Charleston. The ceremony took place outside of the main building, on a lovely balcony overlooking the ocean. Keith and I were stationed on opposite sides of the bridal party, assisting all of the guests with any seating needs they may have. We had one job: keep the front two rows open for family. When a potentially mischievous group of twenty-year-olds sat in the second row, I told them to scram. That row ended up being unused and I looked like a jackass, but I was a jackass who did his job, nonetheless.

There was an acoustic guitarist to the left of the seats playing "Pachelbel's Canon in D." Everything was in place; we were just waiting on the bride. After the second verse of everyone's favorite wedding anthem, Delynn emerged at the top of the stairs leading to the balcony. She walked arm-in-arm with each of her parents and did indeed look more beautiful than ever. I looked at Chris as he watched Delynn walk down the aisle, and I swear I saw a lone tear fall down his cheek.

As soon as Delynn reached the aquarium's equivalent of an altar, the ceremony began. They each recited the vows they had written for each other. In front of their family and friends, they shared the reasons they fell in love and the reasons they would continue to love each other for the rest of their lives. They couldn't stop smiling. Seeing them so happy together now made me realize there was no way the future could be too bad. And even if it was, I'd always have Keith. I looked at my best friend; he looked back at me and grinned.

I'm not sure if you've ever been to the South Carolina Aquarium, but I'd be willing to bet you haven't seen a wedding reception inside it. It was the wildest combination of sea creatures and formal attire, and at the center of it all were two youngsters with a relationship everyone envied.

"They're gonna card you," I said.

"I still have to try," Keith replied.

"Do you really want to break the law at your own sister's wedding?"

"I really want to drink at an open bar," Keith whispered, eyeing the colorful display of liquor bottles stacked behind the bartender. He may not have been twenty-one, but he was taller than half of the groomsmen.

A moment later, he proudly walked back to me with what would be his first of twelve drinks that night. "Told you I could do it," was all he said.

We walked back to the dance floor area. There was a DJ booth set up in front of a wall full of live fish. Standing in front of the booth, with a microphone in her hand, was Kaleigh, Delynn's Maid of Honor. She faced the wedding crowd and shuffled through a stack of papers covered with notes.

"As most of you know, I was Delynn's roommate for most of her college career," she began. "Since Chris went to school in New York, and we went to school here in Charleston, they talked on the phone a lot." A few members of the audience chuckled. "I would occasionally joke with Delynn about whether or not her and Chris were running out of things to talk about. I walked into her room one night and caught her reading a book to Chris over the phone. I knew it was true love as soon as I saw the cover on the book. I won't embarrass Chris by telling you what book it was, but I will say it's a pretty popular fiction book enjoyed mostly by girls."

"Was it *Twilight*?" a drunk groomsman yelled.

"It was *Twilight*," Kaleigh replied, grinning.

"Ahhhhhh!" All of the groomsmen drunkenly cheered and laughed. The newlyweds just shrugged it off. Kaleigh eventually got to the last page of her speech and began to tear up. Delynn wiped a few tears from her own face when she made eye contact with her maid of honor.

Chris's best man's speech was a bit less intense.

"I'm not much of a speaker," he began, "but Chris has been my roommate for the past few years at West Point. He's always been a great guy. This one time, we went out for the weekend, and I left my wallet back home. Chris told me not to worry about it; he would pay for everything. That's just the kind of guy he's always been. Delynn, you picked a winner." We all raised our glasses; I raised my glass of Pepsi, and Keith raised his Long Island iced tea.

After that, we gathered around the dance floor to watch the father/daughter and mother/son dances. Delynn and her father danced to the Beatles' "All My Lovin'," while Chris and his mother danced to Aerosmith's "Dream On." I sat back and enjoyed the music. I've been to several weddings since that day, but Chris and Delynn's reception still takes the cake for the best soundtrack.

Everyone continued to eat, drink, and sing well into the

night. After Keith's tenth drink, he insisted we take several "bro pics," and I obviously obliged (how often were we gonna be in suits at the same time?). Chris and his groomsmen hit their peak drunkenness when they all huddled up in a large circle and sang Toto's "Africa" while wearing ridiculous hats from the photo booth. While Keith went to get another drink, Delynn found me sitting alone at a table, adoring the huddled testament to one of the greatest songs of the eighties.

"Having fun, hun?" she asked. Her dress reflected every color of the rainbow as the DJ's rig of lights danced along the white satin.

"You sure know how to throw a party for only twenty grand," I said, gesturing to the fish in the walls.

She smiled. "It would've been more expensive if the use of the aquarium didn't count as a tax write-off," she said and took a sip from her glass of champagne.

I paused. "You look beautiful, sis."

"Aw, thanks, Cade," she said, reaching out for a hug.

Keith came back from the bar with two Bud Lights. Before he could sit down, his father called him and Delynn over for a family photo. The four of them were gathering in front of the wedding photographer when Keith's father, Paul, motioned toward me. "Get the hell over here, Cade. You're part of the family too."

I ran over with a large grin on my face and joined my family.

The night eventually came to an end. The DJ packed up his gear, and Paul realized Keith was drunk and threatened to punish him (but he never followed through). For the newlyweds' exit, guests lined up on either side of the walkway leading out of the venue and held sparklers in the air, forming a tunnel of sparkling light for the bride and groom to walk through. Delynn has since mentioned that giving sparklers to a sea of drunk people and running past them may not have been the best idea, but the happy couple survived. They were picked up by a small carriage and carted away to their hotel for the evening. I stood next to my plastered best friend and watched them drive away.

"Do you think we'll ever play *Rock Band* together again?"

"Absolutely, brother."

And he was right.

TIMMY & THE LORDS OF THE UNDERWORLD

By Timmy & the Lords of the Underworld

December 2012

"Timmy!"

"I'm not singing that," Chris said.

I sighed. "You have to. It's a classic that reflects one of our absolute favorite *Rock Band* moments."

Keith nodded his head in agreement behind me.

"These should really be songs we all enjoy," Delynn chimed in. "Ones we've played more than all of the rest."

"Okay, fine," I conceded. "Here's the setlist: 'Say It Ain't So' by Weezer, 'In Bloom' by Nirvana, 'More Than a Feeling' by Boston—"

"Oh yeah, that one's a classic," interrupted Delynn.

"—then we go into 'Wanted Dead or Alive' and then 'Who Says You Can't Go Home' by Bon Jovi, the latter being Delynn and I's classic duet."

"Works for me," Delynn said from behind the plastic drum kit.

"Okay, that's plenty. Let's just play and we'll come up with more as we go," Chris said, clutching the microphone.

This was it. This was the last show the Krazy Unikerns would ever play together. Chris and Delynn would be boarding a plane to Germany the very next day, where they would live for the foreseeable future. This was the end of an era; I would no longer spend the holidays in Keith's basement, ecstatic about my *Rock Band* family and lamenting my lack of friends at my high school. The timing was appropriate, seeing as I was now in college and making tons of new friends, but no friends or memories will ever replace the ones I made with my bandmates in the Krazy Unikerns.

We played through all of the songs on expert difficulty. It was kind of surreal—it was almost five years before, to the day, that we had started playing *Rock Band* together in that very same basement. So much had changed in that time, and I couldn't imagine life without my three closest friends. We played like *Rock Band* veterans that night: Keith and I slammed our heads in sync with the guitars on the chorus of "Say It Ain't So," Delynn did a perfect Jennifer Nettles impression during our duet, and we all screamed "WANTED!" whenever Richie Sambora screamed it in "Wanted Dead or Alive."

Unfortunately, like all *Rock Band* sessions, we eventually had to stop playing. It was fitting that we ended with "Say It Ain't So," the very first song we had played together five years before. We put down our instruments and prepared for an emotional goodbye.

"The tour is over, boys," Chris said, smiling.

"It's been a pleasure," I said as I put my hand on Chris's shoulder. "And who knows? Maybe we'll have a reunion show in a decade or two."

"Definitely," he replied, and pulled me in for a hug.

Chris and I then pulled Delynn into our hug. "I'm . . . I'm really gonna miss you guys," I said.

"We'll miss you too," said Delynn. "Just remember: you have a free place to stay in Germany any time." She pulled back from the hug to make eye contact with me. Her facial expression matched everyone else's: a little smile that seemed to convey more gratitude for the past five years than sadness that they were over.

We walked together to the door. "When's the next time we're gonna see you?" I asked.

"It won't be long. We'll come back to visit occasionally," Delynn said.

"We'll see you even sooner if you come to Germany," Chris said, grinning.

Keith pulled everyone together for one final group hug. This would be the last time all four of us would be in the same place at once for the foreseeable future. Though we remained friends for years to come, nothing will ever replace the four of us playing *Rock Band* in Keith's basement.

The band had officially broken up.

TIME WE HAD
By the Mother Hips

March 2013

"Saw a rainbow beneath my feet,
flowing over the filthy street"

My second-to-least favorite quality about myself is that I believe in love at first sight. I'm aware it makes zero sense, and the odds are astronomical, but it's just the way I'm wired. Sometimes when I see a girl for the first time, my brain says, *Yep. You're not going to be able to think about anyone else for the next few months at the very least. And you won't be using me at all during any interaction with her moving forward. Best of luck.*

My least favorite quality about myself is how I involuntarily envision how I'm going to propose to each "love at first sight" girl after six minutes of knowing her.

For Laura, I immediately knew I was going to get my friends to play a small, three-man concert with me at a house party or tiny venue. Our last song would be Green Day's "2,000 Lightyears Away," and during the bass/drum breakdown, I would walk off the stage and pop the question to her in the audience.

I met Eileen in the campus movie theater, Grafton, when we both joined the University Program Board (UPB). I immediately formed my proposal plan: years later, I would invite as many people as I could from the committee initiation meeting to come back to Grafton to surprise Eileen with a huge party and a ring.

For Allison, I planned on taking her to JMU's Taylor Down Under, where we saw our first live comedy show together. I would somehow arrange with the entertainer that evening to let me get on stage and ask Allison to marry me before his or her act.

Needless to say, this has never been a productive impulse.

I had been dating Allison for about six weeks. We listened to music together, got dinner together, played guitar together, and even made out a few times. We didn't have a lot in common, but I enjoyed spending time with her—even though the anxiety I got just from dating a girl made me throw up constantly. I would muster up enough energy to eat about one meal a day, then immediately run to the nearest restroom because I was too anxious to keep any of it down. I lived off soup and apple juice for nearly fifty days.

After almost eight weeks, I was starting to feel more comfortable around her. I was beginning to think we may have a future together that didn't involve so much vomit. I daydreamed about our future while I sat at my desk in my 1 p.m. philosophy class, waiting to take the exam. I hadn't had time to prepare myself for the test due to all of the time I was spending with Allison, so I had planned to study in class right before the exam. But I ended up thinking about Allison instead. I was perplexed as to how anyone dating in college was able to graduate at all.

As the professor began to pass out the exam, I got a text from Allison: "Hey, can you come over this afternoon? I want to talk about something." My heart sank and my head whirled. *There's no way this can be good. The sentence "I want to talk" almost exclusively means either "I'm pregnant," or "I want to break up." And we haven't had sex.*

I replied, "Sure, but just so I can brace myself: is this a good or bad talk?"

Her response was, "It's both good and bad."

I spent about five minutes on my test before I realized I couldn't think about anything other than this talk, so I turned in my mostly blank exam and walked out of the classroom.

Allison lived on the other side of campus, which was about a twenty-minute walk. I put on my headphones and scrolled through my music until I found something heavy enough to take my mind off my problems. I settled on the Deftones' "Headup" and nearly ran across campus. In spite of the music, I couldn't stop worrying. *Why does she want to break up with me? What did I do? I thought I did everything right! I bought her flowers, chocolate, and a stuffed animal for Valentine's Day, and she really liked those. Maybe it was too much? It* was *our first date. . . .* The lyrics to the aggressive nu metal song rang in the background of my paranoia: "This has begun/You seem to have some doubt/I feel you next to me, feeling it/Getting spacy with the common love of music . . ."

I have often attempted to use logic to soothe my paranoia, but it rarely works. I tried it as I trudged across campus. *I have no reason to believe it won't work out,* I reminded myself. *Think back. Why didn't it work out with Kayleigh? Because I was too scared to talk to her ninety-nine percent of the time. I definitely talk to Allison, so no problems there. Check. Why didn't it work out with Penny? Because I never made a big enough romantic gesture. I bought Allison thirty dollars' worth of Valentine's Day presents and asked to kiss her the night of our second date; she knows I like her. Check. Why didn't it work out with Emily? Because I made too big of a romantic gesture. Fuck. Is thirty dollars too much to spend on Valentine's Day gifts?*

I continued to run as fast as my brain generated thoughts. *Maybe it's the fact that I text her every day. Maybe that's too much. I just want her to know I'm thinking about her. Or maybe I try to kiss her too much. Have I been too aggressive? I asked every time before we kissed to make sure it was okay, but . . . maybe that's it! Asking before kissing is hardly romantic. She probably wanted me to be more confident.* I was removed from my trance by a car that honked at me for walking directly in front of it without paying attention. I waved to show my appreciation for not killing me, then went back to losing myself in the music: "Walk into this world with your head up high . . ."

"Hey, I'm here. You wanted to talk?" I asked as she let me into her dorm room. I looked past her to see her roommate folding laundry.

"Hey, yeah. Sorry, I didn't know Angie would be here, why don't we go to the study room down the hall?"

I nodded. My mouth was too dry to form words. I followed her down the poorly lit hall that students paid far too much tuition for. Neither of us said a word; it was like being led to a public execution. I hoped there would be people in the study room, and that she would say, "Oh, I guess I can't do this today! Let's just get dinner and forget I ever texted you."

We entered the completely empty study room; I sat in a rather uncomfortable wooden chair. She sat across from me in a chair also designed for minimal comfort. The room had two windows that let the hue of the overcast weather fill the room. It was the perfect room for receiving bad news.

She sat up straight and folded her hands over her lap. "So I went away this weekend and thought about . . . us. . . ." She said each statement as if it was rehearsed.

"And?" I choked.

"I don't feel like I'm in love with you."

"Allison, it's been six weeks."

"I don't feel like I'll ever be in love with you," she said, looking at her feet.

"Oh," I replied. I looked down at my hands on my lap.

"Yeah."

"Well . . . you said you had good news too?" I asked. I looked up at her with a tiny glimmer of hope.

"Yeah! I still want to be friends!" she said with a smile that would have made you think she had single-handedly ended apartheid.

"Oh. Cool."

"Yeah! We can still hang out and stuff whenever we're both free. My schedule is really busy this semester, but I'm sure we can work something out!"

"Oh, all right. I'm sure we can do that."

"Great! I'm glad we talked!" she said as she stood.

I stood up too. "Cool. . . . Well, I'll see you around," I mumbled.

"Great!" She opened up the door to let me out.

I waved goodbye as I walked down the hallway. I remember it being dark out as I walked home, but I think that's because I blocked out everything around me. I just walked home slowly and tried to process what happened. *What the hell is wrong with me? What did I do wrong? I have no idea how any of this works; people walk all around campus holding hands, falling in love, and having other people fall in love with them as if it's not the most difficult thing to do in the world.*

At times like this throughout my life, I often think back to the episode of *The Simpsons* where Bart sells his soul. He has a recurring dream in which his classmates are rowing boats across a large body of water to some form of paradise. Everyone except Bart traverses the sea with a transparent version of themselves, representing their soul. Bart is left at the shore, unable to travel without his counterpart. That is exactly how I felt in that moment, walking home from Allison's dorm; everyone around me was pairing off with a partner while I stood idle, unable to do what seemed so easy to them.

The last time Allison and I ever spoke was a month later, when she asked me if she could borrow a sled; I told her my roommates and I didn't have one.

WANTED DEAD OR ALIVE
By Bon Jovi

March 2013

"Sometimes you tell the day by the bottle that you drink"

"This song sucks," my father said from the driver's seat.

It was a sunny day and we were on the way to my best friend's house. My father criticized my music taste from behind his sunglasses while snacking on a bag of pistachios. I was controlling the music from the passenger seat with my mp3 player. The new Bon Jovi album had just come out, and like any good fan, I listened to it on repeat. "What's wrong with it?" I inquired defensively.

He took one hand off the steering wheel to wave around while speaking, as he often did when lecturing my sister or me. "The only good Bon Jovi song is 'Runaway.' The rest are garbage."

"You've only listened to thirty seconds of this song—"

"I know a bad song when I hear it." He placed his hand back on the steering wheel.

"Fine," I said, hitting the skip button. "Give Me Novacaine" by Green Day started playing. "How about some punk rock?" I offered.

"This isn't punk rock," my dad scoffed. "They have fireworks at their shows for goodness sake." The glare from the sun bounced off his sunglasses.

"They told George Bush to fuck off in an interview. That's punk rock!" I declared.

He shook his head. "Real punk rock rebels against music, not politics. The Ramones and the Replacements are punk rock."

I threw my hands in the air. "They're rebelling against the thing they love doing? The thing that millions of people worship them for? That's dumb as shit." The car slowed down as we got off the main road and entered Keith's neighborhood. My father continued with his self-proclaimed wisdom.

"It's real, it's scaled down. They're rebelling against the industry that destroys art for the sake of making billions of dollars. The same industry that pays an arm and a leg to give Bon Jovi a chance to put out a thirteenth album."

"You bought me the album!"

"You wanted it as a gift. What was I gonna do, say no? I felt guilty walking out of the store with it, though. I would have rather bought your sister tampons."

I folded my arms. "Whatever."

"We're here. I'm going to pick you up at three tomorrow. Sound good?"

I grabbed my backpack and opened the car door. "Yeah."

"All right, have fun. I love you."

"Love you too." My father and I could argue about anything for hours and then act as if it never happened just seconds later. It's one of the greatest strengths of our relationship.

I walked toward the front door of Keith's childhood home in Alexandria, VA. After I moved to Harrisonburg to attend college, I was unable to visit the house where Keith and I learned how to stay up all night, use Limewire, and play *Rock Band* as frequently as I would have liked, so I seized every opportunity I could. However, this was no ordinary visit.

Allison had just dumped me, and in my distraught frustration at being rejected yet again, I had texted Keith: "I'm sick of feeling shitty about myself. Get a case of beer. I'm finally gonna drink with you." Keith was beyond excited. I was finally ready

to break free from the shackles of my rule-filled Catholic up-
bringing. My mother had warned me about the dangers of alcohol my whole life, but Keith had been drinking since he was
fourteen and he seemed all right. He *had* broken into our old
preschool a few years prior to drink with some friends, which
did lead to his parents receiving a late-night call asking them
to pick him up from the local police station . . . but other than
that, no downsides to alcohol. To be completely honest, in this
particular moment, I would have sooner accepted a five-year
prison sentence than another rejection from a girl.

I knocked on Keith's door, and he opened it seconds later.
He greeted me with his usual celebratory warmth.

"Brother!"

I went in for a hug. "Good to see you, man."

"I've got the goods downstairs," he said, inviting me inside.
We walked downstairs into his basement, and he pulled out a
case of Budweiser from behind his fridge. "As soon as my parents fall asleep, we can drink this whole case!"

I didn't know how much beer I'd be able to drink, but I was
fairly certain it wasn't going to be half a case. "I'll see what I
can do, brother."

After a few hours of *Rock Band*, Keith went upstairs and
confirmed his parents had in fact gone to bed. He returned to
the basement with a grin on his face and brought the case of
beer out from behind the fridge. He was about to crack open
his first beer when we heard a knock on the basement door.
Keith put down his beer and opened the door to reveal his two
friends, Nelson and Jimbo.

"What's up, man!" Jimbo said, grabbing Keith's hand to
pull him in for an embrace. Nelson followed behind him into
the basement.

When Keith enlisted in the Marine Corps, he had met some
very *interesting* people. Some were great, and others . . . not so
much. Nelson and Jimbo were basically the conglomerate of

every douchebag I went to high school with; I had no idea why Keith enjoyed their company.

After they all shared a couple of bro hugs, they walked over to my side of the basement.

"What's up, Cade?" Nelson said, nodding at me.

"Hey, dude," I replied with a tiny wave.

Jimbo shook his head. "Yo, Keith, you only got one case? That's not gonna be enough to get us fucking hammered."

"Yeah, ever since I joined the Marines I need at least a six-pack to even feel a buzz," Nelson said. It was like Testosterone Fest 2k13.

Keith sat down and pulled the case of beer in front of his feet. "Well, this is all I could take without my dad noticing, and since none of us are twenty-one, it's gonna have to fucking do."

Everyone grabbed a beer while I sat in the corner. I was still hesitant; I had been conditioned against drinking ever since I was a child, and it was a lot of guilt to shake off.

After everyone took a few sips, Jimbo looked over at me. "What's wrong, dude? You don't drink?"

In that moment, I thought about Allison, I thought about Emily, I thought about Penny, and I thought about every other girl I had ever been remotely infatuated with. Aside from all the downsides I had heard about alcohol, I had heard one very compelling upside: complete numbness. "Fuck it, I'll have one," I said.

"All right, Cade!" Keith cheered as he tossed me a beer. I took a sip and tried not to cringe. I was tired of feeling shitty, and I came to the realization that I would do just about anything to stop feeling that way, no matter how bad my first Budweiser tasted.

We played video games for an hour, and I finished two entire beers. I didn't feel much different, but I was enjoying myself, which was the goal for the evening. So . . . success!

Nelson had a few more than me. "Jimbo," he said, "you guys have gay-offs over in Iraq?"

"Hell yeah, dude! That shit's hilarious!"

"What's a gay-off?" Keith asked.

"It's when you and one other guy do gay shit to each other until one bitches out," Nelson laughed. He turned to me. "Cade, never challenge me to a gay-off. You'll fucking lose."

"Why would I want to challenge you to a gay-off?"

"Because you'd fucking lose, bitch!" Nelson pulled down his pants and shook his testicles about a foot away from my face. Keith and Jimbo laughed. I wasn't terribly offended; I had seen plenty of drunken scrotum displays in college. At this point I must have seen Gavin's at least four times.

"Why would that be fun?"

"Told you he wouldn't fucking get it," Nelson said.

"Fuck off, Nelson," Keith defended me.

Jimbo changed the subject. "Hey Cade, what are you studying in college?"

"I'm a communications major." I sipped my beer.

"So you do, like, communications for the Marines?"

"No, I do public speaking and stuff like that. Interpersonal, family communication, etc."

"Couldn't you do all of that for the Marines?"

"I don't know, I've never thought about that."

"Well, you fucking should. I got to kill a guy over in Iraq."

"What was it like?" I asked.

"Fucking rewarding. Imagine studying for a communications test for over two years and then finally getting to take it."

"Sounds fucking boring," I told him. I was quickly discovering the alcohol was eating away at my filter. I felt like I should probably focus more on what I chose to say, so as to not offend the greatest minds of our time.

"You're right, Nelson. He doesn't fucking get it."

"Fucking bitch!" Nelson yelled and pulled down his pants to flash us his bare asshole. Keith and Jimbo laughed again. Nelson pulled up his pants and bowed as if he had done something of merit. "Yo, Keith, we should launch some fireworks!"

"Fuck yeah we should!" Keith said, getting up and walking to the door that led to his backyard.

Even in my slightly intoxicated state, I was very opposed to this idea. Keith lived in a neighborhood that could only be described as *full of people*; not to mention his parents were asleep two stories above us. I obviously wasn't going to voice my opinion because I was already watching my words, and I had no interest in finding out what Nelson thought the next step in a "gay-off" was. I followed the three of them as they drunkenly carried fireworks into Keith's tiny yard. Keith grabbed the first one and ignited it. To their credit, drunkenly watching fireworks in suburbia on a weeknight was pretty fucking rad to see. Unfortunately, "pretty fucking rad" breeds noise, and noise breeds . . .

"What the fuck are you guys doing?!" a very large and disgruntled neighbor shouted as he climbed over the fence into Keith's yard.

"Nothing," Nelson said, throwing the remaining fireworks back inside the basement.

"Are you launching fucking fireworks into my backyard!?"

"No, we're just drinking. Mind your own business," Nelson said, approaching the very intimidating gentleman. Keith and Jimbo followed behind him, while I hid behind the safety of the basement door. Fortunately, the top half of the door had a window in it, so I could still see and hear everything going on.

"You better not be lying to me, kid," the neighbor snarled. "I want a real explanation for why I have a fucking bottle rocket in my goddamn yard," the neighbor said as he pushed Nelson.

Keith and Jimbo gasped as they saw Nelson's eyes light up in a fit of rage. "Don't you dare fucking touch me, asshole!" Nelson screamed, staring the neighbor down with the power of a thousand suns.

This was it. Nelson was going to beat the shit out of Keith's neighbor, we were all going to go to jail for underage drinking, and I was never going to be hired by anyone other than Burger King.

My mother had been right all along. In this moment of utmost desperation, I vowed I was never going to drink again.

"Keith, I know your parents. I know you're not twenty-one, and I've got a good feeling your friends aren't either. How would you feel if I woke them up right now and told them what you're doing?"

Keith froze in place. Nelson, however, continued perfecting the role of worst person to speak on behalf of the group. "Why don't you mind your business, asshole? We weren't launching fireworks."

"Why don't you three follow me into my fucking yard, and I'll show you the goddamn bottle rocket?"

"Fine, let's go," Nelson said, now taking on the role of worst person to lead the group into an aggrieved neighbor's yard.

I snuck out of the basement door and made my way over to the fence so I could get a glimpse of the action. I saw the neighbor hold up a bottle rocket firmly in front of Nelson's face. "What does this look like to you?"

"A bottle rocket," Nelson said. His voice had dropped from a yell to something barely above a whisper. He placed his hands in his pockets and looked at his feet.

"That's what I thought," the neighbor said. He moved to stand just inches away from Nelson's face. "What do you have to say for yourself?"

"Sorry . . ." Nelson whispered.

"What was that?"

"I said I'm sorry, asshole!" Nelson yelled as he took a step back.

The neighbor threw the bottle rocket on the ground. "Why don't you boys come inside with me," he said, leading my friend and the two others into his basement.

This was it. My best friend and two other people I kind of knew had pissed off the man living next door, and now he was going to dispense vigilante justice on three kids in his murder basement. *Oh please God, if this guy is gonna go Jigsaw on them, please let Keith survive. If Nelson has to be mutilated, so be it.* I anxiously paced behind the fence for what seemed like hours. But after about fifteen minutes, the three of them walked out of the basement. Not only did they have all of their limbs, but they each had a full fucking mug of beer. They walked back into Keith's yard, but not before the neighbor poked his head out of the basement door and called out, "Thank you boys for your service."

You gotta be fucking kidding me.

Though I was technically speechless, I somehow found a way to ask Keith a question: "How in the *fuck* . . . ?"

Nelson and Jimbo looked at me with raised eyebrows and puzzled faces like I was speaking another language. Then they walked past me back into Keith's basement.

Keith walked up to me. "What's up, buddy?"

"How the fuck did you do that? He was so pissed off at all of us! We were . . . I mean . . . jail!"

"I love you man, but have you ever thought you worry too much?" Keith chuckled, then took a sip of his beer and walked inside.

As Keith opened the door, I heard Nelson brag, "If I wouldn't get court-martialed for it, I would have kicked his fucking ass, dude!" Then the door closed.

I stood speechless for another five minutes, thinking about the desperate vow I had made only moments before to never drink again. Then I walked back inside and cracked open another can of my new favorite beverage.

WAVE OF MUTILATION
By the Pixies

September 2013

"Cease to resist, giving my goodbye"

My favorite show throughout high school and college was *Dexter*. For those of you who haven't seen it, it's a SHOWTIME program about a serial killer who only kills criminals. I began my obsession in the summer of 2009, three years after it was released; once I caught up, I watched every episode habitually the day after it aired. Even though season eight was the worst collection of episodes I had ever seen on television, when the final episode released, I was willing to give my favorite show the benefit of the doubt. Not just because it was the series finale, but because I was watching it with Eileen.

Eileen was the most incredible girl on campus. She was beautiful and didn't flaunt it, smart but wouldn't admit it, and loved *Game of Thrones* more than anyone I've met to this day. She was part of the University Program Board (aka the UPB) with me, and she had told me the previous week that she had just started watching *Dexter*. She finished all of it in less than two weeks. At the time, that was the sexiest thing I had ever heard.

I was spending my Sunday afternoon at work in Grafton, mustering up the courage to text her and ask if she'd watch the finale with me.

I argued with myself over and over.

What if she says no?

Then I'm literally in the same position I am right now, and I'll have a fun time watching it on my own.

What if the finale is bad?

How could it be bad? Showrunners get paid millions of dollars to ensure that shows are at least average; there's no way they'd let the finale of the channel's most profitable show be bad.

By the end of the debate, I liked my odds.

"Hey, any chance you'd wanna watch the *Dexter* finale tonight?" I texted Eileen.

She responded within minutes: "Uggghhhhh, I'd love to, but I have soooooo much homework."

"Screw homework, when you graduate are you gonna remember studying or watching the greatest finale of all time with your friend?"

This wasn't the last time I would use the "What will you remember when you graduate?" argument on Eileen, but it *was* the only time I remember it working.

"Haha, okay that's a good point," she texted back. "How about you come to my dorm at 8? We can grab dinner next door and watch it together."

I felt like I had won five grand from a two-dollar lottery scratcher. I had asked to watch TV with her, and I somehow had finagled dinner out of the deal. I was excited, but I knew I had to play it cool.

"I like food, that works for me!" *Well done, Cade! Everyone likes food, way to blend in!*

I had to text Julian to let him know I was bailing on our plans.

"Hey, I can't watch *Breaking Bad* with you tonight."

"What the fuck, man? Why?"

"The *Dexter* finale is on tonight and I'm gonna watch it with a UPB friend," I texted.

"I can't believe you're passing up a much better show for that shit."

"It's my favorite show, and she said she wanted to watch it with me."

"Ohhhhh, this is for a girl. Why didn't you say so? Remember, you can't come home until you get to second base."

I closed my phone and thought about both the possible implication of Julian locking me out of our apartment and whether or not he knew that he had in fact made an amazing baseball pun, but I quickly went back to thinking about Eileen and *Dexter*.

I met her at her dorm a couple hours later. She greeted me at the door, dressed in a JMU sweatshirt and shorts. Her hair was messy, and she had clearly been studying a while, most likely in a dimly lit room where the laundry hadn't been touched for a few days. She had hypnotic brown eyes that matched her brown hair, and the perfect shade of tan skin. She never wore makeup; I don't know how she did it, but she was always beautiful no matter how she dressed or how stressed out she got over schoolwork.

I was the opposite. I almost exclusively wore things that either didn't match or were out of style. My mother always said women don't care about looks if you have a good personality, but over the course of my life I've come to find she *fucking* lied.

"Hey," she said with a smile. She invited me into her dorm room. She had a couch in front of a small TV, and her desk was littered with accounting textbooks and a Mac laptop with a spreadsheet on the screen.

"Hey! Ready for tonight?" I asked.

"Of course! I just watched last week's episode yesterday," she said, grabbing her wallet off her desk.

"What did you think?" I asked.

She locked her door, and we began walking. "It's not my favorite season," she admitted, "but I'm curious to see where it goes. What's your favorite season?"

"Season four, hands down. John Lithgow was incredible as

the Trinity Killer. I can't watch him in anything else anymore without thinking he's about to butcher someone. *Third Rock from the Sun* is ruined for me forever."

"Yeah, that was a good one," she agreed. "Deb's my favorite character. That's why this season has been rough for me; she just seems so miserable all the time."

"I'm sure they'll give her a respectable ending. She's an important part of the show," I stated. (Spoiler alert: I was completely wrong.)

After more Dexter dialogue, we arrived at PC Duke's dining hall, grabbed our food, and sat down at a patio table outside. I got nachos, and she got spaghetti.

After talking for about twenty minutes about the show, I felt comfortable enough to move past small talk, but I was still a little nervous. "Since we're sharing something as important as the *Dexter* finale," I ventured, "we might as well get to know each other a little better. Tell me about yourself, Eileen." My voice was so shaky you would have thought I was asking a question at my first job interview, but Eileen didn't seem to notice.

"Ummmmm . . ." She looked up and bit her lip. "Well," she looked back down at me and smiled. "I've been to Disneyland twenty-two times."

"Holy fuck, really?" I asked, wide-eyed.

She shrugged. "Yeah. It's the happiest place on Earth. What's your favorite movie?"

I smiled. "*Signs*. The M. Night Shyamalan alien movie," I said. I expected the same backlash I usually received from most people.

She furrowed her brow. "I haven't seen that one. What's it about?" she asked as she took another bite of pasta.

As I explained my favorite film to her, I realized Eileen had inadvertently gotten spaghetti sauce on her chin and didn't wipe it off. Here was this beautiful girl, so genuinely interested in what I had to say about a movie most people disliked that she didn't even realize she had food on her face. I had never seen any other girl talk to me with food on her face. Eileen wasn't like the rest. She was beautiful and smart, but she also got food on her face. She wasn't perfect. She was just a regular person, and I could talk to her like she was a regular person.

"That sounds pretty good," she said. "My favorite is *The Graduate*, although I did just watch *Pulp Fiction* with my friends and that was really great."

"I've never seen *The Graduate*," I said.

"What? It's like the perfect movie! We *have* to watch it."

"Let's focus on *Dexter* first," I said, trying to contain the excitement building in my chest that someone like Eileen wanted to watch movies with me. If she had asked me to play *Rock Band* in that moment, I might have dropped the L word.

We finished our meals and walked back to her dorm. When we walked into her room, she told me to sit on the couch and make myself comfortable, so I did. She grabbed her laptop from her desk and pulled up the link to the episode. She sat close to me on the couch. Really close. I wondered if I should put my arm around her. *No,* I scolded myself. *I'm here as a friend. I'm not going to fuck it up. Tonight is about* Dexter*, not second base.* The episode started. Eileen looked at me and smiled. My neurotic thoughts escaped me all at once as I watched the opening credit sequence to the final episode of my four-year life investment. This was it. This was the last time I would be watching original *Dexter* content.

We didn't talk for the entirety of the episode. We laughed, we cheered, and as most fans of the show can confirm, we made a lot of confused facial expressions. The episode ended after an hour, and we were both speechless.

"That was . . ." I couldn't finish my sentence.

"Bad?" Eileen replied.

"No, not bad . . . I just need to think about it for a while. I'm sure that's one of those endings that will make sense after you think about it for a long time." Again, I was completely wrong. Eileen was right: that episode was garbage. I had just watched the final hour of my favorite addiction and could not have been more let down.

"Why did he become a lumberjack?" Eileen asked.

"Again, I really think it's one of those endings that you have to think about," I said with certainty.

"Well, I guess I'll think about it after I do my homework," she said, looking at the clock on her wall with a defeated expression.

"Yeah, I should head home. Thanks for your hospitality. I had a lot of fun tonight." I smiled.

"Me too! We'll have to watch *The Graduate* soon." She got up and walked toward the door with me.

"Count me in," I said.

I was about to walk out of her room when I had an impulse to say something.

Okay, quick, before you say something, think it through. Why didn't it work out with Kayleigh? Because I was too scared to talk to her. I just had several conversations with Eileen. Check. Why didn't it work out with Penny? Because I went to JMU and was too far away to "be there for her." Eileen currently goes to JMU, so that won't be a problem. Check. Why didn't it work out with Emily? Because I made too big of a romantic gesture. I WILL NOT propose to Eileen right now. Check. Why didn't it work out with Allison? Because I questioned everything about our relationship instead of just being myself and being happy around her.

I looked at Eileen. *Don't think about it, just be yourself. Check.*

"Hey Eileen?"

"Yeah?"

"Earlier at dinner, you had food on your chin."

"Oh, I'm sorry," she said, touching her chin and frowning.

"Nooo no no no. It's not a bad thing. I just . . ."

Tell her it was the most adorable thing you'd ever seen a girl do. Tell her you think she's beautiful. Tell her you'll be thinking about her the entire goddamn walk home.

"I just think we're gonna be really good friends," I said.

She smiled. "I think so too."

"Pleasant dreams, Eileen," I said as I walked out the door.

The entire walk home I kept trying to think about the end of *Dexter;* it was truly the end of an era.

But it seemed like the start of something even better.

SEVEN
By Vagiant

February 2014

"I got your back until I die"

Every thought I had was about Eileen. I was even starting to lose sleep. It was only a matter of time before I would have to shout my feelings from the rooftops of JMU. Delynn had lived in Europe for over a year, and the time difference really affected how much I could call on her for advice in a timely manner. To prevent another Penny/Emily/Allison situation, I had called the only other person I knew who would help me without hesitation.

Emma, my sister, knocked on my door. "Hello, brother."

"Thanks for coming," I said and invited her into my room. "I need your help."

"Of course. What can I help with?"

Emma and I were both raised Catholic; we attended Catholic school from Kindergarten through the eighth grade, and it stuck with us as much as it did any of our friends. We weren't very religious through high school; Emma was too busy seeking attention from guys, and I was too busy hoping that one day I'd be able to talk to a girl I wasn't related to. When I got to JMU, I stopped going to church completely and started questioning everything my parents had raised me to believe. Emma decided to follow me to JMU, but the summer before her freshman year, she had a "revelation." She went on a youth group trip in upstate New York, and while she was there, she got a concussion. During her week-long stay in a nearly comatose state, she claimed she had seen God. When she returned home, she was a *completely* different person. She spent every opportunity she had trying to convert me, but I never bought into it.

But she was always there for me when I needed her.

I sat down on my bed and put my head in my hands. "I feel like my head's about to explode," I told her. "I can't stop thinking about Eileen. I can't eat, I can't sleep, I threw up two days ago because I knew I'd be spending the day with her yesterday. It constantly feels like there's a war going on in my head and I can't do anything right. I have to have a drink to get her off my mind." I gestured over to a bottle of rum on my nightstand. "I just want to say, 'Fuck it,' and tell her how I feel."

Emma looked around the room and back to me. "I'm sorry," she said. "I'm sure this isn't easy, but the best thing to do is take it slow. You remember what happened with Emily? Do you really want to do that again?"

I shook my head. "No, but if I keep holding all of this in, I might actually explode. She's coming over to watch *House of Cards* with me and the guys tomorrow. We're all gonna watch it, then I'll walk her to the bus stop and ask her out on a date. It's that simple."

"I know I can't stop you, but I really think that's a bad idea," she said with a frown.

"Why?"

She moved to sit next to me on the bed. "You'll tell her how you feel, and even if you don't overshare, you'll do something to move too quickly, and it will sabotage your friendship." She paused. "Do you enjoy spending time with her?"

"Yeah, I really do."

"Do you hang out by yourselves?"

"Sometimes. She often invites mutual friends to hang out with us, but I enjoy spending time with them too, so I'm not really bothered by it."

"Just take it slow. Treat her like a friend, and maybe one day she'll be comfortable enough around you to take the next step. Girls wanna marry their best friends."

"That seems wrong."

"It's not. I'm a girl."

"I need a drink—"

"Have you tried prayer?"

I looked at her in disbelief. "What?"

"Praying."

"No."

"Why not? Do you still believe in God?"

"I believe in God, but I don't believe in prayer."

"Why not?"

I sighed and looked at the floor. "I believe everything happens for a reason. Whether you pray or not, the outcome will be the same *every* time. I also can't rightfully pray to a God who makes it possible for me to feel like this. Why would I pray to someone who allows me to have these terrible feelings? Why would I pray to someone who lets parents lose children, or children lose parents? Every day people feel an unparalleled amount of hurt. Why would a benevolent God permit that?"

She smiled as though she'd heard that question many times before. "Bad things make the good things more enjoyable. If you feel that much hurt, it makes the happiness you feel all the better. You couldn't feel happy if you were never sad."

"What do you think about the story of Job?" I said.

She thought for a moment. "I think it's a great story of commitment and faith in God. Satan told God the only reason people believe in him is because they're already happy, so God took everything from Job to prove to Satan that wasn't the case, and Job stuck through it against all odds."

"I think God ruined a random guy's life to win a bet with the devil. Which is dumb."

"There's far more to it than that," she said with a patient smile.

"You're so smart for someone who believes in all of this shit!" I shouted, standing up from the bed. Emma gave me the same look of disappointment our mother had given us when we did something we weren't supposed to do as kids. I sighed. "I'm sorry," I said. "I didn't mean that. I haven't slept in a while."

"I know. I'm sorry you feel this way. But I've given you my advice—you can choose to take it or leave it. God gave us all free will, brother." Emma stood up and walked toward the door. "I'm gonna be late for class," she said, grabbing the doorknob.

"Hey, thanks. It really helps to talk about it."

"Always," she said, and she left the room.

DAY LATE, DOLLAR SHORT
By the Acro-Brats

February 2014

"Day late a dollar short"

Top Five Reasons Why It Will Never Work Out with Eileen:

1. She has a *ton* of attractive guy friends who are super rad. She introduces me to them, and even I think, *Fuck, these guys are hot and cool. I wonder if they like* Rock Band. Then I invite them to play *Rock Band,* and we all have a great time. But they might be trying to sleep with Eileen, and therefore I must hate them.

2. She brings up her ex-boyfriend . . . a lot. At least once every other time we hang out. She'll casually mention how he texted her something funny the other day, or how he was trying to plan a visit to JMU, or how she was thinking about going skiing in Vermont and staying with him.

3. She has severe song ADD. Whenever we're in the car together, she will listen to no more than sixty seconds of a song before she skips it, and it drives me nuts.

4. She comes from a wealthy family. They travel the world frequently, and she's literally been to Disney World dozens of times. My frugal lifestyle

full of Bud Light and Sam's Choice cola would never be enough for her.

5. Because I'm in love with her, and no matter how many reasons I come up with to take things slow, I'd still go on a date with her in a heartbeat, move too fast just like my sister said I would, and permanently ruin any potential shot at a relationship we had.

Fuck, I thought as Bruce walked into the living room on Saturday morning where I was hanging out after being awoken by my infatuation-induced insomnia.

"Hey, man," he mumbled, lightly massaging the side of his head. He grabbed the pot of coffee off the kitchen counter and poured himself a cup. Then he turned off the coffee maker and grabbed himself a glass of water.

"Hey, dude. How was you and Gavin's party thing the other night?"

Bruce hesitated. "It was . . . weird," he said, finally finding the word.

I sat up and closed my laptop. "Why? What happened?"

Bruce peaked down the hall to make sure Gavin's door was closed. "Well, you know how Brie has a thing for me? Something finally happened."

Bruce was referring to a girl he and Gavin had met in their history class. Like most girls, Brie had taken one look at Bruce and melted into a puddle of boy-crazy hormones. Also like most girls, she was nearly guaranteed to be let down by Bruce's shy and non-communicative nature. Nine out of ten times, a girl would see Bruce and immediately feel the need to do *anything* for him, and then Bruce would ruin the opportunities by either being too shy or verbally closed-off. Then Julian and I would simultaneously facepalm in frustration.

"We all got really drunk last night," Bruce continued. "Her,

Gavin, and I. We drank an entire handle of Goldschlager."

"Holy shit," I said, impressed. This was by no means a record for our apartment; we at one point had spent an entire year trying to drink every flavor of Burnette's Vodka that existed (the sugar cookie flavor was fucking gross). I was impressed because Goldschlager was a pretty expensive liquor to buy for only one night of binge drinking.

"Well, Gavin drank more than half of it. Anyway, we were all pretty drunk when Brie invited me back to her room."

"Nice. What did you do?"

"I followed her, and we made out on her bed. Things were about to go to the next level when Gavin decided to walk in."

"No way."

"Yep. It gets worse. He saw us making out and crawled into bed with us. He immediately fell asleep."

"Wow," was all I could say. This story was the most literal cock block I had ever heard. "Gavin's the worst."

"Yeah." He shrugged his shoulders and sipped his coffee. "Oh well, at least it's a good story." Bruce had one of the most forgiving personalities I've ever known. Nobody deserved to have him as a friend.

He grabbed his gym bag. "Welp, time to go work out."

"Aren't you hungover? How can you possibly think about working out?"

Bruce laughed. "If I took a day off every time I was hungover, I'd never go," he said. "I gotta keep up my routine. No pain, no gain!"

I, on the other hand, almost exclusively got my cardio from playing drums on *Rock Band*. "Cool. Have fun, dude."

"Always do," he said and walked out the door.

Shortly after Bruce left, my friend Damon and his roommate Billy walked into our living room with bags of fast food. "Heyooo," they both said as they walked through the door.

"What's up, guys?" I asked.

"It's Saturday. It's fast food and *Frasier* time," Damon said with a grin as he sat on the couch and opened his Hardee's bag.

"Shit, sorry, I forgot. Go ahead and put it on. I'll make my lunch."

I love *Frasier*. Oddly enough, I had never seen it until a year prior to that Saturday, when one morning, Billy had walked into our dorm room and announced, "Hey guys, I just beat Damon in a game of *Frasier*!" The rules of the game, he had told us, were fairly simple: "Whoever laughs the loudest when someone on *Frasier* tells a joke is smarter, and therefore wins!" We had all thought that was a pretty entertaining bit, and I've been a big fan of the show ever since. On most Saturdays throughout that year, Damon and Billy brought fast food over to our apartment and we would binge a few episodes.

After about an hour of Seattle's favorite psychiatrist, Damon took a bathroom break. Billy looked over at me jotting down notes on my "Top Five" list.

"What's up, man?" he asked. "You haven't been laughing at any of the jokes. You're losing *Frasier*."

"Sorry, I'm a bit distracted. It's Eileen."

"Ahh," he said.

Just then, Gavin walked into our living room, also flaunting fast food. "What's up?" he said to both of us as he sat down.

"Just watching TV," I said, not trying to begin a conversation—but I should have known better.

"You're not gonna believe what happened with Brie the other night."

This was a true statement, but probably not for the reason Gavin was thinking. "What happened?" Billy asked.

"So, me and Bruce got a handle of Goldschlager for Brie and her roommate. I offered to pay because I'm a gentleman."

"How chivalrous," I said, hoping the story would end there.

"Anyway, we drank, like, a ton of Goldschlager. We finished the whole bottle. Well . . . *I* drank most of it," he bragged. "Anyway, I threw up in the kitchen sink and Brie came over to help me—she has a thing for me."

"I thought she liked Bruce," I said.

"Nah, she's just really nice to him. I think she's trying to let him down easy. Anyway, her roommate went to bed and she set up a place for me to sleep on the couch, because I was super trashed. Bruce and Brie went back to her room, but I followed. They were just sitting on the bed not doing anything, so I sat down next to Brie and tried to make a move. She was saying super suggestive things and totally wanted to have a three-way; we probably could have if Bruce had a little more experience."

Billy stifled a laugh. I could tell he knew this was a fake story even without hearing the real one.

"So . . . that's all that happened?" I asked.

"Yeah, we just all went to sleep in her bed. It was weird." Gavin finished his story, got up to grab a Gatorade, and returned to his room.

"Should we tell Bruce he could have had a three-way?" Billy asked, smiling.

"I think it's better he doesn't know. This could destroy him," I answered while shaking my head and rolling my eyes. Billy turned back to the TV, and I turned my attention back to my journal.

Billy looked over at me again. "When did you meet Eileen?"

"Like, late 2012. Why?"

"In *Frasier*, it took Niles eight years to win Daphne, you know. Sometimes, waiting is the best solution."

"It sure does make for good television," I agreed. That was comforting. *Maybe I don't end up with Eileen today, or even tomorrow*, I thought. *Maybe it happens eight years down the line, just like with Niles and Daphne.* I put away my journal, started another episode of *Frasier*, and began counting the days until 2020.

CHERUB ROCK
By The Smashing Pumpkins

February 2014

"*Freak out*"

Like many people, I left college with several irreplaceable memories I will carry with me until the day I die. I was lucky enough to go through college with two of my closest friends, I joined an organization full of incredible people, and I got a job at a theater that basically paid me to watch movies and make enough friends to fill a room whenever I wanted to play *Rock Band*.

Also like many people, I have a few regrets (as I'm sure you've come to notice) from the best four years of my life. I don't regret the things most people do, like taking certain classes, making certain fashion decisions, or liking "Call Me Maybe" unironically.

I do regret peeing on Bruce's bed.

Before I get into the story, I would like to make it known that several rock stars have pissed in several places that aren't toilets throughout the history of rock music. The Rolling Stones were fined for urinating on a gas station because Bill Wyman was refused use of the restroom, Slash drunkenly wet the bed nearly every night Guns N' Roses were on tour, and Ozzy Osbourne urinated on a statue commemorating Texans who died at the Alamo in 1836.

I had just recently started a job at the campus movie theater, Grafton-Stovall Theater. I got paid ten dollars per hour to turn on the projector and change the film reels while I mostly just sat in the booth and either watched those movies or did homework. It was the perfect job. This particular day started like most Fridays: I was testing the movies at Grafton when the janitor, Pam, came in. Pam would often watch the movies instead of working, and then make me promise that I wouldn't tell our boss, the building manager, Jeff. It wasn't my money, so I often obliged. After watching most of *Anchorman 2* with Pam that night, I walked back to the apartment to hang out with whoever was around; today it was Damon and Julian.

"Who are we in *House of Cards*?" Julian asked.

"I'm Lucas, Bruce is Stamper, Julian's Freddie, Gavin's Claire, and Damon is Frank," I said.

"Gavin said he was Frank because he's the only one of us who could 'kill without remorse,'" Damon chuckled.

"Jesus Christ," Julian said, shaking his head and preparing to smoke his celebratory pre-weekend weed.

Damon elbowed my arm. "Why do you want to be Lucas, Cade?"

"Hopeless romantic, duh," I replied.

He nodded. "Ah, got it."

Julian took a hit from his vape pen and looked at me. "What about *Frasier*?" he asked, holding the smoke in his lungs as best he could.

"I'm Frasier, Damon's Niles, Bruce is Martin, Gavin's Bulldog, and Julian, you're . . . I guess Roz?"

Julian coughed up smoke. "How the fuck am I Roz?!" he wheezed.

"It's mostly because there's no one else," Damon said with a shrug.

"Everyone else is so perfectly cast," I said, agreeing with Damon.

"Whatever," Julian conceded, standing up. "You wanna get some music going?" He plugged the living room speaker aux cord into his phone.

"I haven't listened to *Tommy* in a while," Damon said.

I shook my head. "The Who is a poor man's Beatles," I declared.

"You say every band is a poor man's Beatles," Damon retorted.

"That's because they are!"

"The Who are great," Julian interjected. "You just need to listen to more of them."

"Where should I start?" I asked.

"'Baba O'Riley' might be my favorite song, but it's too close to call," Damon said.

"I guess I do love 'A Quick One While He's Away,'" I said.

Damon nodded while looking at his phone, "Not bad."

"Mine's 'Boris the Spider,'" Julian said, with glazed eyes and a wide grin.

Damon looked up from his phone. "'Boris the Spider'? That's your favorite?!" He shook his head in disbelief, grabbing Julian's vape. He inhaled, then executed a much smoother exhale than Julian had seconds before. "What time are people coming over, Cade?" he asked, smoke billowing out of his mouth.

"I told them to show up around nine, so . . . a couple of hours." I went to the fridge and started drinking my six pack.

As soon as I opened my Budweiser, Bruce walked through the door with his gym bag and fourth meal of Chipotle that week. "Hey-oooo," he said, throwing his bag down.

"Hey Bruce, what's your favorite Who song?" Julian asked.

Damon laughed.

Hours later, the apartment was full of drunk college students, myself included. I was entertaining everyone with my middle school throwback playlist: Sugar Ray, Green Day, Blink-182, and countless other great bands. Everyone was singing and dancing along. All was well, which is when I noticed that Bruce and Julian had disappeared. Then I realized I had been so busy trying to liven up the party with my playlist that I had lost track of Eileen.

I approached a UPB friend to find answers. "Hey Matt," I

shouted over Tom DeLonge blasting from the speakers, "have you seen Eileen?"

"She was with Bruce, last I saw," he shouted back and sipped his beer.

What the hell would she be doing with Bruce?

I looked all over the apartment, which really was not that big. I ended up finding her standing in front of the bathroom connected to my room. She was with Bruce and Julian, and all three of them were grinning ear to ear.

"We gotcha!" a drunk Bruce shouted, pointing at me with one hand and holding his beer in the other. I pushed past the three of them into the bathroom. My mattress had been shoved into my shower.

Now, if I had been sober, I might have realized that this was a joke that was kind of funny, despite the slight inconvenience. But I was not sober, and I turned full alpha male as a result.

"What the fuck, you guys!" I yelled.

Julian high-fived Bruce. "Got him!" Julian squealed.

I swayed and stared at the mattress. "How the fuck do I get it out of there?!"

"The same way we got it in!" Julian exclaimed, giving Bruce another high five.

"Goddammit," I growled. I turned and narrowed my eyes at them as best I could.

"Don't be a baby," Eileen laughed. "It's a joke." She grabbed Bruce and Julian by the arms. "Let's go get more drinks," she said, and led them back into the living room. I was alone with my mattress, which was now semi-wet from the shower I had taken an hour ago. *This is bullshit,* I told myself. *This is bullshit. This is bullshit.*

I walked back into the living room to find Bruce and Eileen in the kitchen. She was laughing at something he said. I swore in my drunken state I had never seen her this happy.

If that were it, I might have been able to cool off and avoid making an ass of myself. But as I stood there sipping my beer, stewing in anger and contemplating revenge, my friend Abby approached me.

She pointed at Bruce and Eileen. "Who is the guy Eileen's talking to?"

"That's my roommate."

"Holy shit, I've never seen a girl want to blow a dude harder," she said, sipping her beer.

"What?"

"Dude, she's totally into him."

"They're just . . . he's just . . . Ugh," I grunted and stormed off.

I grabbed another beer, went into my room, and chugged the whole thing. I stood there for a minute, staring at my mattress. I attempted to move it back into my room on my own but could not get it past the bathroom door.

"Fuck!" I screamed. I realized I had to pee, and the mattress now blocked the toilet. "Goddammit!" I shouted, punching the mattress.

Then, out of nowhere, I hatched what I considered at the time to be a brilliant idea.

You guessed it. . . .

"Where were you?" Matt asked.

"They put my mattress in my shower," I growled.

Matt chuckled. "Classic college."

"Don't worry, Matt. I'm gonna get them back . . . by peeing on Bruce's bed!" I giggled at the ridiculous notion of pee where it didn't belong. *The irreverence!*

Matt stopped smiling. "Wait, what? That's not a good idea."

"Trust me, Matt. This is gonna work."

"You really should—" he started to say as I pushed past him to get to Bruce's room.

I walked through five people singing "Teenage Dirtbag" on the way to his door. Bruce's was the only door in the apartment that didn't lock, which was lucky for me getting in, but which I promptly forgot when I attempted to lock everyone else out.

Confident the door was secure, I walked to the foot of Bruce's bed, whipped out my unit, and let my sterilized river of beer flow onto his mattress. I don't remember if I was laughing as I did the deed, but I was definitely smiling at the precise moment Eileen knocked on the door and yelled, "Cade, don't!" She walked in to see me with my dick out, pissing all over my roommate's bed. "Oh, great," was all she said before she left the room and slammed the door behind her.

I finished up my business and left the scene of the crime, somehow sure that nobody else in the small apartment would find out what I did. But everyone found out—starting with Bruce, who apparently did not believe Eileen and had to see for himself. When he came back out of his room after investigating, he found me giggling like a schoolgirl and hiding behind Matt. He politely pushed Matt out of the way, punched my arm a few times, and then threw me to the ground—which was very kind, considering what my strongest friend could have done to me. He then walked out onto the balcony porch and slammed the door. The guests had stopped paying attention to the nineties music that was still blasting and instead stared at me.

Someone shouted, "Hey, the drunk bus is here," and everybody left at once to get on the weekend campus shuttle. It was hands-down the worst shindig I ever threw during my time at JMU. Watching everyone leave a party because of something you did is a very sobering experience. Literally. I felt as if hours had passed, and I suddenly realized the stupidity of what I had done. I began to sift through the consequences: Eileen was definitely mad, but I knew she would forget about it in a few days. I was much more worried about my childhood friend, whom I had just dicked over.

I walked out to him on the porch, where Julian and Damon were keeping him company.

"What the fuck was that, dude?!" Julian yelled at me.

It made sense at the time, was my only defense, and I knew it was weak. So, in my drunken state, I said something that made more sense to me, something that is still quoted by my friends to this day: "Honestly, guys, I expected a lot more high fives."

Damon fell to the ground laughing. Julian shook his head and walked inside, and Damon got up off the ground and followed him.

Bruce and I were alone on the porch.

"My bad, dude," I began.

"What the hell was that for?" he asked through a jaw clenched so tight that it looked like it could start a fire.

"You were just with Eileen the whole night, and I—" I choked out every other word. I had no proper rebuttal. I felt like a third grader, being yelled at by the teacher for breaking the rules even though I knew better.

Bruce shook his head. "What?" he shouted. Did you think I was going to take her from you? Do you think I'm that shitty of a friend to sleep with the girl you won't shut the fuck up about?!" He was yelling at a volume loud enough to wake up the entire building. I felt all of Bruce's anger, disappointment, and frustration with every single word.

"No, I—" I started, but then stopped. I stared at a streetlight a couple blocks away. I envied the fly floating around it, free from human drama, free from guilt, free from this feeling in the back of my throat.

"You do this every time with every girl! You put her on a fucking pedestal, and she can never live up to it!"

"I don't—"

"You've been doing it since I met you!" He threw his hands into the air. "You somehow make yourself think that a girl is so perfect that nobody can compare! You have to have *that girl*. If Jessica Alba or Margot Robbie walked through the goddamn door you would still choose Eileen! And every time it happens, you do the stupidest shit. You ask girls out in front of an audience, you talk about fucking marrying them after knowing them for three weeks, and you piss on your goddamn friend's bed!" His face was inches away from mine now; I could see every bead of sweat on his face.

I took a step back and tried to lighten the moment. "In all fairness, I was just commenting on the fact that Eileen went to a wedding that had a guitarist which I would also want at our wedding should we ever get marr—"

Bruce cut through my convivial smokescreen and continued to yell. "You want to know why you and Eileen won't work? Because she's never going to live up to the perfect fucking exaggeration of a goddess you've created in your head!"

"I do really like her though," I said quietly to the top of my shoes.

"You don't even have anything in common! You don't share any interests! She came to hang out with me because she said Blink-182 sounded too much like 'screamo' for Christ's sake!"

I shrugged, still looking down. "Opposites attract." I was nearly out of every go-to cliché counter for this argument—not that any of them would have worked in the first place.

"This happens every time. You act like a fucking moron, she finds someone else, and then Julian and I have to pick up the pieces." Bruce slammed his hands on the balcony railing. Then he was quiet.

"Yeah . . . you're right," was all I could say. I had been doing this all my life. What does it say about me as a person that I'd be willing to damage one of my best friendships for a girl I'd only known for a few months? "Maybe I should take a break from Eileen for a while."

Bruce stood there, out of breath, staring off the balcony. "Don't ever let a fucking girl come between us again," he said and walked inside. I stood outside for a bit longer. Then I walked to my room and passed Bruce making a bed on our couch.

By the time I got to my room, I realized that I had completely forgotten about my mattress in the shower. I was 110% sure nobody in the apartment would help me get it out at this point, so I did what any man would do in that situation: I slept on the mattress in my bathroom. I was able to pull the mattress out of the tub and onto the floor of the bathroom, but it would not lie completely flat, so I slept at an angle for most of the night. I contemplated moving to sleep on the floor of my bedroom, but I couldn't come up with enough energy to make that move. I slept for only a few hours and woke up with my foot in the toilet.

When the sun came up, I was blessed with a few seconds of not remembering the previous night before I was pummeled with regret for the rest of the weekend. My first thought was, *Fuck. Why did I do that?* and then, *Well, at least it wasn't as bad as asking Emily out live in concert . . .* I looked at my phone to see a text from Keith that read, "Dude, you pissed on Bruce's bed? That's fucking hilarious!" I could not take always having a cheerleader in my corner for granted.

I washed Bruce's sheets, bought him a fifth of liquor, and apologized later that day.

He just smiled and said, "Shit happens."

SUFFRAGETTE CITY
By David Bowie

March 2014

"I can't take you this time, no way"

Following the desecration of Bruce's bed, I really wanted to re-evaluate my "relationship" with Eileen. I decided to refrain from texting her until I could figure things out. I knew it would be difficult, seeing as we normally texted each other nearly every day, but I felt it was necessary.

After a brief two days of self-reflection, she texted me out of the blue and asked to get dinner. I immediately obliged. I told Eileen about my heart-to-heart with Bruce and how we patched things up, leaving out every detail of my feelings for her. I told her it was a drunk mistake that I would never make again. She laughed the unpleasantness away and then apologized for the mattress prank. Before I knew it, everything was back to normal, and we were thick as thieves again.

A few weeks later, we found ourselves on a long late-night walk together.

"I really have to pee," Eileen said, walking at an increasing pace.

"It's only three miles. If you want, you can go behind a dumpster while I stand on lookout."

"I'm not peeing behind a dumpster. That's fucking disgusting."

"Then there's not much I can do for you." I shrugged.

"What if we find a random party and use the bathroom there?"

"That's a weird reason to show up to a stranger's house. Plus, what if they're murderers?"

"At this point I'm willing to take that chance. I see one up ahead." Eileen pointed out a lot of people gathered around a front stoop off in the distance and assumed at least one of them belonged to a building with a toilet in it. "I'm going to see if these guys will let us use their bathroom," she yelled back to me as she sprinted away.

Women are strange, I thought, and walked behind a dumpster to piss.

Eileen and I had attended a fellow UPB member's twenty-first birthday party earlier in the evening. That is, until the cops showed up to stop it. The music was very loud and happened to disturb some jerk who liked going to bed at midnight on a Saturday and probably also hated the sound of other people having a good time. It didn't help the birthday girl that most of her friends were under twenty-one, Eileen included. Instead of waiting for a taxi or bus like the rest of our friends at the party, Eileen had drunkenly muttered what her mother would do if she found out she had been arrested for underage drinking and had run as far away from the scene of the crime as possible. I had decided to follow her as she semi-drunkenly sauntered down the street.

Eileen returned from the stranger's bathroom.

"How was it?" I asked.

"Fucking gross. The floor was sticky, and the toilet wouldn't flush," she said, her nose wrinkled.

"Sounds worse than the dumpster. Their parents must be so disappointed in their inability to keep a bathroom clean for drunk strangers."

"I know mine would be."

"What are your parents like?" I asked.

"They're divorced."

"I know, I mean your mom and your stepdad."

She smiled. "They like clean bathrooms."

"Don't we all. What are they like?"

"Why?" she asked.

"Because we have a four-mile walk home. I'm just trying to start a dialogue."

"Oh, alright. Umm, they're really happy together. My mom told me last Christmas that the goal to finding your soulmate is finding the most boring person possible. No drama, no flair, just marital bliss."

"Really? Do you believe that?" I asked, surprised.

"I have no reason not to. What are your parents like?"

"Regular parents, I guess. They met in high school and they've never been with anyone else since. They fight sometimes, but so does everyone."

"What do they fight about?"

I shrugged. "Mostly how they don't go out anymore, how they can't afford to go on a cruise; you know, mostly middle-class family stuff."

"My parents fought a lot before they got divorced. Funny thing is I don't really remember what they fought about."

"Whenever my parents fought, I would lock myself in my room and listen to *Abbey Road* from start to finish. They never had a fight that lasted longer than the record."

She looked over at me. "What's *Abbey Road*?"

"It's the Beatles' last album they did before they split up."

"Oh gotcha. I really like that *Across the Universe* movie they made. Although I think the actor in that movie sings the songs better than the Beatles do."

Isn't it crazy that on any given day, you can be completely in love with someone and hold them in the highest regard, and then on a different day they can say something that makes you want to throw up in your mouth a little bit?

"Do you believe in love at first sight?" I asked.

"Not really. I like the idea of it, but it just seems impossible. Do you?"

"Yeah. It's how my parents met. Ever since my dad told me that story, I've never thought about love differently. You just see the person you're meant to be with, and you know."

"I don't think that's possible," Eileen said as she pulled out her phone.

"Don't you believe you could meet someone who makes you feel different than anybody else? Even if you just knew this person was important *before* you began a relationship with them?"

Eileen didn't respond. She was staring at her phone. I carefully peeked over and saw that she was texting her ex-boyfriend, Drew. "Sorry, what did you say?" she asked.

"Nothing important."

"When I started dating my ex-boyfriend, it wasn't love at first sight. We just spent a lot of time together and both liked being around each other."

It always sucks to hear a girl you're in love with talk about how much she cared about another man, no matter how wrong her views of the Beatles are. "But then you broke up," I reminded her.

"Yeah, because we went to different colleges twelve hours apart."

"If you didn't go to different schools, would you still be together?"

"Maybe. Our parents and siblings both talk about how we're gonna end up together one day."

"Do you think you will?"

"I don't know," she said, looking off into the distance with a truly perplexed look on her face.

I spent the rest of the walk trying to think of ways to change the subject, but failing.

IN BLOOM
By Nirvana

August 2014

"Tender age in bloom"

There we all were: the fourteen members of the University Program Board's Executive Team from 2014 to 2015. We were hired to lead the 120-plus member organization, which put on a wide variety of entertainment events for James Madison University students every year. Everything from movies like *Whiplash* or *Captain America: The Winter Soldier*, to comedians like Jay Pharoah or Michael Ian Black, to musicians like X Ambassadors and Foo Fighters—UPB did it all. I had the enormous responsibility of directing the Film Committee, ordering and scheduling movies for JMU's on-campus movie theater, Grafton, and being a "role model" in some way or another.

Though I became closer to some members of the UPB than others, from that first day on I would always view the other thirteen members of exec as great friends who helped shape me during the most influential year of my life.

It was the first day of our exec training. Our program leader, Maris, had summoned us all to meet at noon in a parking lot at the center of campus to start a week-long team building retreat. We gathered, fourteen near-strangers who would soon become inseparable companions. The only people I knew at that point were Nora and Jessica, because I had worked several UPB events with them the previous year.

"Hey, old friend," I said as I approached Nora.

"Hey!" she said as she hugged me. "How was your summer?"

"I worked at Grafton all summer and lived off of twenty dollars' worth of groceries every week," I said, proud of both my employment and frugality. "How about you?"

"I got an internship as a physical therapist. Very time-consuming, but I still found enough time to hang out with my boyfriend and family."

Our conversation was interrupted by an approaching Maris. The fourteen of us quieted down and awaited instructions.

"Hello, everyone! Ready for an exciting week?" Maris asked, smiling.

I didn't know much about Maris, but I did know that previous members of the board were not fond of her; I was told she was bossy, condescending, and uptight. I wasn't one to pass judgement, though—the same thing was said about Severus Snape, and he ended up being a good guy.

Maris directed us toward a large van, which we all piled into. Despite the van's size, fifteen adults in one van was still a tight fit. I sat next to Henrietta, who I had come to know from our occasional conversations in the UPB office over the past couple of years.

"Hey, so I listened to your suggestion and started watching *Arrow* this summer," I said to her. "It was great!"

"Right?? Season two was soooooo good! And Deathstroke was such a great villain! I hope they keep up the quality of the show; that season will be hard to beat."

"Are you stoked for the ropes course?" I asked.

"I guess. I really don't know what to expect. I've never done a ropes course before. Never been crazy about heights."

"Eh, I'm sure it'll be fine."

I looked around the van to get a better gauge of the people I would be working with for the rest of the year. I recognized nearly everyone, but I didn't know much about their personalities. Directly behind me, in the middle of the van, sat Griffin, whom I had met a few months before when I was short a dollar to get a bus ticket to D.C. He had kindly given me the dollar, and to this day he has not asked for it back. Griffin was a tall guitar lover with long, dark, curly hair; I didn't know it at the time, but I soon discovered he could shred on a real guitar almost as well as I could on a fake one.

Behind Griffin were Violet and Nicole, both friendly lovers of indie/alternative music, and best friends since the seventh grade. Violet had long blonde hair, pale skin, and a smile that could light up a room; Nicole had dark hair which she sometimes dyed red, a passion for flannel shirts, and one of the most contagious laughs in the world. Nicole laid her head on Violet's shoulder and fell asleep for most of the ride.

Tommy sat next to them, and all I knew about him at the time was that he would be my bunkmate during this weeklong retreat. He was short, tan, and had his hair cut short at all times. Next to Tommy was Layne. Layne was the only one in the group who was an outside hire, which meant he was the only person who was not in the organization prior to joining the executive team, and therefore nobody knew him at all. He was tall, with short blonde hair, blue eyes, and the demeanor of a high school jock.

Lenny was the looks of the team; he had the face of a country music star and the body of a college athlete. Several girls joined the Special Events Committee simply because he ran it. I immediately assumed he would be a douche as a result, but nothing could have been further from the truth.

When we got to the ropes course, Maris told us to leave all of our possessions in the van. I was uncomfortable with this because I had six bucks left on a Target gift card in my wallet and a phone that I never wanted to part with in case a celebrity liked one of my tweets, but I told myself to suck it up for the sake of my new board position and the sweet, sweet $400 stipend I would be awarded with at the end of the semester.

We all gathered around the gate leading to the ropes course, and an employee greeted us. "Hello, everyone!" he chirped. "We're very glad to have you all here!" He was very short and had one of those twirly mustaches like a villain in a silent film. "Now, who here has done the ropes course before?"

No one raised a hand.

The University Park ropes course was something many students fantasized about doing but never did. I had had several intoxicated conversations with my roommates about how we were totally gonna "actually sign up and do it this weekend," but then we'd wake up hungover and spend our Saturday watching a series of whatever terrible movies were on TV.

Our ropes guide coughed. "Okay, not a lot. That's totally fine. A majority of our climbers are first-timers. What we're gonna do first is pair up into two groups. Then we'll climb to the first platform, one group at a time."

The concept was easy enough. We climbed a seemingly endless rope ladder one by one to meet our group at the starting platform at the top. As soon as I finished climbing and arrived at the platform, I looked at my fellow board members and had a sudden epiphany: I was terrified of heights.

"You good, Cade?" Lenny asked. He must have noticed the concern all over my face.

"Yeah, man. Toootally fine," I promised. I was doing everything I could to avoid peeing my pants in fear.

"Okay everyone, put on these vests and attach the hook on the back of them to the metal line above you. As long as you're hooked on, you won't have any problems with falling," the mustached guide said, clearly underestimating the power of gravity.

I put on my vest and hooked myself to the metal line. There was no turning back now. I considered the option of crying until they pitied me enough to let me down, but no matter how glorious the ground would be, I couldn't cry in front of my comrades.

I remember three things and only three things from the entire experience:

1. It lasted *two hours*.
2. One of the exec members, Cheryl, fell halfway through the course and slammed her leg on a wire, giving herself a nasty metal blister that she had for weeks afterward.
3. I had never been more frightened in my entire life.

I felt as if every step I took could be my last, but I never shared it with anyone. I just kept my cool, hoping to impress my new team. They were there for me every step of the way. Every time I had to jump, shimmy, or climb, I had a teammate there to help and support me. It was an odd feeling: to have people you could undoubtedly rely on after knowing them for only a short period of time.

We eventually made it to the end of the course. I couldn't believe it; I had made it past every obstacle with my group and kept my composure the whole time. I couldn't keep from smiling ear to ear.

"Okay, Cade, you and Henrietta are next," our guide said.

My smile fell away. "Next for what?"

"You guys have to slide down the rope to get back to the ground."

"Oh." I looked down. "Is there, like . . . a ladder?"

"Nope. It's a zipline, and it's the only way off the course." He smiled, and his mustache curled up to touch the sides of his nose. "Is there a problem?"

I swallowed. "No no no, not at all."

I had just spent the last two hours trying to stay *on* small platforms while hanging from a thin metal rope, and this guy was now expecting me to jump *off* of the platform, using just that thin metal rope. *Fuck.*

"Ready, Team Arrow?" Henrietta said, grinning.

"Just another day in Starling City."

I closed my eyes and jumped.

A moment later, I lay peacefully on the ground; I had never been more appreciative to be once again on Earth's floor. Shortly after I recovered from my state of rational fear, we loaded back in the van and went to our hotel where we would be staying that night. We all enjoyed dinner and swapping stories about our experience defying gravity.

By the end of the night, we were all gathered in a circle in a conference room attached to the hotel. Maris sat at the front of the room, while everyone in the circle faced her. After we all settled in, she began to speak.

"After I saw everyone on the ropes course, I found this quote that really resonated with me," she said, lifting her phone. "'When you find people who not only tolerate your quirks but celebrate them with cries of 'Me too!' be sure to cherish them, because those weirdos are your tribe.'"

"Awww! Maris, I love that!" Nicole exclaimed. Everyone else around the room nodded with approval.

"I hope you all learned a lot from the course and are starting to understand what this week is about," Maris added.

If this week was in fact a deep glimpse into Cade's darkest fears, I was not looking forward to spider day or murder-clown weekend.

"A big part of being on a team is being there for each other at all times, knowing everyone's strengths and weaknesses, and knowing what you need to do for these people in order to ultimately fulfill the needs of the group. So, tonight we're going to continue our team building week by sharing our weaknesses. I want everyone to keep in mind that everything said in this room stays in this room. I want you all to think about a certain darkness that you carry around. A darkness that you rarely share with others, maybe never share with others. Only talk about what you're comfortable with, but remember: you're in a safe place."

I could go into detail about what everyone said, but I made a promise that night that I would never speak of their "darkness." A lot of the people in that room shared *real* stories. Some stories made us laugh, some made us cry, and some made us stare at the person in empathetic disbelief.

Before I knew it, it was my turn to share—and for the opportunity to fully immerse myself in the group, I didn't hold back.

"Umm . . . here it goes, I guess. I met my best friend Keith when I was five. I moved away a year later and started going to Catholic school, where I met five friends I still have to this day; two of them have been my roommates throughout college. I loved those eight years in private school. We were inseparable. A lot of people complain about how middle school was full of some of the worst days in their life. Not me. Every day was another day in paradise with people I loved. Whenever I was apart from these friends, I always had Keith to visit. It was the perfect eight years, and I wouldn't change a thing.

"Then I had to go to public high school. None of my friends followed me; we all went to different schools. For the first time in my life, I felt alone. I got bullied a lot: people made fun of me, people stole my lunch, people beat me up . . . sometimes they'd even throw rocks at me outside while teachers weren't looking. My dad was sympathetic, but he always treated each situation as if it was more or less supposed to happen. He said that bullies built character and made me stronger. Thank God for my mom, though. She knew how bad I had it. Every time I'd come home with a sad story, it was like it had happened to her, as if my abusers had damaged a piece of her. I once caught her crying to Dad about me being 'stuck at that school.' She would always do the best she could to make me feel better. She bought me whatever video games I wanted and invited my private school friends over every weekend, so it never got too unbearable, and I still got to visit Keith over Christmas and the summer.

"Anyway, Keith and I started playing the video game *Rock*

Band with his sister and her boyfriend during my freshman year. It was honestly some of the best times I had in all of high school. I remember waking up every morning and getting on that goddamn school bus, putting my headphones in and closing my eyes to picture Chris, Keith, Delynn, and I playing whatever song it was. It would get me through the rest of the day. I counted down the days until the four of us could be together to play *Rock Band* again. It got me through some tough times, but as a whole, high school didn't really get better.

"Then in my senior year, I had my first girlfriend. Everything was great for a seemingly endless time. I had never felt this way about anybody before. One night, she told me she had cheated on me. I was absolutely destroyed. It ruined the last shot I had at looking back at high school in a positive light.

"Finally, those four years ended, and they had that cliché assembly for all the seniors. You know the one: all the popular kids sit together, all the geeks sit together, all the stoners sit together, and we all watch a twenty-minute slideshow with pictures of everybody in your graduating class while 'Good Riddance' by Green Day and 'Closing Time' by Semisonic and 'Graduation' by Vitamin C all play on repeat. I sat by myself and watched that shitty summation of four years for the entire twenty minutes, and I didn't see a single picture of myself. The feeling that I had had for the entire four years finally came back in one full-circle realization: *I feel like I don't exist.*

"Every time I had that feeling, I thought back to the first night Keith, Chris, Delynn, and I played *Rock Band.* The tour mode in the game kept making us play 'In Bloom' by Nirvana and 'Say It Ain't So' by Weezer over and over again. We got sick of the songs after playing them ten times in a row. We never wanted to hear them again. But now I can't listen to either of those songs without wanting to go back and play them all over again. Over and over again. Just to be back in that basement with my friends. We were a group, and I felt like I belonged . . . just like I felt with you guys at the ropes course today. So . . . I really want to thank you for that."

I quieted down. The rest of "my tribe" was looking at me with big smiles on their faces.

Jessica nodded at me and realized it was her cue to start talking.

GIMME SHELTER
By the Rolling Stones

September 2014

"My very life today"

I got acclimated to my new job on the exec board very quickly. An average day would begin with class, then I would wander over to Grafton and test the movies for the week. We showed two movies—one at 7 p.m. and one at 9:30 p.m.—four nights a week, Wednesday through Saturday. I would have the film reels/Blu-rays/hard drives delivered to the UPB office early in the week, then I would take them over to Grafton to test them out on the projector.

This process usually took a few hours, so unless the movie was really good, I'd often end up doing homework. The janitor, Pam, would usually clean around the same time; I would frequently find her "taking a break" to watch these movies in their entirety. Whenever I found her sitting in the theater, she would look at me and say, "Just taking a break dear! Hope you're having a good week!" She was always polite about it, so I would just smile, nod, and let her be.

After I tested the movies, I'd head back to either the UPB office or class, depending on the day. When I finished that, I had to stop by Grafton one last time to make sure Pam locked the doors.

One Tuesday afternoon, on my way back from office hours, I looked inside the Grafton glass doors to see Eileen.

"Hey, you," I said as I opened the door. "To what do I owe the pleasure?"

"Oh, hey," she said. She sounded surprised to see me. "I was just collecting the theater ticket numbers from last week so I can put them in the report for the meeting this week. I wasn't sure if you were still in the booth testing the movies." Eileen was one of the UPB committee chairs that dealt with finance. She reported her sales figures to the exec team and we used the data to schedule more events pleasing to students.

"I was already up there earlier. I had office hours this afternoon, so I had to do that. Oh, by the way, exec is coming over to my apartment tonight to play *Rock Band* if you want to come."

She smiled. "I'll see what I can do, but I'll probably be studying all night. My major is a bitch." Suddenly, she dropped her bag off her shoulder and lay down on the floor of the theater, looking up at the ceiling. "I'm so exhausted," she sighed. Eileen was enrolled in the most difficult business course at JMU, and it had been eating away at her social life. This was one of the few times I had seen her all year since the semester started.

I lay down next to her. "I know the feeling," I said. "I just had to watch *The Fault in Our Stars* and *A Million Ways to Die in the West* back to back."

Eileen rolled her eyes. "I pity you so much," she said, smiling.

I rolled over on my side and propped my head on my hand to face her. "Will you have time for me in your busy schedule this semester?"

"Of course. Are you still going to want to hang out with me even if your exec friends are more fun?"

"There's only one Eileen," I promised.

Our conversation was interrupted by the sound of knocking on the glass doors. We looked up to see my sister Emma smiling and waving. Eileen and I got up quickly, and I ran to open the door.

"Hello, brother," Emma said, opening her arms for a hug.

"Hey," I said, with less enthusiasm than her currently chipper demeanor.

Emma turned to Eileen. "Hey, Eileen. How are you?"

"I'm good!" Eileen said with a smile. "I do have to get going, though." She picked up her bag from the ground and brushed off her jeans. "Believe it or not, I already have a test first thing next week."

"How do your teachers sleep at night?" I asked.

"On a huge pile of money, probably. They all have high ranking business degrees that say they're better at investing than either of us, at least."

"Have they spent thousands of dollars on the world's greatest video game franchise?"

Eileen laughed and shook her head as she walked out. "I'll see you later, Cade. It was good seeing you again, Emma."

Emma gave her a cheerful "You too!" and a wave.

"*Rock Band* party tonight! Be there or be square!" I shouted after Eileen. I then turned back to my sister.

"How are you two?" she asked.

"Always great," I said half-heartedly before changing the subject. "What brings you to my movie theater?"

"I'm on my way to my youth group meeting. Want to come?"

"I watched a couple Flanders-heavy episodes of *The Simpsons* this morning, so I'm set."

She smiled and sighed. "Thought I'd offer. Any good movies playing this week?"

"You'd probably like *The Fault in Our Stars*. It's basically *The Notebook* except it doesn't make me wish I had cancer."

Emma rolled her eyes. "You're so dramatic," she said. She was always less offended by my jokes than most people, which made it easier to talk to her about really anything, despite our differing opinions.

"The nurse just looked at them and assumed they were dead at the end! She didn't even check their pulses!"

"If that's what you took away from *The Notebook*, you probably weren't paying attention."

"Ryan Gosling climbed a fucking ferris wheel! He could have died! You know if that happened today, Rachel McAdams would immediately text all of her friends about a crazy guy stalking her."

"Your favorite movie is *Signs*! You don't have a lot of room to argue."

"Aren't you going to be late to your Kool-Aid drinking party?"

Emma looked at the clock on the wall. "Oh, good call. Have fun at your party tonight, brother. Sing 'Here It Goes Again' for me."

"Always," I said as she left.

SHOULD I STAY OR SHOULD I GO
By the Clash

September 2014

"Exactly whom I'm supposed to be"

The second most selfish thing a person can do in life is to start a band. You spend six months learning an instrument, get with a couple of other guys or girls with a similar musical skill level, and ask all of your closest friends to watch you play in your garage, your basement, or the lobby of an Applebee's. Your friends and family have to sit through your forty-five-minute set, comprised mostly of terrible songs you think are good because you spent weeks writing them, and usually one mediocre cover of Tom Petty or the Goo Goo Dolls that everybody knows the words to and can briefly participate in. Your friends will sit there in agony waiting for your set to be over, wishing that you had asked them to help you move furniture into your new apartment instead.

The first most selfish thing a person can do in life is start a *jam* band. You spend six months smoking weed and playing an instrument with a few other stoners and then ask your closest friends to listen to you play a thirty-five-minute bass solo. This is infinitely worse than a regular band, because you aren't even giving your friends a basic song structure they can follow along with. They have no idea how long they are trapped in the drug-addled purgatory you have created. And they can't even sing along—all they can do is awkwardly sway. I'm not denying the incredible amount of talent every member of the band Phish has, but if you have a set with multiple thirty-minute windows where I have nothing to sing along to, I'm gonna have a bad time. Trey Anastasio, you're an incredible guitarist; write more choruses and catchy hooks so I have something to do at your concerts other than ecstasy or LSD. (I'd also like to challenge you to play your song "Wilson" on *Rock Band* against me and beat my high score, but that's another discussion.)

The best part about *Rock Band* is that *anybody* can play. It's an all-inclusive activity that allows the non-music-savvy people of the world to share their favorite songs with friends or strangers. *Rock Band* creates an atmosphere where anyone can play guitar, drums, or bass and feel like a goddamn rock star. If the microphones are all claimed, anyone is invited to sing along in the background to the choruses we have all sung in the shower or car at some point in our lives.

You can really tell a lot about someone by the *Rock Band* song they choose to play. I decided the best way to get to know my UPB exec team was to invite them over to my apartment to enjoy my favorite video game. After spending a month with my new UPB family, we were becoming more inseparable each day. The ropes course had brought us closer together, and working in a student office every day only strengthened our bond; the logical next step was *Rock Band*.

When the game came out in 2007, it was one of the most popular gifts under everyone's Christmas tree that year. Prior to that holiday, I was the only one of my friends planning on getting it. But lo and behold, that very morning I received texts from both Bruce and Martin that they got *Rock Band: Special Edition* as well. Keith bought it immediately after I introduced it to him for the first time, and every kid I sat next to in every high school class that wasn't talking to me was talking about playing *Rock Band* to somebody. The game's popularity only increased leading up to the release of *Rock Band 2* the following fall. By Christmas 2008, everyone had some form of *Rock Band* and dreams of being a rock star. Between 2009 and 2010, Harmonix released *The Beatles: Rock Band, Green Day: Rock Band, Lego: Rock Band* (the franchise really knew how to dig its way deep into my heart), and several other iterations of the video game for handheld devices.

The party started to end by late 2010, with the release of *Rock Band 3*. People had already been playing the game far less when Harmonix decided to spend millions of dollars engineering the option to allow real guitars, keyboards, and electronic drum kits to be playable in *Rock Band 3*. It seemed like nobody wanted this option, and the majority of fans started throwing away their plastic instruments over the next few years. But not me. I played every instrument into the ground and then I bought new ones to replace them. I bought the brand-new songs they released almost weekly until my library had hundreds of options to choose from. Then in college, I started hosting *Rock Band* parties. People were intrigued by the concept immediately: "Wait, this is the game that I used to love! Why did I ever stop playing it?"

I hosted my first *Rock Band* party of the year a few weeks into the semester and decided to invite several members of my film committee and my exec team. Though not everyone I invited made it, we had about forty people in my tiny-ass apartment living room playing *Rock Band* on a far-too-small TV screen with the volume all the way up. But nobody cared about the setup; everyone was just baffled at my extensive 800+ song library and excited that I was able to provide free beer.

After a couple of hours, I got drunk enough to climb on top of the tallest piece of furniture and get everyone's attention. Billie Joe Armstrong has a great stage bit when he tells everyone to "shut the fuck up for a second," then lowers his hands. He slowly lifts them back up, and the audience gets louder and louder as his hands rise higher and higher.

"Everyone! Shut up for a second!" I said as I lowered my plastic guitar. The room quickly quieted down.

I then inched my outstretched arms slowly up, closer to the

ceiling every second. And oddly enough, the other drunk people were the first to catch on. I raised my hands above my head to an orgasm of noise and enthusiastic drunk chants. I had come a long way from having a few friends to play with in high school to an entire room full of people literally looking up to me at my own *Rock Band* party. After I did this bit a few more times, I cued up the song "Basket Case" and jumped around from couch to couch while playing.

After my routine, I decided to give someone else a chance to choose a song. "Anyone else want to pick one?"

"'Mr. Brightside'!" Layne shouted after chugging a Keystone Ice.

"The Killers it is!" I shouted back as I cued up the song.

I learned a lot about my exec team that night. Nicole's favorite song of the evening was "Rebel Girl" by Bikini Kill, which meant she really liked music. "Rebel Girl" isn't a song that comes on the radio, it's a song you discover through years and years of listening to other bands. I respect her admiration for it. Tommy chose "Nightmare" by Avenged Sevenfold, which meant he was a metalhead—he enjoyed the heavier side of music and probably liked mosh pits or going to the gym. Violet chose "Fix You" by Coldplay, which meant she loved sheer fucking beauty. Jessica followed my lead and stood on the couch to sing "Total Eclipse of the Heart" by Bonnie Tyler, while the rest of the girls in the room sang along at the top of their lungs. I assumed she loved sleepovers as a child and karaoke as an adult. Lenny chose "Free Bird" by Lynyrd Skynyrd, which meant he was drunk and ready to party.

My biggest takeaway from the evening, though, was how much fun everyone had playing a whole bunch of plastic instruments they had each probably thrown away at some point in their lives. None of my exec team thought I was weird for playing an old game, but instead they celebrated me for it. It felt really good to finally have a band like the Krazy Unikerns again.

BLITZKRIEG BOP
By the Ramones

March 2015

"They're all revved up and ready to go"

As I've mentioned several times, I was not popular in high school. This means I missed out on every teenager's rite of passage into adulthood: a proper spring break. For those of you out there, like me, who never went on a high school spring break vacation, apparently it goes like this: you get a group of about ten-ish people (fifty-fifty guy-to-girl ratio if possible), you chip in about two hundred bucks, you all rent a beach-adjacent house, and you go crazy for a week.

In high school, while I gazed upon all of the popular kids' Facebook photos for an entire week, I couldn't help but feel envious of a seemingly necessary milestone in one's life.

Fortunately for me, my life was once again fixed by my UPB exec team. During the JMU spring break of 2015, Violet, Layne, Griffin, Lenny, Lenny's girlfriend, Susan, and myself all chipped in and rented a house at Myrtle Beach for a week of nonstop debauchery. What transpired there was the stuff of legend; the problem is, we were all so drunk that none of us remember all of the details.

Here is what I know for sure:

1. Lenny lost at beer pong one night and had to streak naked around the house. We all saw his dick.
2. Lenny's girlfriend, Susan, who none of us knew

very well, ended up being the life of the party all week long. We knew for sure she was a keeper when she drunkenly danced with a vacuum cleaner.

3. Griffin and I shared a bed and fell asleep listening to Noel Gallagher's *Chasing Yesterday* album every night.

4. Layne wore a tank top for seventy percent of the trip that said "VP of Hazing" on it in big letters. He made all of us beer-bong a Kirkland Light at least one time during the trip.

5. In order to get back at Layne for all of the hazing, Griffin and I bought a fifth of Whipped Cream Burnett's Vodka and hid shots all around the house. The house rule for the week was that if someone intentionally hides a drink and you find it, you have to drink it. Layne found ten Burnett's shots before 9 a.m. the next morning and threw up very shortly after.

6. One night, Layne bought everyone a Four Loko after finding out that nobody there had ever tried one before. He recommended drinking the entire can in one hour to ensure maximum intoxication. Several of us said, "Fuck off, Layne," and proceeded to play a drinking game where we all inadvertently drank our Four Lokos in thirty minutes.

7. I bought one forty-ounce Bud Ice for every day of the week and drank one with my dinner each night. I hate myself for that.

8. While walking around the town of Myrtle Beach, we found a used clothing store to look around in. Violet found an old hat from 2008 that bore the *Rock Band* logo, and I immediately bought it. To this day, I wear it every time I play *Rock Band*.

Aside from all of these wonderful memories, there is one night I remember vividly: it all began with a new Nickelback single and the one person in the world who could be excited about a new Nickelback single.

"It's out, everybody!" Lenny shouted as he scrolled through Spotify on his phone. It was Tuesday afternoon, and much like every other day, we were all a little hungover. We let out a groan in unison, but it didn't prevent Lenny from playing the song over the speakers.

"Ooh this one has a *funky* beat to it!" he said. In his defense, it *was* interesting that we were twenty seconds into a Nickelback song and not one of us had punched Lenny in the throat out of frustration.

Then the vocals kicked in.

Griffin stood up, grabbed Lenny's phone, and threw it across the room. "It wasn't bad until Chad Kroeger opened his goddamn motherfucking cock-sucking mouth!" he shouted in anger. We all laughed, including Lenny.

"So, what's the drinking game for tonight?" Layne asked.

"I'm still kind of hungover from last night," Susan said, picking up Lenny's phone for him. "Why don't we just watch a movie and drink casually like we've been doing all day?"

"Great idea! A movie drinking game!" Layne shouted with a vexatious smile. Everyone groaned again, but Layne was unfazed. "What's in the house DVD collection?"

"*Jaws* and *Good Will Hunting*," Griffin said, sorting through the cabinet.

"I wonder what a *Good Will Hunting* drinking game would be like," I said.

Lenny looked up from his phone. "I found rules for a *Jaws* drinking game," he chimed in. "You drink every time someone says 'chief,' every time you hear the theme song or see a fin, every time you hear them reference 'the Kitner boy,' every time you see a gun fired, or see someone attacked by a shark, or see blood . . .

also, you have to finish your drink every time someone says, 'We're gonna need a bigger boat,' or, 'Smile, you son of a . . . '"

"Oh my god," Violet said, laughing, "we're all gonna die."

"You got a rule against breathing as well?" I asked.

"This sounds fucking awesome. Let's do it," Layne said, cracking open a Four Loko. Everyone else grabbed their respective drinks. I grabbed a Bud Ice.

We were about half an hour into the movie when I finished my forty and had to crack open a Corona. Everyone was already very drunk. I threw my empty bottle across the room in a fit of drunken frustration, which everyone took as a funny joke instead of a cry for help or an indication to stop playing. I lay on the ground and closed my eyes for what I thought was a moment, but the next thing I knew, I awoke to *Bob's Burgers* on the TV.

I looked around the room. Lenny and Susan were asleep next to each other on the couch behind me. Griffin was sitting in a recliner in the corner, drinking something out of a brown bag. He was the only other person awake in the room.

"What happened to the game?" I asked.

"You fell asleep like twenty minutes into the movie," Griffin said and took another swig from the bag, "and everyone was feeling pretty tired, so we started watching TV. Layne and Violet wandered off together, so it looks like the rumors are true."

"I had a feeling they were a thing," I said as I finished a yawn. "I wish my intuition for dumb drinking games was that strong." I sat up slowly and turned to face Griffin.

"You totally won *Jaws* MVP, by the way," he laughed. "How about some fresh air?"

We sat down at the picnic bench in the back yard. It was the perfect mid-sixties temperature with a nice breeze coming off the water. The rest of the houses on the street were completely dark and quiet. It was like our tiny palace of indecency was in an invisible bubble that gave us immunity from bothering the neighbors—which we especially appreciated at that moment as we began to hear faint, emotional grunts coming from Violet and Layne's room. "I guess I'll have to give the *Jaws* drinking game date method a shot next time Lindsey comes over," Griffin said, grinning.

I shrugged. "Worst-case scenario is you get to drink a lot, which is always a win. How's that going, by the way?"

"Well, I've been talking to her a lot recently. I really like her, so I'll probably ask her out and take it from there."

"Seems like a solid plan," I said.

"What about that girl Laura you told me about? Is she still dating that guy?"

I had met Laura through a mutual friend; she was a short, cute blonde girl with glasses and a shy demeanor. We were coincidentally in two classes together, so I was able to form a friendship by asking her to help me with various assignments. She had a boyfriend she had been seeing for two years, so I didn't get my hopes up for romance. That is, until a few days before we left for spring break, when she told me they had broken up.

As much as I cared for Eileen and still thought about ending up with her, we both failed to keep the promises we had made to each other nearly half a year prior, in Grafton. She was unable to make time for me due to her classes, and I had made a much bigger effort to spend time with my exec friends than for her. We still saw each other, but it was exclusively in a group or professional UPB setting.

Laura was the first person I had met in a long time who made me feel like I could move on to someone else.

"She actually texted me a few days ago saying she broke up with him."

Griffin raised an eyebrow. "Do you like her?"

"Yeah, I think she's really cute, and she has good taste in music. We got lunch the other day and talked about mix CDs the whole time."

"You should send her a text." He lifted his brown paper bag for another sip.

"Right now? It's 12:30 in the morning. Isn't that a weird time to get a text?"

"Don't think about it, just do it." Griffin pulled out his phone. "Watch. I'll call Lindsey right now."

"Really?"

Griffin held up his phone to show me that he was indeed calling Lindsey, then put the phone up to his ear. "Text Laura, dude. You'll be happy that you did." He walked to the other side of the yard to talk to Lindsey.

I sat and stared at my phone for nearly the entire duration of Griffin's phone call. Despite his advice, I couldn't help but worry about sending a girl I was romantically interested in a text after midnight. Every time I tried to convince my brain it was a good idea, it would fire back with, *You just thought it was okay to drink every time you heard the word "chief" in* Jaws. *Fuck you.*

After nearly thirty minutes, I heard Griffin wrap up his phone call; not wanting to let him down, I panicked and texted Laura, "Hey, what's up?" at 1 a.m., just as he walked up to me.

"What did she say?" he asked.

"She didn't respond. Guess she's asleep," I said.

"Proud of you, dude. Let's go crack open another beer and fall asleep to Noel Gallagher."

SABOTAGE
By the Beastie Boys

April 2015

"I can't stand it"

"You wanted to see me, Professor?"

"Yeah, Cade. Come on in."

I stepped into Professor Vedder's office. I still needed eighteen credits to graduate, so for my last semester at JMU, I needed to add one more class to my already full course load. I ended up taking a random creative nonfiction writing class.

It turned out to be the best course I took at JMU.

"I brought my paper," I said as I sat in the chair facing my professor's desk. "I don't think it's as good as the last one, though."

"You've set quite a high bar for yourself," he said. "Everyone in the class seemed to really enjoy your first piece. Where did you get the idea?"

"My friend Jessica suggested it, actually. The Beatles' *One* album has probably been the most influential record in my life, and she suggested I make each song a story."

He turned his chair to face the bookshelf behind him. "I'm gonna give you a book to read. Have you heard of Rob Sheffield?" He picked up a book and turned back around.

"No," I admitted, as he handed me a book. I read the title out loud: "*Love is a Mixtape*. What's it about?"

He grinned. "You're gonna like it."

"Always appreciate a good recommendation," I said, storing the book in my backpack.

He looked back down at my paper. "So, if this isn't as good as your last piece, what's wrong with it?"

"The last one was a memoir, so I could just be myself. You wanted this to be a journalistic piece. I felt more restricted with my writing, and I think my creativity suffered."

"It's always good to challenge your writing style. It makes us all better writers. Let's take a look. . . . "

Cade Wiberg
ENG 391
4/9/15

Mr. Big Sean

The University Program Board has been responsible for bringing alcohol alternative programming to JMU since 1973. Within the organization, there are five committees that have brought several reputable acts to JMU throughout the years, including performances by Maroon 5, Boston, the Offspring, Aziz Ansari, James Taylor, Macklemore, Third Eye Blind, and, for some reason, Snooki. Every year, the Center Stage Committee is responsible for two shows in Wilson Hall, the Madipalooza lineup, and the large-scale concert that takes place in the Convocation Center at the end of the year. The amount of work that goes into this final event is unparalleled by any other event on campus.

Big Sean, this year's Convo artist, performed on April 2. I wanted to go out of my comfort zone; not only to work a concert for the first time, but to see a live rap act as well. I asked a fellow member of the Executive Board, Nicole Dawson, the head of the Center Stage Committee, if I could follow her around during the show and write about everything that went on. She ecstatically approved the idea and told me she could not wait to read it.

I remember when Nicole was hired last year; I was so excited when I found out. I liked Nicole as a person, but I especially liked Nicole's taste in music. We had interacted a few times before she was hired; we talked about bands like the Fratellis, Cage the Elephant, and Panic! at the Disco. We even spontaneously sang "Eight Days a Week" together one night when we ran into each other at Applebee's karaoke. Since I first came to JMU I had longed to see a well renowned rock band perform, and the closest I got was Passion Pit. I knew Nicole was the person to bring rock and roll back to JMU students, and she did not disappoint. The only problem was the students did not approve of anything she and her committee brought. The Canadian pop rock outfit Magic! was brought to Wilson Hall in the fall; granted they were no Led Zeppelin, but it was a start goddammit. The attendance at the Magic! show was low and led to budget cuts for other events throughout the year. However, this did not deter my hero Nicole and her committee from spearheading a show called *Frost Fest* last February. The bands Grizfolk, X-Ambassadors, and The Mowglis filled Wilson with a variety of epic Alt. Rock for three straight hours. The venue was more than half empty. Nicole and her committee put countless hours into preparation, marketing, and working these shows and all they got was rude, if not hateful comments on Facebook, Twitter, and my eternally least favorite form of social media, Yik Yak. If you are unfamiliar with the art of Yakking, it is an app where you can anonymously say anything about anyone, and anybody within a ten-mile radius can read what you say. This way you can say terrible things about good people while anonymity protects you, your basement, and your precious Cheetos. After multiple complaints, Nicole and her committee decided they owed it to the students to bring a rap act to the school. They landed on Big Sean and it sold out in less than a day.

I was born into the wrong time period.

3 p.m.—Set Up

I showed up to the Convocation Center right after my last class of the day on Thursday. Other volunteers had been there since 8 a.m. setting up the stage and awaiting other orders for the million things that needed to happen to make the show go on. Nicole was going to be late; her event planning professor would not let her miss her class for the biggest event of the school year. He clearly did not teach a class on irony. I stood next to the other volunteers, all anxious for the night to happen. They were all talking about what to do when they met Big Sean, someone shouted above all of the other voices, "Be sure to call him something professional, Big Sean is not a formal name for addressing him." I had no idea what that meant, but I looked forward to meeting Mr. Big Sean.

5 p.m.—Security

Nicole showed up around 5, ready to put on a show for 3,200 intoxicated students. Lines were already forming outside of the entrances two hours before doors opened. Several students sat outside the doors, pre-gaming with unlabeled plastic bottles. Police surrounded the entrance accompanied by drug dogs to make sure there weren't any problems before the show started. Nicole told me I could get some good inspiration for my piece if I worked pre-show security. I happily accepted and followed four other committee members outside to Big Sean's tour bus. Our job was to make sure the performers were not harassed by students so drunk they seemed passionate or students so passionate they seemed drunk. I stood outside of the largest vehicle I had ever witnessed; spanning fifteen parking spaces was Big Sean's bus. I was so curious as to what was inside, but before I could give it any thought, Mr. Big Sean himself stepped outside of the portable mansion. The committee members were very professional and gave an acknowledging wave or nod in his direction. He approached all of us, gave all of the girls a hug, and gave me a firm handshake. He was very polite, saying things like "Thank you all for having me," and "I'm so excited to be here." He then pulled out his phone and paced around the tour bus while he made a call. Several of the girls claimed he was talking to *Ariana Grande*, but I didn't know who that was, so I continued to be the best bodyguard I could be.

Several students began to gather around the perimeter we had set up around the bus; I kept telling everyone to keep their distance, but Big Sean insisted they get a photo with him. I didn't want to upset Nicole, but I also didn't want to upset the talent, so I let a few people take a picture with Mr. Big Sean. After about forty minutes, Big Sean said he was going to go back in his bus so we told all of the students to patiently wait in line with all of the other fans too drunk, timid, or naive to walk the hundred yards from the line to Big Sean's tour bus. Big Sean approached me and thanked me for my hard work; he shook my hand and went into his bus. I felt terrible. Over 3,000 people had paid hard earned money and showed up three hours early just to get a glimpse of this modern-day icon, and I felt no different shaking his hand than I did shaking hands with the dry cleaner who fixed my dress pants earlier that week. It made me think somehow somewhere one of my idols was suffering from unappreciation, and I just couldn't bear that. I shrugged off the thought of Matthew Bellamy paying for a sandwich with his own money while I walked back toward Convo for the pre-show security briefing.

6:30 p.m.—Pre-Show Security Briefing

In order to maximize safety and the overall success of the event, the program board hires outside security to work the event with the students. I would like to think that I could prevent a JMU linebacker from storming the stage, but fortunately, I didn't have to thanks to outside help. Each group of student volunteers was paired up with an actual security guard and sent to their designated locations. Nicole wanted me to be a stagehand, which meant I got to lift equipment on the stage with professional stage crew workers and then watch the show from the barricade, the last defense between Big Sean and five hundred inebriated students. I went to my post, lifted my share of equipment, and then approached the barricade to meet the security guard I was paired with. I never got his name, so for the sake of the story we will call him Gorby because I've always wanted to know someone named Gorby. I introduced myself and shook Gorby's hand; he was a middle-aged man, not that intimidating in the looks department, and fairly small. He told me this was the first time he had worked a concert here at JMU; we weren't so different after all. He told me about some of the jobs he had worked in the past; he was apparently a regular at John Paul Jones Arena in Charlottesville. I told him where I was from, and he told me he worked a county fair in my hometown and he hated it; we were getting along great! After laying the groundwork of our new friendship, Gorby began venting his personal feelings about the show. He said, "Shows these days aren't about music, they're about getting wasted and doing hard drugs with your friends while a beat plays in the background, all in the name of grinding on a stranger." He clearly had some strong reservations with rap music; I began to wonder if he had lost a loved one in a grinding accident.

Students began to flow in; based on all of the horror stories I had heard from previous years, they all seemed pretty tame. Nobody was starting fires, vomiting profusely, or doing heroin as Gorby anticipated. But the night was young and there was still plenty of time for people to chase the dragon. Gorby leaned back over to me to strike up another conversation; apparently we hadn't conversed enough. He asked me if I had ever been to The Tilted Kilt; I hadn't, but my friend Billy once playfully described it as *'Hooters, except with buttholes.'* He then began to describe his meal, which I thought was unnecessary, but he did it anyway. He finally ended his description with, "But you don't go there for the food, now do ya?" He then looked out into the crowd at a girl wearing very little clothes as she approached the stage. Gorby let out a twelve-syllable *damn,* and I began to feel fairly uncomfortable with my middle-aged counterpart.

8 p.m.—The Show

After an hour, the venue was nearly full; the people in the front of the pit were being crushed against the barricade by the people behind them. So far nothing crazy had happened, Nicole texted me saying someone with cheap seats tried to run into the pit but was immediately stopped by the cops. How anticlimactic. The opening act, Ground Up, was about to perform; I had carefully lifted several speakers and placed them on the stage while the actual tour support arranged them into precise positions. Nicole got on the stage to give her speech about the organization and why everyone was here. I stood behind the barricade, subconsciously holding my breath to show that I sympathized with the people in the very front. Nicole got off the stage and the lights went out. Everyone went crazy. Ground Up took the stage and opened with DMX's "Party Up (Up In Here)," and immediately the crowd lost control. Everyone was jumping up and down and yelling; so far it seemed no different from the hundreds of rock concerts I had been to. A fight broke out between two girls in the right-front of the pit; Gorby took charge and jumped on the barricade. He then pointed and yelled at them repeatedly until they stopped. A rather lame way to stop a fight—I expected a WWE match and I got a pissed off lunch lady. And to think I once looked up to you. The police pushed through the pit and grabbed one of the girls; she was fairly tall with a long wingspan that definitely benefited her in the fight, but it did her no good in handcuffs. The other girl left the pit crying; the police paid her no heed; she was clearly the victim.

The band finished in thirty minutes. I ran to check in with Nicole before I had to carry Big Sean's equipment to the stage. She told me nothing much else crazy had happened; some guy in the back row threw up on five seats in front of him, which made it difficult to sit in them. I thanked her for the intel and ran back to do my stage crew duties. Most of his gear was already set up earlier that day; I was shocked at how someone who didn't play an instrument could have so many amps. Granted I had never worked backstage at a show before, but this had to be more equipment than most musicians need. After I set up everything, I returned to the barricade. Gorby had sensed some distance between us and told me I had to move back five feet so I wouldn't get in the way of the *actual security.* I reluctantly accepted and positioned myself in front of a stack of bass amps. I put in earplugs and waited for Big Sean to take the stage. Nicole went back on to the stage to give her spiel, while I gazed into the pit. It looked uncomfortable; girls were on guys' shoulders against Gorby's will, the people in the front row had an iron barricade shoved in their stomachs and chests, and I saw a couple unlucky people crammed into other people's armpits; however, still no fire or heroin. Nicole descended from the stage, the lights went out, and everyone went crazy as Sean Michael Leonard Anderson took the stage. *"Heeeeeey JMU are you ready to party!?"* Dammit if they were not indeed ready to party.

Everyone screamed and the first song began. A strong sensation punched me in the back; it was the bass speakers. I have seen P-Nut play a ten-minute bass solo, I've been in the front row while Arin Ilejay played a double bass drum for ninety minutes, but nothing I had ever experienced could prepare me for the sensation I felt that night. I can't even describe it now; I felt as if the bass amps had transformed me into Dr. Manhattan and I could transcend space and time with ease. I felt like I was being ripped apart, and I also felt like I had chosen a bad place to stand. Damn you, Gorby. I couldn't hear Big Sean. It was like I was in a car with the speakers blown out and turned all the way up. It sounded like he was singing to me through a tin can from a mile away. After a minute, the vibrations were so uncomfortable they forced me to cough. I ran to the bathroom to compose myself. I washed my face, wet my hair and decided to find a better location to stand. I went to find Nicole to make sure I didn't miss anything else crazy. She had nothing much to report. Apparently, some student said "Fuck you" to a volunteer, and they responded, "No it's 'I Don't Fuck with You,' get it right!" I didn't get it at first, but Nicole explained it to me, and I chuckled.

I returned to my command post. The crowd was eating every word he *sang*. When the Beatles started performing in Hamburg, they played ten-hour sets; some of which consisted of ninety-minute guitar solos. This means the Beatles had to not only learn instruments, but play them for long periods of time; what a hassle. Big Sean had the luxury of a large speaker system and a computer with all of his songs pre-recorded on them. This gets all of the clutter of instruments off the stage, to make room for the man in a lion suit. I shit you not. A man dressed up like a lion and pranced around the stage with Big Sean for the entire second half of the set. The crowd had lost it, and it was all due to a furry costume. Mike McCready once played an eleven-minute guitar solo; Kirk Hammett, almost thirty. Fuck that. Give me a guy in a lion suit. That's where I want my money to go.

Big Sean played for about eighty minutes and the students ate up every second of it. He was only contracted to play for one hour; he must have really enjoyed the crowd. He came out to do an encore. I think he said something about never having played this song before, but I couldn't hear him. After the encore, the students filtered out, leaving behind sweaty rags, pieces of clothing, and enough airplane bottles to fill a bathtub.

10:30 p.m.—The Cleanup

After every Convo artist performs, it is a tradition to take a picture with the artist and the committee in it. Big Sean happily posed with the committee and hugged all of the members after it was over. He thanked everyone for an amazing turnout and all of our hard work; he sure was graceful. He then returned to his tour bus and was attacked by a swarm of college students. His tour support successfully defended him and sent the drunkards and fangirls on their way. I had been dreading the cleanup all day; we had to wait for tour support to remove Big Sean's millions of amps, and then take the stage apart. But first we had to clean up the seats. I was actually intrigued by that part; at last year's concert when Juicy J played, they found airplane bottles, cocaine, and tampons soaked in vodka for a festive alcohol enema. No such luck this year. The craziest thing we found was an airplane bottle of cake batter flavored vodka, and that wasn't nearly as crazy as the person who decided to drink it.

At midnight, there were still students gathered by the front entrances thinking Big Sean would have been bold enough to not only walk through the front entrance but leave ninety minutes after his bus did. After two hours of intense manual labor, the stage had yet to be taken apart, but on the plus side, pizza had arrived. The program board pays for all of the volunteers to eat pizza in exchange for all of their hard work. I had two slices of cheese courtesy of Papa John, and then joined the stage disassembling team. By the end of the night, I was so drowsy from waking up to go to an 8 a.m. class, standing all day, and transcending dimensions via the bass speaker, I apparently ran into my friend Pete, who was also volunteering that day, and told him the bass speakers were such an experience, but before I could describe it to him, I walked away disoriented. He told me the next day. After we finished taking apart the stage, Nicole invited me to go to IHOP with her committee, but I told her I simply did not have the energy. I got home at 2:30 a.m. and collapsed in my bed, thinking about modern music and cursing Gorby's name.

The Next Day

We did it. We finally did it. We got complimented on Yik Yak. The University Program Board woke up to find several positive Yak's including, *UPB stayed up until 2 cleaning convo, that's dedication thank you guys we love you,* and, *Thank you UPB for all you do and dealing with drunk people!* I reflected on the show; though Big Sean was not my favorite musician, he sure did know how to entertain a crowd, and sometimes that's the hardest thing for a musician to do. I was most impressed with Nicole. Even though it wasn't her favorite type of music, her passion for the event and the student body fueled her interest in it. And I will always look up to her for it.

"What's so bad about that?" Professor Vedder asked.

"I don't know. I just felt like my Beatles paper with all the short stories was better. Plus, a lot of people in class told me I was too critical of other music in my last one, and I feel like I'm more critical here."

"That's good. Be critical. Critical is unique. Critical is entertaining. Writers get jobs as critics because they don't say things like, 'This song is neat,' or 'Season eight of *The Simpsons* is really solid.'"

"Season eight of *The Simpsons* is really solid, though," I laughed.

My professor smiled. "True," he said. "Don't let negative feedback deter you. Write for yourself, not for others."

I'll never forget that advice.

ORANGE CRUSH
By R.E.M.

April 2015

"I've got my spine, I've got my orange crush"

After an unbelievable amount of effort and planning, I had finally done it: I had finally crafted the perfect plan to kiss Laura for the first time. I wasn't going to let another opportunity slip through my fingers. This was going to work. Foolproof.

Things had been going well with Laura: we had seen a couple movies at Grafton together, we had been out to dinner a few times, and we texted frequently. We even had a show we were watching together: Judd Apatow's classic sitcom about college, *Undeclared*. Earlier in the week, I had mentioned that Keith was visiting, to which she had responded, "I'd love to meet him." Without hesitation, I had invited her to join us that coming Friday, and she enthusiastically agreed to hang out with my roommates, my best friend, and me.

Finally, it was Friday. Keith would arrive at my apartment in a few hours, we would enjoy a standard college Friday night, and then we would spend most of Saturday recovering from that standard college Friday night. Then I'd go to work at Grafton, where Laura would meet me. We'd finish my shift together, then I'd bring her back to my apartment, introduce her to my best friend and my roommates, play a little *Rock Band*, then walk her home. Based on the data, I was confident she would have such a good time and be so charmed by the evening that she'd let me kiss her when I dropped her off at her apartment. It was guaranteed to work.

Not only had I come up with the best plan of all time, but Marvel had released season one of *Daredevil* on Netflix that very day, and I was able to bask in unfiltered, unadulterated, comic book violence while I waited for Keith. *It can't get better than this*, I thought . . . just before I received a phone call from my best friend.

"Hey," Keith sighed. "I've got some bad news."

My heart sank. "What's wrong?"

"My car is totaled."

"Oh, fuck. Are you okay?"

"Yeah, I'm fine. I ran over a fucking puddle, and somehow water got in the engine and totaled my car." Keith always had a passion for souped-up speed machines, while I preferred the speed limit and seatbelts. It normally wasn't a problem . . . until this very evening, when he drove a sports car low enough to the ground that a puddle could destroy his engine.

"Shit, that sucks. Where are you?"

"I just got towed about two hours away from you. Near Richmond. I'm not sure how I'm getting home, but I'm not gonna be able to come up this weekend."

My heart sank even further. I had no car, so not only did I have no way to help my best friend, but now my perfect plan was ruined. Would Laura even want to come over if Keith wasn't here? I had no way of knowing. "Sorry to hear that, brother. I'm just glad you're alright."

"Yeah, I'm fine. I'm sorry to let you down. I know you were excited about introducing me to Laura."

"Don't worry about that. You'll meet her someday," I guessed.

"All right, man. I'm going to drown my sorrows at a bar. I'll talk to you later."

"Sounds good, dude."

I hung up the phone and walked over to the fridge to crack

open a beer. Keith wasn't the only one who needed to drown his sorrows. I opened a Bud Light and heard the door to the apartment swing open. My fellow *Frasier* fanatic, Damon, walked through it. "Hey-oh," he said, casually sauntering into my living room.

"Hey," I said.

"You started drinking without me?"

"Keith totaled his car and is stuck in Richmond for the entire weekend. I couldn't afford to wait for you."

"Well, shit. You wanna go get him?"

My heart leaped out of its sinkhole. "Wait . . . for real?"

"Yeah. Could be fun."

I wanted to tell Damon I loved him and that if I had my way, I would be kissing two people for the first time this weekend. But I just said, "Sweet! I'll call Keith."

"What's up?" Keith answered.

"Great news! We're coming to get you! Me and Damon!"

"For real? Oh, wow . . . you guys just made my night! I've got a hotel, so why don't you both stay here, and we'll drive back in the morning?"

"Works for me," Damon said, eavesdropping on the apparently loud phone call.

"We'll be there in two hours, bro!"

I hung up and filled a backpack with liquor and a change of clothes.

"How the hell am I most likely to get divorced?!" I asked toward the end of our car ride to meet Keith.

"Gavin just asked me and Bruce who we thought was most likely to get divorced," Damon defended himself. "I obviously wasn't going to say either of them and start an argument, and you weren't there, so it was an obvious choice."

"Well, surely they asked you to defend your decision."

Damon nodded. "They did."

"What the fuck was it?"

"You're a hopeless romantic."

I threw my arms in the air. "How is that bad?! It means I'm passionate about the girls I'm into! I'm like Ross from *Friends*!"

"Ross has been divorced three times!"

I crossed my arms. "You know, I actually don't care for that show. I prefer *How I Met Your Mother*."

"Never mind. That's the real reason you're getting divorced."

"Fuck *Friends*! It's so goddamn mediocre, and everyone eats that shit up because it's safe to like. It's the Mumford and Sons of television shows."

"*How I Met Your Mother* is so much more mediocre!" Damon argued. "I can understand how you might like the characters better, but it's the most cliché garbage on TV. It's not even remotely funny."

"We just watched an episode of *Friends* where Monica and Chandler talk about a racecar bed or some shit. I've seen plays funnier than that, honest to God. Plays!"

"I don't have the whiteboard and several hours necessary to explain how wrong you are."

I shook my head. "This isn't even the right argument," I remembered. "There's no way in hell I get divorced before Gavin. He thinks Aerosmith is better than the Beatles."

"That *is* pretty damning," Damon admitted. "Find out where Keith is and tell him we'll be there in ten minutes."

I pulled out my phone to text my non-biological brother. "We're close to you. Where should we meet?"

He quickly responded: "Drinking in a gloomy bar until I forget the fact that I destroyed my first car."

"Where?"

"Red Lobster."

Damon and I pulled into the Red Lobster parking lot

across the street from the hotel we would be staying in. Inside Red Lobster, we received a warm greeting from the hostess, who directed us to the bar. There, we found a down-and-out Keith, who had at that point consumed over two-hours' worth of beer and cheddar biscuits.

"Hey, brother!" he shouted with a hug. He moved on to hug Damon and thank him for the spontaneous rescue. "Hey, man. It's been ages. I really can't thank you enough."

"It's no problem. I was in the mood for a road trip," Damon said with a mellow smile.

"How about I buy you two a beer?" Keith offered.

Damon and I graciously accepted the offer and asked Keith to help us continue our debate on divorce.

"Wow, I'm pretty hammered. Why the hell did you buy that shit?" Keith said with a look of disgust.

"We always drink 151 when we hang out. It's tradition." I gestured over to the bottle on the nightstand, The three of us were sandwiched together in a queen-sized bed in our hotel room. It wasn't an ideal sleeping arrangement, but we were too drunk to care about mild discomfort.

"It's a dumbass tradition. Stop buying it."

"You were the one who got me into it!" I pointed at him and laughed.

"I'm not a teenager trying to blackout anymore." Keith pinched some chewing tobacco from his tin and inserted it between his lips. It was a habit of his I already hated, and it didn't help that we were sharing a bed. Damon was asleep to my left, while Keith was spitting dip into a water bottle on my right. Aside from my current situation, the room was quite tolerable—if you avoided the bathroom covered in mysterious brown stains.

"This was a surprisingly fun night," I said.

"Hell yeah it was. I miss the good old days where we'd hang out for weeks at a time. Seems like just yesterday we were playing *Rock Band* with Chris and Delynn."

I nodded. "I miss them. I think I'm going to spring for the plane ticket and visit them in Germany this summer. Laura's studying abroad in Europe, so I'm hoping I can somehow take a train or something and surprise her."

"Wow, this girl must really be something special," Keith said with a mouthful of tobacco.

"I've never felt this way about anybody. Not even Penny. There's just something about . . . whenever we spend time together. She's just . . . cool. I can't really describe how . . . I don't really know what I'm saying."

Keith laughed. "I can't wait to meet her."

"She's excited to meet you. I just really want to impress her. I really suck at getting girls to think much of me."

"Why? You're great at making friends, and that's a skill you shouldn't take for granted. You've been the most dependable person in my life for almost twenty years. Not just me; as soon as you moved away, you found five more friends you still have to this day. Fuck, you've lived with two of them for the past four years. You met fucking Damon like two years ago, and he just drove you two hours spontaneously for no goddamn reason."

"He did get free booze and a shitty hotel room. Don't sell yourself short."

Keith rolled his eyes. "All I'm saying is, every time you make new friends, you don't forget the old ones. You just add them to the group. I've always felt comfortable hanging out with any friends you've ever had. Don't try to be someone different to impress Laura. Just be yourself."

I smiled. "Remember how we met?"

"Yeah. It was the first day of preschool and you were sitting in the corner like a sad little bastard with no friends, and I asked if you wanted to play."

"Thanks for that."

"Anytime, brother," he said, and we both began to let our drunken brains descend into sleep.

Everything was in place: Damon had dropped me off at work and taken Keith to my apartment. Keith was still pretty upset about totaling his car, but Bruce and Julian told me they would show him a good time and buy him a case of beer to distract him from his troubles. All I had to do was hang out in Grafton, wait for the movies to end, then bring Laura back to my apartment.

I was in the Grafton projection booth watching more *Daredevil* on my laptop when I decided to text Julian.

"Hey, man. Just wanted to remind you I'm bringing Laura back tonight. Nobody is plastered to the point of embarrassment, right?"

Daredevil was in the middle of kicking a drug dealer off of a roof when Julian responded: "Yeah, everything's fine. Keith, Bruce, Gavin, Damon, and I are just playing drinking games. Nothing to report."

I had not factored in our consistent controversy creator, Gavin, also spending time with us that evening. Though it had been a while since he drank a near-full bottle of Goldschlager and prevented Joey from hooking up with his crush, I could not guarantee he wouldn't do the same thing again after he had a few drinks in him. This was an unexpected wrench in an otherwise thoroughly devised and therefore flawless plan. I began to worry Gavin may screw it up.

My new-found anxiety was interrupted when Laura walked into the booth. "Hey, you," she said, smiling. She wore a seemingly new black skirt and a sleek blue shirt with transparent sleeves that clung to her arms and glimmered in the light. She looked fucking incredible.

My brain immediately spiraled. *Surely, she's not dressed like this for my benefit; maybe there was a deal at. . . a popular clothing store. Wow, you can't even think of the name of a clothing store because you only buy clothes at concerts.*

"Wow, you look great," I said, still in disbelief as I stood up to hug her.

She shrugged. "I figured it was a special night. I know Keith means a lot to you, so I wanted to make a good impression."

"I'm sure he'll appreciate that," I said casually, instead of the "Marry me!" I wanted to shout from the top of my lungs. "I do have to warn you: my friends can get a bit rowdy. I hope it won't be too much of a bother."

"I have a brother; I know what your gender is like. Honestly, if they aren't getting blackout drunk and watching porn, I'll be a little disappointed."

I thought about how frequently *both* of those things happened in my apartment and prayed that this wouldn't be one of the nights Gavin decided to brag about how much he could drink and masturbate. "Wanna watch *Undeclared*?"

"Love to," she said, smiling.

After several episodes of *Undeclared,* the film in Grafton had ended, and we were ready to lock up the theater and drive back to my apartment. I texted Julian to let him know we were coming back, and to make sure everyone was behaving themselves, but I never got a response. The night was off to a perfect start so far; I couldn't let the friends (and Gavin) I loved so dearly (and tolerated) ruin my shot at my first kiss with Laura. When we pulled into the driveway of my apartment, we got out of Laura's car and walked up the three flights of stairs it took to get into 1825 J.

I turned to Laura just outside the door. "Again, I have to warn you: it could be a war zone in there."

"Bring it on," she said, flaunting the sexiest smile I had ever seen.

I opened the door to my apartment to find . . . nothing happening at all.

"What the hell?" I said out loud, looking around. I investigated further to find my best friend asleep on the living room couch, Damon passed out shirtless on the other couch across the room from him, and Julian asleep in his room with the lights out. Gavin and Bruce were conversing on the porch. I poked my head out to assess the situation.

Gavin saw me first. "Cade's here!" he shouted drunkenly. He peered over my shoulder at Laura standing behind me. "And he brought a friend!"

"What the hell happened?" I asked.

"Well, we were playing drinking games, and Julian got upset for no reason and locked himself in his room. Keith drank an entire case of beer and fell asleep, and Damon drank a lot of liquor quickly and passed out several hours ago."

I pulled out my phone to see if Julian had ever responded to me. He had, in fact, but I had missed it. The first text read, "Everything's fine, we're playing a drinking game where we go around naming the world's most dangerous blank." The second text read, "Gavin's being a dick. He keeps giving shit answers, but he won't admit he's wrong." The third and final text read, "THERE'S NO WAY KITE-SURFING IS THE WORLD'S MOST DANGEROUS SPORT! I'M GOING TO BED!"

My apartment wasn't just underwhelmingly calm; it had turned into the most boring place on Earth, against all odds. I had promised Laura a fun night, and it was imperative I deliver. I walked back into the living room where Laura stood in between two couches with an unconscious boy on each.

"Can I get you a drink?" I asked her.

"Um sure, what do you have?"

"We have Orange Crush in the fridge as far as mixers go, and pretty much anything you could want in the liquor cabinet."

"Do you have any gin?"

"You want Orange Crush and gin?" I was surprised.

"I'll drink anything with gin." She grinned.

"Fair enough. I'll grab you a glass."

"Great. Can I use your bathroom?"

"Of course," I directed her into my bedroom and pointed to the bathroom inside.

As soon as she shut the door, I sprang into action. I ran to the kitchen and made Laura's drink, then grabbed a bottle of Bacardi 151 and ran back into the living room. I poured a swig of the rum into Keith's slightly open mouth.

He shot up, his eyes wide. "What the fuck was that for, ass-hole?!" he choked out.

"You fell asleep," I told him. "I need you awake so you can meet Laura."

"Fuck that, dude. I'm tired as shit." He yawned and lay back down again.

Before I could shake him, Bruce and Gavin came in from the porch, and Laura returned from the bathroom. I returned to playing it cool and handed Laura her drink.

"Laura, these are my roommates Bruce and Gavin . . . and the one passed out on the couch is Keith."

"He doesn't look like the pictures you've shown me," she said, tilting her head to the side and looking at the couch.

"Oh, sorry, no . . . the passed-out guy *without* a shirt is Damon, and the one *with* a shirt is Keith. Sorry, I should have been more specific."

Bruce gave a polite wave to Laura while Gavin reached out to grab her hand. "It's lovely to meet you," he said, kissing her on the knuckle.

She pulled her hand back and lightly rubbed it, a puzzled look on her face. "Likewise," she said politely.

"I really wish Keith was awake so you could meet him," I said.

"Oh, you want Keith awake?" Gavin interrupted. "Piece of cake." With a lady in the room, it was Gavin's goal to establish himself as the alpha male, so he did what any drunk show-off would do in this situation: he lifted up the couch. Keith rolled right off it onto the coffee table, then onto the floor.

"What the shit, Gavin?" Keith mumbled from the floor.

"We have a guest! You're being rude," Gavin said, grabbing another beer from the fridge in the room.

Keith sat up on the carpet, rubbing his eyes. "Goddammit, I was fucking asleep!"

I looked over at Laura. She didn't seem too turned off by the situation. She seemed almost entertained. My confidence grew.

"Hey," I suggested, "why don't we play some *Rock Band*?"

"This is bullshit," Keith grumbled, but he stood up. "Just give me the drums." He grabbed a glass from the kitchen and came back for the 151. I handed one guitar to Bruce and the other guitar to Gavin and set up a chair next to the drum kit for my best friend. I grabbed a microphone and sat on the couch next to Laura so we could sing together.

She shook her head. "Oh, I don't know if I can sing," she said. "I'm not very good."

"That's what the alcohol is for," I said, and stood up to make myself a rum and coke. "I'll even let you pick the song."

"Hmm . . . I don't know." She sorted through the songs while Bruce, Gavin, and Keith set up their instruments. But soon she quit scrolling and sighed. "You like Green Day, right?" she yelled to me. "Just pick a Green Day song I know."

I walked back into the room with my drink. "Works for me," I said, cuing up the song.

"No hard feelings, right Keith?" Gavin asked, adjusting his plastic guitar strap.

"I fucking hate you," Keith growled back. Bruce laughed.

The intro acoustic guitar riff to "Wake Me Up When September Ends" rang throughout the apartment. Laura and I began to sing the iconic middle-school anthem; she was half-smiles half-self-conscious, but at that moment she was the cutest girl I had ever seen.

When the chorus came around, Keith sang over us, "He woooke me uuup, Gaaavin fuuucking suuuuuucks!" Everyone in the room laughed at the top of their lungs; even Keith couldn't help but grin at the reaction he had not expected to receive. When the eponymous line came up in the song, everyone other than

Gavin sang Keith's new lyrics in place of Green Day's, and luckily Gavin just laughed it off and continued playing bass. This became a theme of the night: every time the chorus of any song came around, Keith replaced the lyrics with variations of "I hope you die, Gavin," or "I hate you, Gavin." Each time, we would all laugh and sing Keith's new lyrics.

After about half an hour, Gavin wanted to change it up.

"Mind if I sing, Cade?"

"Sure thing. Go for it," I said, handing him the mic.

He pulled the mic up to his lips. "Keith, hit me with 'Tears Don't Fall' by Bullet for My Valentine," he demanded. "Time to get my scream on." He pulled his shirt off and threw it into the corner of the room. Laura laughed. There was a split second where he heard the laugh and looked across the room at his shirt with uncertainty. This clearly was not the reaction Gavin was hoping for, but he shook off his doubt and started to flex while swinging the mic around. Keith cued up the song, and Gavin reached out his hand to me. "Come sing with me, brother," he implored. "Let's duet this shit."

"I think I'm gonna sit this one out," I said, smiling at Laura.

"Your loss. Let's do this, boys," he said, continuing to swing the microphone around like Robert Plant.

Bruce began to play the chilling guitar intro to the heavy metal number. I turned to Laura, hoping Gavin wasn't about to start a mosh pit in our living room.

She clinked her empty glass against my Beatles pint glass. "You have some drinking to do," she said with a grin on her face. "I'm the guest. I can't get drunk before you do."

At this point, I had drunk enough to finally ask the question that had been on my mind the past forty-eight hours: "If I drink to the Beatles logo on my cup, can I kiss you?"

I held my breath. *This is it,* I thought. *All of the effort I put into this weekend—this is the moment where I find out if she dressed like this for me or because she got a great deal on clothes somewhere.*

"You can kiss me right now," she said, with the same grin on her face. And I did.

Laura kissed unlike any girl I had kissed before her; she was filled with passion and she kissed with her whole body. We kissed for several minutes while Gavin, Bruce, and Keith performed a screamo song right next to us. It was a surreal moment that I'll never forget. When the chorus came up, Keith improvised anti-Gavin lyrics and we all sang them and laughed. Then Laura and I kissed until the song was over.

"Are you sure you don't want me to drive your car back? I really didn't drink much," I asked as I walked Laura home at the end of the evening.

"Don't worry about it. I'll just come back and pick it up tomorrow and maybe hang out for a bit, if . . . if that's alright with you."

"Of course. I guess I'll see you then," I said as we arrived at her front door.

"I . . . I had a really fun time tonight," she said softly.

I went in for one final kiss and said goodnight.

The following morning was like any other Sunday morning. A majority of the apartment was hungover; Bruce and I discussed the highlights of the previous evening to the people who missed out, while Keith wallowed on the couch.

"I'm never drinking 151 again," he said, slouching in his seat, using his smartphone to figure out how he was going to report for duty in North Carolina in twenty-four hours.

I grabbed a glass of water from the kitchen and sat down next to him. "Thanks for coming up, dude. Sorry about your car."

"Eh, shit happens. Anything for you, brother."

I took a sip from my water and immediately felt odd. *Weird. I didn't drink a lot last night. Why do I feel so . . .* I threw up in my cup. I filled it to the brim, but miraculously managed not to get any on the couch.

Keith thought it was the funniest thing in the world. "Holy shit, dude! I guess I'm not the only one who drank too much last night!"

Unfortunately for me, it was something much worse than a hangover. It was love.

EPIC
By Faith No More

April 2015

"You want it all, but you can't have it"

My anxiety hit new heights with Laura. Whenever I was with her, it was like some wonderful, euphoric drug. Whenever I was without her, it was pure hell. Every thought I had just added to the chaos: *She's cheating on you just like Penny! She'll get bored with you before you know it! You're gonna fucking blow this!* I was getting two to three hours of sleep per night. Every day I'd wake up, go to class, walk to Grafton, try to take a nap in the projection booth, wake up again, try to stay awake for my UPB office hours, then go home and wait for her to either text me or respond to my texts. I had to play it cool and not send too many texts, but I also had to let her know I was interested; it was a fine line that I didn't navigate very well.

I decided this had gone on long enough, and it was time I got some additional help managing the chaos in my brain. Fortunately, I had an entire exec team to call upon if I needed anything.

"Violet, meet me in Grafton. I need help with something," I texted.

"Okay, I'll head over there after class," she said.

Violet walked into the booth an hour later. "What's up?" she said. She took off her backpack and sat down.

"I really need some Laura advice," I said. Fatigue was all over my face; I wore the same Nirvana shirt and dark-washed jeans from the previous day. If Violet had just met me for the first time, she might have thought I was a drug addict.

Violet smiled. "Okay, lay it on me."

We sat in two computer chairs behind the large projector in the Grafton projection booth. It was always the most peaceful place to do homework, watch Netflix, or have heart-to-heart conversations. "Well, as you know," I began, "we were talking for a while, then we went out to dinner and the movies a couple of times, and just a couple of weeks ago, we made out. We've been hanging out even more for the past two weeks; sometimes we make out, sometimes we just talk, sometimes we just lie there and listen to music."

She raised an eyebrow "It sounds like everything is going well. What's the problem?"

"I just don't know what my next move is. I want to be in a relationship with her, but she's mentioned she doesn't want anything serious since she just broke up with her boyfriend. Also, she's studying abroad in Europe for six weeks this summer, and she says she wants to 'spend time finding herself' which I assume she wants to do alone." I placed my elbows on my knees and slouched over in my seat.

"So, she just wants to be casual?"

"I don't know. I'm getting a lot of mixed signals. I feel like she'd be in a relationship with me if I made one huge romantic gesture," I said, looking at the floor.

Violet shook her head. "I'd say take it slow and keep pursuing her. Let her know you're interested, but don't make her feel like she needs to marry you."

I looked up at her, then came up with another question. "Is it weird that she still hangs out with her ex-boyfriend?"

"How much?"

I looked back down at my feet. "Like a lot. Probably as much as she hangs out with me."

"Hmmm . . . I don't know. Some people realize they're better friends than significant others. I dated my first boyfriend for two-and-a-half years, and we tried to be friends after we broke up."

"Did it work?"

"Not really." She paused. "We don't talk anymore."

"Fuck. Just what I needed." I looked at the small smiley face on the wall of the projection booth Laura had drawn a few days prior.

"That doesn't mean that Laura's situation is the same," Violet said, placing a comforting hand on my shoulder. "She could totally have just wanted to be friends with him when it didn't work out the way she wanted it to romantically."

"Or she's still fucking him."

Violet was a bit surprised by this comment. "That's a bit pessimistic, don't you think?"

I sighed and looked at the floor. "Not pessimism, just déjà vu." We were both quiet for a few seconds. Then I broke the silence.

"How are you and Layne doing?"

"We're doing pretty well, I guess. It's still new, but we're enjoying it." Violet was great at listening to other peoples' problems without turning the focus to any aspect of her own life. I will always value her friendship for that.

"I'm happy for you both," I said sincerely.

"Thanks," Violet said and stood up. "I should get back to the apartment. Nicole and I are going out for drinks later if you want to come."

"Thanks, Violet. Maybe I will," I said with my first smile of the day. It felt good to know that no matter how rough life got, my friends always had my back.

"Cool," she said, opening the booth door. She paused and turned back around to me. "Are we still doing a campus crawl next week?" she asked.

I nodded. "Yes. For sure."

"Great. Text me later." She walked out of the booth.

I went downstairs and bumped into Pam the janitor, who was

playing *Candy Crush* on her phone instead of cleaning the theater. She looked up at me as if I had startled her.

"Oh, sorry, sir! I'm just taking a break. Don't tell anyone, right?"

"Mum's the word, Pam," I said, having too much on my mind to give the smallest of fucks about Pam's work ethic. I walked into the theater lobby and lay down on the table where we sold popcorn.

My phone vibrated, and I answered it.

"Hey, G-dad."

"Hiya, pal!" G-dad said with his usual warm enthusiasm. "I saw you called earlier today."

"I wanted to wish you a happy birthday," I said. My grandmother had once told me I was the only grandchild to habitually call G-dad on his birthday. She said it meant a lot to him, so I kept it up. "Seventy-seven years young, if I'm not mistaken?"

"That's correct, and I don't feel a day over forty."

"You don't look it either, G-dad."

"So . . . what's new with you? Ready to graduate?"

"Absolutely not. I've never been less ready for anything."

"Well, I'm sure you have a job lined up for after college."

"I'm a communications major. I don't even know where to begin looking for a job. Plus, I don't have a car, so I have to find somewhere to work within walking distance." I began to realize my anxiety over Laura had slowly crept its way into all of the other facets of my life.

"I'm sure it's not all bad. Your mother tells me you have a girlfriend now. What's her name?"

I had told my mother about one date I went on months ago, and she told the whole family I was in a formal relationship. Being young, stupid, and in love, I decided to play along with the charade, even though Laura and I weren't Facebook official. "Her name's Laura, G-dad."

"Ah, a great Catholic name," he said. I could feel his smile through the phone.

I laughed. "I'm sure she gets that a lot. She said she's coming to my graduation party, so you might get to meet her."

"Excellent. I look forward to it."

"Sounds good, G-dad. I gotta go home and eat dinner. Happy birthday."

"Thanks for calling. Talk to you later."

I hung up my phone, grabbed my stuff, waved to Pam, still playing on her phone, and walked home.

I looked at my phone as I walked. *To text her or not to text her, that was the question that was consuming every fucking one of my brain cells. If I don't text her, she could forget that I'm interested in her and immediately fall in love with someone else. If I text her, she could see it as neediness for attention and be totally turned off by it.* We had texted each other every day for the past eighteen days. *What happens if I don't talk to her for a day?* I wondered. *Will she forget I exist? Will she think I'm bored with her? Fuck!* I know now that my logic didn't make sense, but love isn't the most rational or thought-out of life's experiences. Right when I began to feel a brain aneurysm coming on, I received a text. It was from Laura.

"Hey! Do you want to help me study tonight?"

Don't seem too eager, don't seem too eager. . . .

I waited a full forty-five seconds before I responded: "Sure! Where at?"

"I was thinking of your room? If it's okay. I don't want to intrude."

Holy fuck, there is a God.

"Yeah, that totally works for me. Thirty minutes?"

"Perfect! I'll see you then."

Holy shit Holy shit Holy shit Holy shit. She wants to study? In my room, of all places? At 11:30 p.m.??? Is this it? Are we going to have sex? I had nearly gone my entire college career without having sex, and in the final minute of the final quarter, I was being thrown a Hail Mary pass. I had a theory: If I didn't have sex in college, I would grow up into a weirdo who had never had sex, and it would only become more and more socially unacceptable and therefore difficult for me to lose my virginity at all. If it didn't happen now, I had a good shot of turning into Steve Carrell in *The 40-Year-Old Virgin*.

But I had strong feelings for a girl, I was pretty sure she felt the same way about me, and she was on her way over to hang out in my room after midnight on a Wednesday. This was it. It had to be.

I opened the door for Laura. She came in wearing her backpack and carrying a large blanket.

"I hope it's not weird that I brought my blanket," she said. "I usually carry it around with me."

I didn't know what to think of that statement. I had never seen her carry this blanket around, nor had I ever heard of anyone taking a blanket with them to a study session in the history of college academics. Was she sending me a signal? *God I'm so bad at this.* "Oh, no, I don't mind," was all I could say, remaining neutral on the blanket issue.

"Cool. Do you only have one chair in here?"

"Oh, sorry. I can grab another one from the living room."

"Don't worry about it. Let's just sit on the bed."

I was wrong about God existing; in his place was a puzzle master, hellbent on getting me to make an ass of myself in front of a girl who may or may not want to be intimate with me. If I sat on the bed and made any sort of move to initiate intercourse, there was a good to fair chance Laura would say, "Oh, no. You misunderstood. I just wanted someone I could make out with a couple times before I went on vacation." Then she'd tell all of our friends how much of a pervert I was.

"Oh, all right," I said, grabbing my laptop and sitting next to her on the bed.

"You want to listen to music?" she asked.

"Um, yeah." I turned on my speakers, plugged in my laptop, and shuffled my twelve thousand songs, hoping music would make my move for me. *Come on, shuffle,* I silently prayed. *I've never needed your guidance more than now.* The first song to come on was

"Break Stuff" by Limp Bizkit. *All right, shuffle, you can fuck right off.* I skipped the song. It was followed immediately by the Beatles' "Helter Skelter." *Ugggghhhh, the one time you guys don't write a love song. SKIP!* The third song was "Crash Into Me" by Dave Matthews. *I'm not losing my virginity to the fucking Dave Matthews Band.* The fourth song, "The Change," was a song from Evanescence's self-titled record. *This was released nine years after "Bring Me to Life" was relevant. Why the fuck do I have this?*

"You know, we can listen to more than five seconds of each song," Laura said as she gently brushed her hand against my neck and face.

Fortunately for me, the fifth song was "Swallowed in the Sea" by Coldplay and was therefore safe to play all the way through. "Okay," I said, turning to her.

She smiled back at me and went in for a kiss. I kissed her back. Her hands began to move up and down my body. I mimicked her motions so I wouldn't seem like the inexperienced Catholic boy my mother wanted me to be until I got married and magically inherited sexual prowess from Jesus on my wedding day. We kissed for several minutes; I was beginning to think she didn't even want to study at all, which I realized was a bit of a shame because I had a shit-ton of work to do before I graduated in less than two weeks. After a very enjoyable thirty minutes, Laura made an attempt to make the moment even more enjoyable and moved her hands below my waist.

Oh fuck! This is it, boys! Battle stations! I thought, readying my body for what it had wanted to do since I saw the sex scene from the 1985 film *Teen Wolf* in middle school. Her hand went into my pants. *This is it, this is it, this is . . . wait, what the hell?*

My body was prepared, but there was one member of the team—the most important member—who wasn't reporting for duty. *You've got to be fucking kidding me. You used to show up when the pizza delivery person was a chick. Why the fuck are you doing this to me now?!*

Laura looked at me. "Is something wrong?"

"What? No, why?" I asked, hoping she wouldn't notice I didn't have an erection.

She quickly took her hands off me. "Sorry, I didn't mean to make you feel uncomfortable."

"Laura, no, no, no, no, no! That's not at all what the problem is. To be honest, I don't really know what the problem is."

She looked into my eyes for several seconds and realized I was telling the truth. Then she smiled. "Oh, I know what it is."

"Really? Oh God, please tell me."

"You're nervous."

"What?"

"You like me, and you want to make a good first impression. It's all right. I like you too."

"Well, that's . . . wait, really?"

"Well, yeah. I enjoy spending time with you. I think you're funny, and it's a plus you have good taste in music."

"I just feel like . . . I let you down."

"You didn't let me down," she said, going in for another kiss. I kissed her back. "We can go slow if you want to. I brought beer. Would you like one?"

I had never wanted a beer more in my life.

Hours later, we both lay in my bed, listening to music—slightly buzzed, with our bodies intertwined and our clothes still on.

"Tell me something else I don't know about you," she prodded.

"When Keith joined the Marines and went to bootcamp, I sent him a letter once a week. He said he cried when he read the last one, and you can never tell him I told you that."

Laura smiled from ear to ear. Her head lay on my pillow, inches away from mine. "You seem like you're made up."

"How do you mean?"

"I've never met another guy like you. I don't think I've even met a person like you."

I chose to take this statement as a compliment. "Thanks, you seem like you're made up too."

"I like made-up people better than real people," she whispered behind a sleepy grin.

"I sometimes think that's the whole point of life. Finding someone who doesn't seem real and makes you want to be different than the real people who are boring."

Laura laughed. "You should put that on a t-shirt."

I smiled back. "I just drank more than you."

"I only brought three beers, and I've had two of them! You're practically sober," she said.

"Hey, it's your turn. Stop changing the subject. Tell me something I don't know about you."

Laura paused. "Gus . . . my ex-boyfriend . . . he was abusive." She began to tear up. "When he got mad, he would yell at me and throw beer bottles at my car. Sometimes, he would slam my head against the headboard when we had sex. I constantly worried about what he would do next." She continued to cry. The stain on her pillow grew by the minute.

This was a complete shock to me—I was near speechless. "Laura . . ." I said, brushing tears from her eyes. "I'm so sorry. I had no idea, I mean . . . you still hang out with him and all."

"It's because I'm scared of what he'll do to me if I stop."

As if I needed another reason to hate this fucking guy. I had wanted to dispense vigilante justice on him when I thought he just had a crush on Laura, but this was exponentially worse. "I'll talk to him. I'll tell him if he ever—"

"You can't tell *anyone* I told you!" she begged, and more tears escaped her blue eyes. "That's the most important rule of the secrets game."

"Laura, this isn't a game. You could get hurt. Or worse."

"It's so hard. He's still my best friend. I know it's weird, but it's just how I feel. It's . . . hard to change that. He hasn't done anything to me since we broke up. I think if I just stay friends with him, he'll eventually find someone else and leave me alone."

"Laura . . ."

"You promised! You can't tell anyone. Just like I won't tell Keith about the letters."

"I mean . . . one of those saves someone from mild embarrassment, and the other saves someone a lot of physical and emotional pain."

"Please. You can't," she said, letting one more tear out.

I sighed. "Okay, I promise."

"Good." She sniffled. "This isn't exactly the first-time activity I had in mind for us tonight," she said, a smile spreading across her tear-stained face.

"You know . . . I've never shared a bed with a girl. It's really nice."

"Never? Not even with Penny?" she asked.

"Not even with Penny."

"Glad I could be your first then," she said, bringing her body closer to mine.

"Me too." I put my arm around her.

We lay together for two pleasant hours before we had to get up for class.

DETROIT ROCK CITY
By KISS

May 2015

"I hear my song playin' on the radio"

"What if the door's locked?" I asked.

"It's not," Violet whispered. Her face lit up as she pulled the door to my sophomore-year dorm building open. We both stepped inside.

"Okay, what are the rules again?" I asked.

She laughed. "We've been over this already. How drunk are you?" she asked.

"The normal amount?"

Violet rolled her eyes. "We have to take a shot in every room on campus we lived in, worked in, or took an important class in."

"What if we can't get in the room?"

"Then we go on to the next one." She peered down the hallway. "Which one of these is your room?"

"The end of the hall," I said.

It was surreal being back in my dorm after two years. So many things had happened in this very hallway. Like the time Billy got naked and ran into our room as a prank. Or the time Julian and Bruce walked into Billy's room naked while he was having sex with his girlfriend for the first time. Or the time Keith visited, only to get blackout drunk and fall asleep in the room directly above ours. He had been missing for an hour when we found him sleeping on a pile of laundry in the middle of a room that belonged to three girls we had never met. Good times.

"This one?" Violet asked.

"That's the one," I said and knocked. A frat-dude-looking stranger opened the door.

"Who are you?" he asked.

"I'm here to drink in the room," I muttered, drunk, shy, and still confused regarding the rules of what we were doing.

Violet laughed. "We're doing a campus crawl. My friend here used to live in this room. Can he have a drink in here?"

"Campus crawl? Why didn't you say so? I'll drink one with you!" the stranger said. He reached into his fridge and threw a Keystone Ice to me, which I drank quickly, wishing this poor underaged kid had better beer hidden in his room.

After a few more stops, we headed over to reunite with Tommy, Henrietta, and Nicole, who had gone to their own individual dorms and classrooms. I was thankful to be drinking with close friends, as opposed to my recent habit of drinking alone while thinking about Laura . . . who immediately texted me as soon as I had this thought.

"Looks like fun!" she responded to a picture I had sent her of Violet and me. "Promise you'll come be on my campus crawl next year when I graduate?"

"Wouldn't miss it for the world, baby," I promised.

We approached a drunk Tommy and a concerned Nicole, the latter of whom was looking at a very wet Henrietta.

"What the hell happened?" Violet asked.

"I fell in the fountain next to the Quad," Henrietta said, laughing.

We all shared a laugh as Tommy drunkenly stood up from the steps in front of Wilson Hall, flaunting his bottle of Jack Daniels. "So where to next?" he slurred. We all moved to the grassy comfort of the lawn and sat down briefly to collect our bearings.

"I think we hit all of the stops on the list," Violet responded.

The alcohol began to jog some mental cogs in my brain, and out of nowhere I came up with what I thought was the best idea of all time: "Let's go to Grafton. I've got the keys."

I watched everyone's faces light up and a near-unanimous "YES!" was released into the air. We had all spent so many hours of our UPB exec career working and attending events in this building; what a perfect way to close out our senior year campus crawl, making popcorn and taking shots on the stage of our favorite JMU landmark.

On our walk over to the building, I received multiple Snapchats from Julian, Gavin, and Bruce, who were on their very own campus crawl. The best video I saw was probably Bruce in the lobby of Harrison Hall, ripping a yearbook in half and cheering as the fragments hit the ground.

When we arrived at Grafton, I unlocked the doors and did a quick sweep to make sure the coast was clear. I turned on all the lights, let my companions in, and locked the doors behind us. We wheeled out the popcorn machine and began chugging beers in the theater. I went into the projection booth to turn on the theater speakers and made a playlist comprised of songs quintessential to our exec board experience: "Sonsick" by San Fermin; "Naked" by X Ambassadors; "Reflections" by Misterwives; "Rude" by Magic!; hell, we even threw on "Photograph" by Nickelback to honor Lenny, who was currently studying for an exam he had at 8 a.m. the following morning.

Nora saw the Snapchats and Instagram posts of our drunken debauchery and found her way to the building. She walked in to see all of her friends dancing to classic UPB jams and throwing popcorn into the air. It occurred to her that because she would be president of the exec board the next year, she should probably walk away and wash her hands of any potential trouble we could get into (as if there could be any consequences to our actions—we're twenty-two and invincible, baby!). She left the building chuckling.

I went back into the booth and aimed spotlights on the stage, highlighting Henrietta, Nicole, and Violet. Their silhouettes bounced off the stage curtain as they danced to alt-pop masterpieces; it was like something out of a goddamn indie film. I went to join my friends on the stage and looked out over a sea of empty chairs. In that moment, I wished more than anything that I could go back to that sad bastard high schooler, sitting alone on the school bus, knowing exactly where it was taking him but still hoping that maybe today would be different—that today would be the day he would make friends or get a girl to acknowledge his existence. I wished I could go back and tell him that he'd be celebrated one day, that he'd throw the best *Rock Band* parties the world had ever seen, and that no matter how bad life seemed, it would get better.

Then I'd tell him, "We made it. We finally made it."

BALLROOM BLITZ
By Sweet

May 2015

"So frantically hectic"

The day after the campus crawl, I had sobered up and returned to feeling awful. In fact, I couldn't remember a time when I had felt worse. Laura had just started spending the night at my apartment, so I was getting two hours of sleep per night when she was there, and even less when she wasn't. My body was on the verge of shutting down; my brain constantly felt like it could snap in half at any moment. I started bringing beer to work so I could focus without suffering intense anxiety attacks. My grades took a serious plunge; on top of my exec internship and my job at Grafton, I was taking six classes, and every single one of them took a back seat to Laura.

Despite all of that, I had finally made it to what I thought would be the last class of my college career. Seventy-five minutes later, I would be done with school forever. My History of Rock professor from my sophomore year taught a class on entrepreneurship in the music industry. Thinking it would be a cool career path, I had foolishly made the music industry my minor, so I needed this class to graduate. I was failing . . . hard. Our final project was to find a business in the industry, research it diligently, put together a thirty-page business plan for it, and then pitch it to the class.

You'll never guess what I chose.

"The company Harmonix is located in Boston. It has brought

us countless hours of entertainment in both the music and video game industries. From the creation of the revolutionary music game known as *Guitar Hero,* to their launch of the infinitely more popular *Rock Band* franchise, Harmonix changed the music video game biz forever."

I stood in front of my whole class looking how I felt: near death. I was running on two hours of sleep and was probably still drunk from the night before. It was really fortunate I knew *Rock Band* like the back of my hand; I would have looked and sounded like a complete idiot on any other topic. "*Rock Band* launched in 2007, selling millions of copies worldwide. To date, over thirteen million copies of *Rock Band* titles have been sold, netting over one billion dollars' worth of sales. Over four thousand songs representing over twelve hundred artists are available in the franchise library, and over 130 million song purchases have been made since the game launch. I've got to be responsible for at least two million of them." I paused and glanced around the room. Nobody laughed. "After a brief two-year hiatus from releasing new content, the franchise is scheduled to return this fall with the release of *Rock Band 4.* It has the potential to be a huge release after their content dry spell."

One of my classmates raised his hand. "Do people still play that game?" he asked.

"I definitely do, and I'm sure other people do as well. Harmonix said they tracked at least two hundred thousand users still playing last month alone."

"How many people want to invest in this company?" Professor Childress asked. Nobody raised their hand.

"You're missing out," I tried to say confidently, but I'm sure I just looked and sounded like a tired wreck.

"It seems nobody is playing your game anymore. Interesting choice of business model," the professor said as he jotted something down on a piece of paper. "I've seen enough. You can take a seat."

I received the first and only F of my college career in that class. I sent Professor Childress an email begging him to reconsider, and told him how I needed this class to graduate, but he just responded a week later with, "Sorry, you deserved that F."

I ended up having to drop my minor and take an online class in "romantic communication" over the summer in order to graduate. I chose that subject so I could maybe learn how to communicate with Laura better and understand how to be in a real relationship.

At the end of my presentation, I sat back down at my desk, waiting for the feeling of defeat to wash over me. But I was too tired to feel anything. Right before I fell asleep listening to my classmates present their business models, my phone exploded with texts. Before I could understand what was happening, I had forty unread messages and twelve new emails, all relating to the campus crawl the previous evening. I left the final in-person class of my entire school career in a panic and hurried to Jeff's office.

I ran along the campus sidewalks I'd walked up and down millions of times, through the buildings I'd studied in for hours, smelling the undeniable stench of dog food in the air as I had countless times before. I ran past Wilson Hall, where the UPB crew and I had hosted artists like Magic!, X Ambassadors, and the Mowglis. I ran past Mr. Chips, the convenience store that sat in front of a creek that Julian, Bruce, Damon, Billy, and I would jump across after we saw movies at Grafton. I ran past "the quad," the long, grassy lawn on campus where the douchebags gathered to play shitty reggae pop on acoustic guitars, hoping they could get a girl to talk to them.

And along this entire beautiful race through a campus full of memories, only one thought filled my mind:

Shit shit shit shit shit shit shit shit.

My phone vibrated.

"Hello?" I wheezed.

"Hey, Cade. How are you?" Violet asked.

"Fucking fantastic."

"So . . . you read Maris's email?" she asked.

"I read the email, I read the texts from you, and I read the forty messages in the group chat."

"Should we be worried?"

"Worried about what? Getting expelled? Or going to jail?"

She was quiet for a moment. ". . . So, what's the plan?"

I slowed down as I neared my destination. "I can't think clearly. I got no sleep last night. I'm just gonna talk to Jeff and then meet up with you guys. Hopefully that will smooth over the situation."

"Okay, good luck," she said and hung up.

I wandered into my boss Jeff's office as I had so many times before, under better circumstances. He was sitting at his desk looking at his computer screen, with his back to the door. His office was a small nook in the back of the building, and his desk took up three quarters of the space. He always kept two empty airplane bottles of Fireball Whiskey in the back corner on a shelf. I had no idea why he never threw them away.

"Hey, Jeff," I said. "What's the good word?"

He turned around to see me and frowned. "Sit down," he grumbled. "I see you got my email."

"Of course." I actually had not received his email. The one I had read came from the equally authoritative Maris, whom Violet had referred to earlier.

"I don't get it, Cade. I've been your boss for two years. You've been my best employee. Nothing like this has ever happened before now." I had never seen Jeff without a smile before, so this whole "smoothing over the situation" thing was off to a rough start.

"I don't know what to say, Jeff. We're seniors. We graduate Saturday and we just wanted to do something spontaneous," I said, mustering up as much sincerity as I could.

Jeff was about to say something but then he choked a little. I could see a lone tear forming in his eye. It wasn't a good sign.

"You're a good kid, Cade, but you made a dumb decision. You

call it 'spontaneity,' but I'd call it 'throwing your goddamn college career away.'"

I was at a loss for words.

"I'm really, *really* sorry Jeff," I tried. "I'll never do anything spontaneous again."

We gathered near a dining hall patio about thirty minutes later to discuss how we were going to confront Maris. The tension was high.

"My parents are gonna fucking kill me!" Henrietta panted. "Did you see that email? Maris said she could expel us!"

"Maris won't do shit," Tommy said and leaned back in his seat. "She's just trying to scare us."

Violet stood up. "Shut up, Tommy!" she yelled. "This is your goddamn fault in the first place! You were the one holding your fucking Jack Daniels bottle in every picture we took!"

Tommy sat up and put his hands in the air. "It was a campus crawl! We're supposed to get fucking wasted in public! I paid tens of thousands of dollars to study here. The least they can do is calm the fuck down and not expel me! Plus, it was Nicole who posted all of the photos to social media."

"Everyone calm down," I begged. "It could be worse."

"How?!" Henrietta practically shrieked.

"Jeff could have fired me, but he didn't. Now I can pay rent this summer." I looked around. My friends were truly devastated. I had only known them for a year, but it was the best year of my life, and I had grown very close to them in a short amount of time. I looked around at a hopeless Henrietta, Tommy, Nicole, and Violet. It absolutely killed me to see them this distraught.

"Do you guys remember what Maris told us at the beginning of the year?" I asked them.

"Don't get blackout drunk and trash campus?" Henrietta said, staring at the ground.

"No," I said, and stood up. "At the very beginning of the year, she gave us that quote that I thought was really lame at the time, but it actually describes us very well."

"What was it?" Nicole asked.

"'When you find people who not only tolerate your quirks but celebrate them with cries of "Me too!" be sure to cherish them, because those weirdos are your tribe.'"

For the first time that day, I saw them all smile.

As I sit here writing this book, I'm looking directly at a framed picture I keep on my nightstand. There are four pictures in the frame: the first is the UPB logo with the UPB motto, *College is more than just classes*; the second photo is the entire exec team standing together right after we finished the ropes course; the third photo is of all of us standing together after the Big Sean concert that we put on; and the fourth photo is the inscription of the same quote I had reminded them of on that day after the campus crawl. Looking at these photos now, I remember what it was like to be amongst people who celebrated the *Rock Band*-loving, movie fanatic, constantly-referencing-things-few-people-understand nerd I was. I've had great relationships since then, but the relationship I had with my exec team will never be replaced by any new co-worker, friend, or romantic interest I'll ever meet. I'll hold onto these pictures of the UPB forever, along with the perfect memories of good times (and bad) that come with them.

HIGHWAY STAR
By Deep Purple

May 2015

"I've got everything"

As Tommy, Henrietta, Nicole, Violet, and I all sat in the UPB board room waiting for our inevitable doom, I thought about everything that had led us to this moment. I thought about how, just mere hours ago, we thought it would be a good idea to do a campus crawl, which led to us thinking it would be a good idea to drunkenly break into Grafton and make popcorn one last time, which led us to playing music over the loudspeakers and dancing on the stage.

Everyone was in a somber mood. We all knew we were in trouble, but how *much* trouble? Would the law get involved? Would I go to jail for getting drunk, as my mother had warned me several years prior? I looked at my phone. I realized this was the first time in months I wasn't anxious about texting Laura back. I thought, *Log this for future reference: if you're nervous about talking to a girl ever again, just break the law and get caught. The text anxiety will disappear, guaranteed.*

I thought about Laura and how I hadn't gotten any sleep for the past two weeks. That's probably part of why I had thought this was a good idea. Or maybe I didn't care. Laura had slowly become my everything, and I had stopped giving a shit about any other aspect of my life.

That is, until it was all about to fall apart.

The tension in the room was smashed when Maris opened the door to the office. She calmly sat down in the seat at the head of the table. It was like some *Game of Thrones* shit; one of us was going to get beheaded.

Maris looked at all of us silently for a moment. When she finally spoke, her voice was low and quiet.

"I feel betrayed, hurt, and let down," she began.

Words were out of my mouth before I could stop them. "Maris, we completely understand. We did a terrible thing and—"

"I don't need you to validate my feelings!" she snapped at me.

Oh fuck, this is bad! I thought as I mentally placed myself back in my metaphorical guillotine and shut up. In that moment, I felt like I deserved the absolute worst, and I was confident I was going to get it.

"This morning I woke up to an Instagram post showing several of you standing on the bridge next to East Campus. Tommy was holding a handle of Jack Daniels."

We all side-eyed Tommy, but nothing would sting more than what Maris said next.

"I then received a call from Pam, the Grafton custodian. She said the building was littered with popcorn when she came in the next morning, and she had a strong hunch about who it was."

Pam. The janitor who never did her job. The person who told me not to turn her in for watching several movies on the clock. I had gone to painstaking efforts to ensure every beer can and liquor bottle was picked up and removed from the theater; I was certain there was no evidence of us breaking the law. However, I did not account for popcorn left on the ground, or for Pam actually doing her fucking job. I had half a mind to tell Maris what *real* betrayal felt like, but I knew it would just land us in more trouble.

"Why did you get drunk in Grafton?" she asked.

"We were doing a campus crawl," Violet choked out as she looked down at the conference table.

"What's that?"

Henrietta looked up at Maris. "It's when you take a shot or drink a beer in every class, dorm, or important building in your college career right before graduation," she elaborated. Her voice grew more faint with each word, as Maris's unwavering glare of disappointment persisted. By the end of her sentence, Henrietta's eyes were back down on the table.

"And why did you think that was a good idea?" Maris asked.

"All of the seniors do it," Tommy said. "We spent this whole year busting our asses with UPB, our jobs, and our classes. I feel like it's only fair we got a chance to let loose for once."

We turned to Tommy with our eyes wide. Was he trying to make the situation worse?

"You all graduate in two days," Maris continued. "I am completely within my right to not only call the police, but also send an email to the administration and ask them to suspend your graduation."

The silence in the room was deafening. I don't know if it was the lack of sleep or the recent Laura-related binge-drinking that had destroyed many of my brain cells, but I decided to say something.

"Maris, this year was the best of my life." Everyone turned to me with a look of confusion, but I proceeded. "If you told me in high school there would be a time when I could spend every day with people who not only accept me, but *celebrate* me, I would have called you a liar. I'm never going to work with a better group of people."

"You don't know that," Maris said skeptically.

"I do. I promise you I do. I spent every day of high school wishing I was somewhere else. *Anywhere* else. But this year, I never wanted to be anywhere else when I was with these people. In high school, I told a random kid I liked Panic! at the Disco, and he punched me. I told Nicole the same thing, and she asked if we could sing their songs at karaoke together. In high school, I told a girl I liked comic book movies, and she never spoke to me again. Violet, Henrietta, and I got together once a week to watch a show about the Green Arrow. In high school, I didn't have anyone to play *Rock Band* with; in college, everyone wants to play every weekend. It's not just everyone sitting at this table. I feel this way about Griffin, Layne, Jessica, and the rest of exec. I know we fuc—sorry, I know we messed up, but we did it together. We even turned ourselves in together. We're more than a team, we're a family. You were right all along, Maris: these weirdos are my tribe."

I never once saw Maris prominently display emotion throughout the entire exec internship; not even the first night when she told us all to tell our darkest secrets and shared hers as well. But for the first time all day, her look of disappointment vanished as she closed her eyes and took a breath. A look of calm washed over her.

She sighed. "Are you all actually sorry?" she asked.

Everyone nodded.

"You're not just saying it so I'll let you go without punishment?"

Nicole was the first to respond. "Maris, I think we all feel genuinely terrible. I wouldn't even know how to begin faking an apology to you."

"Jeff is making me pay for the cleanup bill," I chimed in, "which is more than fair. We've really learned our lesson."

"Okay," was all Maris said after that.

And that was it. Maris let us go, and we went on to graduate and never tell any of our parents we almost got expelled two days before graduation. (Sorry, Mom and Dad!)

Violet drove me home that day. We were too shocked to say much at first, but by the end of the drive, we opened up.

I spoke first. "That was crazy," was all I could think to say.

"Yeah," she replied.

"I really thought we were going to jail."

"Yeah." She sighed and laid her head back on her seat. "It's been a really long day."

I looked out the window at the cars driving by. People were just carrying on with their lives like it was a regular day. Students were drinking in their front yards on Fraternity Row, laughing and shouting on their balconies and chugging cheap beer through funnels. It seemed like everyone we passed was smiling. What did I have to do to be happy like them? "God, I feel terrible," I groaned. I turned to Violet. "What do you want to do tonight?" I asked.

Violet thought for a moment. Then she shrugged and smiled at me. "Eh," she said, "let's just get drunk again."

I couldn't help but smile back. To be happy, all I needed were my friends. "Sounds good to me."

After the Krazy Unikerns broke up, I thought I would never again meet a group of people who celebrated every facet of who I was. But then I met my exec team. All of the highs and lows we endured over the year just brought us closer together, and I'm still close to most of them as a result. As time goes by, it becomes harder and harder to remember how happy people once made you feel, especially if you don't spend as much time with them as you once did. If you ever meet a person or group of people who celebrate you for *you,* realize how important they are and never take them for granted. No matter how much life tries to make you, *never let them go.*

PLEASURE (PLEASURE)
By Bang Camaro

June 2015

"Let your feelings come alive"

"So, what does she mean to you?" Delynn asked, sipping a glass of delicious and affordable German wine.

"I'm in love with her," I explained. "I've never felt this way about a girl." I sipped my equally delicious and affordable beer out of a cold stein. The city of Baumberg was full of scenery, and the temperature was a crisp mid-sixties, but all I could think about was how good my authentic German Pilsner tasted.

I had gotten a lot of graduation money after I finished my last semester at JMU, and rather than save for my future, I had decided to spend all of it on a trip to Germany. Chris and Delynn were stationed there for three years after Chris had received a promotion in the Army, so I had a free place to stay during my trip abroad. Unfortunately, Chris was spending the summer building houses in Africa, so it was just Delynn and I for ten days, which was only half of the Krazy Unikerns' original lineup.

Mostly, I had spent $1,300 and traveled halfway around the world to get my mind off Laura. Since she had left for her study abroad program in Europe, each day I had spent in Harrisonburg without her would go as follows: wake up an anxious wreck after about four hours of sleep, try to play video games and realize I couldn't focus, write songs about Laura until lunch, try to keep my food down when I ate lunch, try to watch TV then quit watching TV when the most minute of details reminded me of her, finally text her when the pressure became too unbearable, start drinking promptly at five, and wait for a response until bedtime. Sometimes she would text me that she missed me, sometimes she would say she wanted to be left alone, and sometimes she wouldn't respond at all. I even resorted to praying, but it felt insincere, and I was almost positive that God wouldn't care about the desperate cries for help from a sheep who strayed from his flock long ago.

Fortunately, the trip to Germany was doing a pretty good job of distracting me; on this side of the globe, I only thought about Laura for about a third of the day.

"How long have you been dating?" Delynn asked.

"Well, we're not formally dating. We had a class together, she broke up with her boyfriend about four months ago, and we just started hanging out after that. We really clicked."

"Has she said she loves you?"

"Yes . . . I mean, she was drunk when she said it, but it still counts."

Delynn shook her head. "That doesn't count," she said.

"Of course it does! Drunk actions are sober thoughts," I responded confidently placing my beer stein back on the table.

"Oh, I'm sorry, what was the last rational decision you made after drinking twelve shots of tequila?"

I ignored Delynn. "It was the *way* she said it. We spent our last day in Harrisonburg together doing . . . *everything*. She invited me over to her place, and we nearly spent the whole day in her bed—"

"Okay, okay! I don't need to hear all of the details," Delynn said, shriveling her face in disgust and holding her hand up to stop me.

"We told each other we would have one final day together

and then just go our separate ways for the summer. If we're both single and have feelings for each other this fall, we'll give it a shot."

"So . . . you're not in a relationship."

"You didn't let me finish. We parted ways and didn't talk for almost a week, then out of nowhere she sent me a Facebook message that said, 'Would you be mad if I told you I love you?' and that's all I could think about for the rest of the night. I told her I loved her too, but then when she woke up the next morning, she explained that she had gotten blackout drunk and didn't remember sending the message."

"I don't know," Delynn said, furrowing her brow. "You don't see that one in a ton of rom coms."

"Don't be such a pessimist. Do you know how big a deal those words are? Why would you say something as serious as 'I love you' if you didn't at least mean it fifty percent?"

Delynn looked down at her wine glass and didn't reply. After a few moments, she looked up from her glass. "Have you talked since then?" she asked.

"Well, yeah, about every other day or so. Her birthday is coming up and I told her I was going to write her a song."

"How's that going?"

"I recorded it before I left. Her birthday is the day I go back, so I'm going to email it to her from the airport."

Delynn smiled. "She'd be stupid not to fall in love with you."

"Thanks, sis. You know, I did the math: Laura is only an eight-hour train ride away from here."

"I've already bought you like two hundred euros' worth of beer. I'm not spending any money on a train ticket."

We both laughed and agreed to spend more money on alcohol.

DANI CALIFORNIA
By the Red Hot Chili Peppers

June 2015

"Too true to say goodbye to you"

During our time together, I gave Laura three mix CDs: *Best Mix Ever Vol. One*, *EuroLaura*, and *Charlottesville*.

The day before I had left for spring break in 2015, I had invited her over to play *Rock Band*, and we ended up talking about mix CDs for an hour. I promised her right then and there I would make her the best mix CD she had ever heard. I had spent what little downtime I had during my vacation making her this CD, and this is what I came up with:

1. Crazy One - Rivers Cuomo
2. When I'm With You - Best Coast
3. Whistle for the Choir - The Fratellis
4. First Day of My Life - Bright Eyes
5. If I Had a Gun . . . - Noel Gallagher's High Flying Birds
6. Songbird - Oasis
7. Rosie - The Kooks
8. I For You - The All-American Rejects
9. She's Always a Woman - Billy Joel
10. Jesus Christ - Brand New
11. I'm on Fire - Bruce Springsteen
12. Fields of Gold - Sting

13. In the Aeroplane Over the Sea - Neutral Milk Hotel
14. Swallowed in the Sea - Coldplay
15. Unsteady - X Ambassadors
16. Reste Avec Moi - Codeine Velvet Club
17. Linger - The Cranberries
18. Dreaming of You - The Coral
19. Friday I'm in Love - The Cure
20. National Anthem - The Gaslight Anthem
21. Rocks and Razorblades - Next Bus to Wrongtown
22. In My Life - The Beatles

As soon as I gave it to her, she went home and immediately put it in her DVD player (the only device she had that still played CDs) and listened to the whole thing in eighty minutes. Then she texted me saying it was in fact the best mix CD she had ever heard.

I gave her *EuroLaura* the day before had she left for Europe, and wrote the Kooks' lyrics "I see the sun rising, and all you see is it fall, fall, fall" on the disc. I had filled the CD with long-distance love songs and spent the entire summer listening to them, hoping she was also listening to them and thinking of me.

1. 2,000 Light Years Away - Green Day
2. Jet Lag - Simple Plan
3. Here Without You - 3 Doors Down
4. Across the Sea - Weezer
5. Back to Me - The All-American Rejects
6. God Only Knows - The Beach Boys
7. Please Mister Postman - The Beatles
8. She's Got a Way - Billy Joel
9. We Are Nowhere and It's Now - Bright Eyes
10. Warning Sign - Coldplay
11. Earth Angel - Death Cab for Cutie
12. Carry You - Dispatch

13. All I Have to Do Is Dream - The Everly Brothers
14. The Girl I Can't Forget - Fountains of Wayne
15. Ole Black 'n' Blue Eyes - The Fratellis
16. See the Sun - The Kooks
17. Run - Snow Patrol
18. America - Simon & Garfunkel
19. I'll Follow You - Shinedown
20. The Calendar - Panic! at the Disco

The third CD was named *Charlottesville* to commemorate a spontaneous trip we took to its namesake. We listened to it on the way there, we listened to it on the way back, and then we used it as background music for . . . other things . . . when we got back to my apartment's parking lot.

1. Calico Skies - Paul McCartney
2. Things I'll Never Say - Avril Lavigne
3. You're All I Need - Mötley Crüe
4. Babydoll - The Fratellis
5. If That's What It Takes - Bon Jovi
6. Moshi Moshi - Brand New
7. Mean Ol' Moon - Amanda Seyfried
8. Action Cat - Gerard Way
9. Stray Heart - Green Day
10. Waiting for You - Grizfolk
11. Madness - Muse
12. Always - Panic! at the Disco
13. Married with Children - Oasis
14. Skin - Sixx: A.M.
15. Make a Plan to Love Me - Bright Eyes
16. Lost in You - Three Days Grace
17. Hesitate - Stone Sour
18. Fix You - Coldplay

I know what you're thinking: *Why the hell do these mix CDs*

have Bon Jovi, Simple Plan, and goddamn Avril Lavigne on them?
First of all, I'm a big fan of songs with a catchy hook. Second off,
go fuck yourself. You think you're hot shit because you like Arcade
Fire and are too good to throw on a fucking Shinedown record
once in a while? I can like Talking Heads *and* put Mötley Crüe bal-
lads on my mix CDs, so piss off. The goal of these mixes was to fill
mine and Laura's heads with catchy melodies that we couldn't get
out of our brains, hoping that the songs would bring us thoughts
of each other.

Once you get a good chorus stuck in your head, you'll either
obsess over it, or it will drive you absolutely insane—and honestly,
isn't that all love really is?

I hate airports. On my way back from what was arguably the
best vacation of my life in Germany, I had what was *definitely* the
worst airline experience in my life. I saved a hundred bucks on
tickets by accepting an eleven-hour layover in London. I didn't
think much of it when I bought them, I just thought I'd be happier
with the hundred bucks than without it.

This was not the case.

I got to London at 10 p.m. only to find out the airport closes
at midnight. I couldn't pay for a hotel because I only had American money, but mostly because I only had six dollars of American
money. I had to go through the security check where a man with a
thick British accent asked me if I had Ebola eight times. He then
made sure I was an American citizen and not just some European
moocher trying to cash in on that sweet, sweet U.S. healthcare
system. As soon as I got past the interrogation portion of my trip,
I had to run and catch what ended up being the final Metro ride
of the night, which transported me to the only part of the airport
where travelers were allowed to sleep. I got there right at midnight,
found a bench between two homeless people, and set my backpack

down, firmly establishing eminent domain. I then began to write a very important email—an email that I was very nervous about sending.

Laura's twenty-first birthday was in one hour. I had promised her the best birthday gift she could ever ask for and told her I would send it via email right at midnight. Mix CDs would no longer cut it; I decided to spend many of my anxious days and sleepless nights back home writing her a song, a song that would finally explain to her how much she meant to me. It was called "Dizzy Lung."

I don't know if you've ever written a song *for* someone, but I assure you it is infinitely harder than writing a song *about* someone. I had written countless songs *about* Eileen and other girls I had feelings for; all I had to do was play chords and talk about what was going through my head. Easy. Writing a song *for* someone is an exhausting procedure where you pour everything you've got into one little piece of "art" and hope that the person you're gifting it to feels a level of joy comparable to the level of emotion you're tearing from your soul in order to write it. It was a simple song with a simple chord progression, but it said everything I wanted to say. The difficult part of this whole thing was seeing whether or not she felt the same way I did.

I connected to the airport Wi-Fi and attached my recorded song file to the email. I then got on Facebook and messaged Laura. She was currently in Italy, and the clock had just struck midnight there. It seemed as if she had been waiting for me online, because I got a response about ten seconds later."

"Hey!" she messaged back.

"Happy 21st birthday, Laura! I hope you like your present," I typed, and I clicked send on the email.

The song was around four minutes long, and I waited anxiously for her to tell me what she thought. In the meantime, my brain told me what *it* thought: *Ugh, it sucks,* my brain said. *She hates it. You wasted your insomnia on this bullshit when you could have been drinking or watching* Reno 911.

Then after almost the exact length of the song, she wrote back. "Cade! It's perfect! I absolutely love it!"

"I'm glad," I replied. I probably added a dumb emoji as well.

"This is the nicest thing anyone has ever done for me! I love you! I love you! I love you! I'm in love with you!"

After several weeks of wondering if she felt the same way about me as I did about her, I was elated to see the words. It was kind of a strange sensation; if you had told me three months before that this was going to happen, I would have shouted from my balcony how happy I was. I would have run through the town of Harrisonburg *A Christmas Carol*-style, hugged everybody, and thrown what little money I had at all the children and elderly. I was that happy in that moment, but after three months of anxiety-induced insomnia, the happiness translated to a wave of calm. I finally felt at peace, and that was arguably just as good of a feeling. I remember how I had overstepped my bounds with Penny, so I responded to Laura with a suave, "Haha, glad to hear it. I feel the same way."

We talked for a little bit longer, mostly about how much we missed each other. Then she said she had to go to sleep to be ready for the big trip her group was taking in the morning (I don't remember where). I didn't want the conversation to end, but I said goodnight. And for the first time all summer, I felt optimistic. Laura was *the one*. She had told me she loved me; there was no way to misinterpret that. Everything in that moment, in that *shitty* airport with the *shitty* layover and my *shitty* bed for the evening, was absolutely perfect. I fell asleep on the bench listening to "Dizzy Lung" on repeat. It was the best night's sleep I had had all summer.

REPTILIA
By the Strokes

July 2015

"Yeah, the night's not over"

"What do you mean you don't want me there?" I asked Julian. "I thought you wanted my help."

Julian, Martin, and Damon were standing together on the other side of the room. "It's our first time," Julian said. "You're totally gonna fuck with us and ruin our trip."

The summer had been rough. On top of missing Laura an unfathomable amount while she was away, most of my friends had moved out of town, and I still didn't have a plan for my future after JMU. I spent most of my nights playing *Rock Band* with Martin and Damon and drinking enough brandy to forget about how far away Laura was. I was anxious all the time, so I drank all the time; the only reasons I survived that summer were because of my friends and *Rock Band*.

"I'll just sit in the corner and play video games! I'll be quiet!" I pleaded.

"Dude, we're doing acid for the first time. We don't want to have a bad experience, and since you're not doing it, you might give us one."

LSD was on Martin, Julian, and Damon's college bucket list. Martin had recently procured some from the shady parts of the internet, and they were all excited to try it out. I had (and still have) never done drugs, and I wasn't about to start with acid. Damon and Martin had told me I could hang around while they did it, but Julian had a different plan when he drove into town that night.

"I . . . really don't want to be alone tonight. . . ." I admitted quietly, not breaking eye contact with my shoes.

"Why?" Julian asked, talking for the three of them. Martin and Damon stood behind him with their hands in their pockets.

In hindsight, I probably could have told them the truth: my relationship with Laura had turned me into an anxious alcoholic, and my friends were the only things helping me cope. But I knew I would lose my mind if I told them the truth and they still chose the drugs.

"I'll be bored."

"You can handle being bored for a night. We're gonna hang out tomorrow," Julian said as he led my only friends in town out of my apartment. "We'll all get lunch at noon, dude. We'll see you then."

Martin and Damon waved goodbye as they followed Julian out of the apartment, then shut the door behind them.

I cracked open a beer and immediately jumped into playing video games; the anxiety multiplied ferociously when I didn't have anything to take my mind off Laura. I thought about how I hadn't talked to her all that much in the few weeks since her birthday when she told me she loved me. She had recently returned home from her study-abroad trip, and she didn't respond with any more than a brief sentence whenever I asked her about her trip or if she wanted to talk. I figured giving her some space would be best for the situation, but so far it had been absolute hell for me.

I grabbed another beer and was about to pull out my guitar to play some sad bastard songs when I heard my phone vibrate. I ran over to the couch where I'd left it. The message was from Laura.

"Hey," she said.

I waited for what I thought was an appropriate amount of time to respond, which ended up being forty-eight seconds. "Hey!" I replied. "How's unpacking going?"

"It's okay. Hey, can we talk?"

"Sure! Do you want me to call?"

"No, my phone charger is broken. I'm texting from my computer."

I thought this was an odd excuse, but I decided not to mention it. "Oh, okay. What's up?"

"I can't do this anymore."

"What do you mean?"

"Listen, you're really great. You're like the nicest guy in the world. You called and texted me every night when I was getting acclimated to studying abroad, and that was SUPER helpful. You wrote me a song for my birthday, which I really loved."

I began to realize the direction of where this conversation was headed and attempted to respond before she could finish her train of thought: "I know you don't want to be in a formal relationship, and I'm totally fine with that. I'm sorry if I've been coming on too strong in the past few weeks. I just missed you," I said.

It didn't help.

"Gus just bought us tickets to go to Boston for my birthday. I'm going with him."

"Gus . . . your ex-boyfriend?" I typed. Every second waiting for her to respond was an eternity. My addiction could have been measured with how tightly I gripped my phone, or how I didn't blink while I waited for the screen to refresh.

"Well, we never *really* broke up officially."

There was very little furniture in the apartment after my roommates moved out, so when I felt like I was going to collapse after reading this text, I sat down on the hardwood floor with my back to the sliding-glass porch door. The air conditioning vent blew on the door all day and night; it felt like leaning against an iceberg. I put my phone on my lap and stared at the screen. I was destroyed. I felt like I was in a dream. But I quickly found out there were still parts of me left to be obliterated. "You told me he was abusive."

"I know. I lied."

I shook my head. Was this real life? I felt like Rob Stark at the Red Wedding. I felt like Dexter when he found Rita in the bathtub. I felt like Brad Pitt when he found out what was in the box. I didn't know it was possible to feel this way in real life, just television. "Why?"

"You paid attention to me. It felt really good knowing you cared so much about me. Gus just wasn't treating me like you were at the time."

I was completely lost. "You told me you loved me."

"I was drunk."

"What about the song I wrote for your birthday? You said it was the best gift you've ever received."

"Gus got me shells from our favorite beach back home for my birthday. They really meant a lot."

I had no idea what to say. I had no idea how to feel. She had lied to me. She was lying the whole time. She lied about liking songs more than shells, and about her ex-boyfriend abusing her, and even about him *being* an ex-boyfriend. And now she and her *real* boyfriend were taking a trip to Boston. Fucking Boston! The home of Harmonix and the *Rock Band* headquarters! My fucking mecca of all places! After months of not sleeping, not eating, and being blindly in love, it turned out it was all for nothing. Laura had just wanted attention. I didn't respond to any other messages. I threw my phone at the couch and sat there. I didn't know if the sharp chills were coming from the cold glass pressed against my back or from the shock of heartbreak. For the first time all summer, I didn't feel the immediate need to drink my troubles away. I just sat still and felt it all. Paralyzed.

I don't know what to call what I felt other than "devastating sadness." But if I was to try to describe it, I'd say it was kind of like a lightning storm in my chest. Before this moment, I thought it was stupid to call it "heartbreak," considering nothing happens to your heart. It continues to pump blood, as usual. But suddenly I could feel every tear, every crack, every fracture in the center of my chest. For hours. It didn't go away. I was completely alone. It's kind of funny, the feeling of loneliness; I knew I had neighbors close by in the apartment next door, and there may have even been a party going on on the floor beneath me. But in that particular moment, there was *nobody* for miles. I was the last man on Earth.

When Penny had dumped me, my father had often tried to cheer me up by telling me the popular post-breakup-optimist-expression, "There are plenty of fish in the sea." This is undoubtedly a true statement; however, in a way, it's also a lie. People are unique. No two of us are the same. No matter how hard I scoured the planet, I would never find someone with Laura's exact smile, or someone who blushed the way she did whenever I made her a mix CD with a fucking 3 Doors Down song on it. There were plenty of fish in the sea, but there was only one I wanted.

I couldn't shake the feeling of having nobody around. I looked around my empty apartment, which Bruce, Julian, and Gavin had all moved out of. I couldn't stand the open emptiness of it. I walked over to my bedroom closet and closed myself in.

I sat there in that tiny space for at least an hour. I didn't feel anxious anymore, but in that moment, I would have traded what I felt for all of the anxiety in the world. I didn't think about much else other than Laura in that time, but I do remember having one brief moment of clarity.

Remember this feeling, I thought. *You've never felt it before, and hopefully you'll never have to feel it again. But you should remember it.*

THE ELECTRIC VERSION
By the New Pornographers

July 2015

*"Power and blood will pulse through your song,
just as long as it sounds lost"*

Dizzy Lung
By Cade Wiberg

I fell in love at a wedding
I wasn't even the groom
She whispered my name and I melted in place
I said I wanna be there for you

She's really close with her family
I've got a sister or two
Won't you tell me stories about your plans and schemes
And how I wanna be there for you

She wants to write all her novels
I want to write out of tune
I'll never say what she's got me doing
But I will say I'll be there for you

I'm out of breath when I see you
My dizzy lung I can't move
But maybe someday, I'll take your breath away
Because I wanna be there for you

I wrote a song for her Tuesday
By Friday I had thirty-two
She hung up the phone and said she had to go
Before I said I'll be there for you

When I sleep alone, I get nervous
I wake up in a sweaty pool
If you break my heart, I'll go move away far
Until I need to be there for you

And if I ever break your heart
I just don't know what I'd do
I'd go on hoping that you'd be there for me
Because I'll always be there for you

I'm overwhelmed by this feeling
My dizzy lung, I can't breathe
But maybe someday, I'll take your breath away
And then you'll always be there for me

And all the days they will pass by
And all the seasons will soon
I'll be there up to the thirty-second of June
And then after I'll be there for you
And then after I'll be there for you
And then after I'll be there for you

CREEP
By Radiohead

July 2015

"Whatever makes you happy, whatever you want"

My phone said 6:57 a.m. I was already awake; my head had hit the pillow at midnight, but I had lain there in a purgatorial state for seven hours. Though Laura had dumped me mere hours before, it felt like an eternity had passed. Time didn't matter in purgatory. After a few hours, I tried to jerk off to get my mind off my current situation, but it didn't work. I listened to "Sparks" by Coldplay nearly thirty times. I had never really cared for the song before tonight, but something about it numbed the pain ever so slightly. It was as if the peaceful chord progression and somber, lovesick chorus was a portal capable of taking me back to a time when I didn't feel unequivocal despair. I couldn't enter the portal, but I could look through it and remind myself that life was once sublime. After tossing and turning for hours without a second of actual sleep, I opened my eyes and stared at the ceiling for ten minutes before my alarm went off.

I got up, walked into the kitchen, and cracked open a beer. I'd earned it; you don't realize how long the night is until you stay awake for the entirety of it. I walked into the living room and stared into space while drinking my beer. No more JMU, no more Grafton, no more exec, no more *Laura*. I opened my laptop to write a note.

The top five *best* sad bastard albums of all time:

1. *I'm Wide Awake, It's Morning* by Bright Eyes: Truly the best collection of sad songs you will ever hear, written by the incredibly talented Conor Oberst, *Wide Awake* is a folk masterpiece. If you can listen—like, *truly* listen—to the song "Lua" without shedding a tear, you're a better man than I. During the last few days of college, when I was overwhelmed with school, love, and giving up sleep altogether, I would sneak into Grafton for an hour and close my eyes while I listened to the entire album. It epitomized all of my feelings at that time perfectly.

2. *The Devil and God Are Raging Inside Me* by Brand New: Jesse Lacey, the lead singer/songwriter of Brand New, named this album after talking to his friend in a bar. Both Jesse and his friend had crippling anxiety, so Jesse asked his friend to describe what the anxiety in his head was like. His friend responded, "It's like the devil and God are fighting in my head all the time." I told my dad this story once and he wrote it off as hyperbolic. "Surely no feeling of anxiety can feel more powerful than our Lord and Savior fighting ultimate evil," he said. But I can say from first-hand experience, I have felt the devil and God raging inside of me.

3. *Disclaimer II* by Seether: Penny and I used to sing the song "Broken" by Seether together all the time; Amy Lee of Evanescence is featured on the track and sings a hauntingly beautiful duet with Seether's lead singer, Shaun Morgan. When Penny dumped me for another man at the "peak" of

my high school career, I bought the whole album as a coping device. It's all I listened to for about a month. The twenty-song record has a wide range; everything from soft first-date songs to heavy mosh rock, and the lyrics cut deep on every track. Most people write Seether off as dumb hard rock, and the band often gets lumped in with fucking Papa Roach or some shit. *Disclaimer II* will always be a sad bastard ode to my youth. If you've never heard this album, I assure you it's not what you're expecting from a band like Seether.

4. *Ghost Stories* by Coldplay: Often described as Coldplay's worst album by fans, *Ghost Stories* never really got much attention aside from the abhorrent cancer of a single "Sky Full of Stars." The album was written right after Chris Martin and Gwyneth Paltrow got divorced, and it feels as if the songs were written by the bummed-out lead singer, recorded, and then thrown together on an album in no particular order—just a random collection of very sad songs that don't quite fit together, and for some fucking reason, "Sky Full of Stars." I literally boycotted this album for six months because that radio single was so bad. They're a collection of songs that will randomly come up on your shuffle twice a year that remind you that even though life goes on, heartbreak never permanently goes away.

5. *These Days* by Bon Jovi: *These Days* is nothing like any other Bon Jovi album; take it from an expert fan. These eighties rock gods carried it with them into the early nineties with their album *Keep the Faith*. Then, after their greatest hits dropped, they didn't really have a direction to go in. Bassist

Alec John Such left the band a few months later, and Jon Bon Jovi started writing mellower, more intimate songs. An album centered around loss, heartache, and infidelity was the product.

I closed my laptop and got up to replace the beer I had finished.

LEARN TO FLY
By Foo Fighters

July 2015

"Looking for a sign of life"

"You must be so excited that Laura's back! Will you get to see her anytime soon?" my mother asked over the phone.

"As soon as I buy a car," I said, hungover as shit. I wasn't ready to break the news to my mother that Laura and I were over. I was still struggling to believe it myself.

"I finished reading her blog the other day. It sounds like she had quite the trip!"

Laura had written a blog documenting her entire study abroad trip, and my mom was so excited at the prospect of me having a girlfriend that she had read the *entire* goddamn thing. Every post. Documenting nearly two months of travelling. I didn't even read the whole fucking thing.

"Yeah, it looked like fun," I agreed.

"How's the job hunt coming?"

As good as my relationship with Laura came to mind. "It's alright. I have an interview today," I lied.

"Good for you," she said.

"I'm going to be late. I should go."

"All right, say hello to Laura for me!"

"Mom, you haven't even met her."

"Whose fault is that?" she asked.

"I have to go. I love you. Bye," I said, hanging up the phone. I love my mother very much, but the pressure she sometimes put on my sister and I to get married and have children was a bit much to handle. Especially considering how hungover I was.

I missed my exec team more than anything; it seemed as though we had all parted ways at a time when I needed them most. Though there were a few of us still in Harrisonburg, we all had different obligations and responsibilities that didn't involve spending every waking hour with each other. Jessica was busy taking grad school classes to be an elementary school teacher, Nora became the new president of UPB and was even busier organizing a new exec team for the upcoming school year, and I had a floor covered with beer cans and liquor bottles I needed to clean up and half a season of *Everybody Loves Raymond* waiting to be watched.

But after two straight weeks of grieving over Laura, I decided to stop drinking all day and to get back on my feet—both literally and figuratively. I had no job and no car, and I had fallen asleep while drinking a piña colada the previous evening. It was time for a change.

The first step was to find employment. I was no longer a student and was therefore relieved of the two best jobs I'd ever had: my exec internship with UPB and my gig as a student projectionist at Grafton. I didn't know where I was going to get a job, but I had just signed a year-long lease and spent the remainder of my student loans and exec stipends on a trip to visit Delynn in Germany. I had one hundred bucks to my name and a month to come up with August's rent.

One of my friends mentioned her brother was a house manager at Court Square Theater downtown. I had never been, but movie theaters were all I knew, and this was the only one within walking distance of my apartment. After the phone call with my mom, I decided that I would take a walk downtown, get some fresh air for the first time in two weeks, and hopefully find employment. *I'm gonna need this,* I thought, as I grabbed a beer out of the fridge. *How can I get a job without liquid confidence?* I quickly finished my Corona and left my apartment.

My walk to what I hoped would be my new career was mostly through campus and therefore quite enjoyable. As I mentioned before, JMU has the most captivating campus. It provided a very pleasant scenic ambience for my many walks through it. As an added bonus on this particular day, the chicken plant wasn't emitting its regular pungent smell of dog food, so everything was coming up Cade. That is, until . . .

"Cade!"

I heard the piercing shout of a girl's voice from across the quad. I looked to see two girls walking toward me, one of them waving. I will concede I have a few faults: 1) I'm frequently too nice; 2) I occasionally become a microphone hog when I play *Rock Band* drunk; 3) my vision is terrible. I could have used glasses in this particular moment, but I could not have been less able to afford them. I waited patiently for the blurry blobs to become clear, and when they finally did, I felt a paralyzing pit grow in my stomach.

It was Laura.

I didn't recognize the girl she was with, and I didn't care. All I could think about was how destroyed I had felt for the past two weeks, and how the one person solely responsible was walking toward me. *She's gonna want to see that you're miserable,* I told myself. *Whatever you do, do NOT tell her you ate pizza from underneath the couch last night and cried while listening to "Linger" by the Cranberries.* She approached me and reached out her arms for a hug. I put on a synthetic smile and hugged her back.

"What are you doing here?" I asked with a flawless plastic smile. "The fall semester doesn't start for another few weeks."

"My friend, Sierra, is touring colleges." She gestured to the teenage girl next to her. "I told her I'd bring her here!" she said, beaming like a ray of sunshine instead of the heartbreaking harpy she was. "What are *you* doing here?"

I live here, you idiot. "Oh, I'm actually on my way to a job interview at the theater downtown. It's for a managerial position so it's kind of a big deal." I shrugged. *That's it, keep lying until the job becomes a reality!*

"Oh wow! Good for you!" They both smiled at me.

"How's . . . um . . . do you miss Europe?" I searched my mind to find words for a conversation I wanted absolutely nothing to do with.

"Every day. Wanna see my tattoo?" she said, lifting up her sleeve.

I don't remember what the tattoo was, but I do remember she had called me a few weeks ago from Italy and talked about the tattoo for three hours.

"Wow, it looks just like (insert whatever the tattoo resembled here)," I offered. I didn't want to stick around for too long and accidentally reveal I wasn't going to a job interview, or that seeing her made me want to drink non-stop for another two weeks. "Well, I gotta go," I lied. "I don't want to be late."

I turned to Laura's friend. "Choose JMU," I told her. "It'll be the best four years of your life."

Sierra smiled, but before she could respond, Laura interrupted. "Sounds good! It was great seeing you!" She led a waving Sierra back toward her tour.

I felt defeated. My liquid confidence had drained, and I desperately needed a friend. Fortunately, I knew of one close by. I quit my walk toward the theater and headed back to campus.

Griffin had the summer job of being Maris's assistant, which meant he was in the UPB office twenty hours a week. I stopped by as frequently as I could but setting foot in that office brought back too many pleasant memories I knew I would never get to relive. I knocked on the door.

"What's up, man?" Griffin greeted me warmly, and we both wrapped our arms around each other.

"The usual," I said. "How's work?"

"Eh, the same. Maris just made me sort the office supplies for next year's exec, but I get to listen to Gary Clark Jr. while I do it, so it's pretty great."

"Nice. How are things with Lindsey?"

"Last week when she came to visit, we ate pizza, watched *How I Met Your Mother*, and listened to Noel Gallagher, so . . . really great. Laura just got back from Europe, right? Have you gone to visit her yet?"

"We . . . actually . . . we broke . . . well, she dumped me."

Griffin raised his eyebrows. "What? When?" he said.

"Like a couple weeks ago. I didn't want to tell anyone and make a big deal out of it."

"Shit, dude, I'm really sorry. I really thought you guys had something. You must be devastated."

"Eh, I'm hanging in there." (Hard cut to me pacing around my house while listening to "Total Eclipse of the Heart" on repeat.) "I did actually just run into her on the quad. It was kind of awkward."

"Quick: don't think about how awkward it was," Griffin said, "that'll only make you feel worse. Think happy thoughts." He slapped me on the back. "There are plenty of fish in the sea."

I tried not to sigh out loud.

"You can have any girl you want. If she doesn't realize you're great, one of the coolest fucking guys I know, then she's objectively wrong."

Griffin did his best, but I was beyond repair by then. "I guess. I just wish we could go back in time to a few months ago when we were on exec and everything was perfect."

"I feel you, dude. I know what will cheer you up. How about I buy us forties and we watch X-men movies?"

"Yeah. That sounds amazing."

BLACK HOLE SUN
By Soundgarden

July 2015

"In my eyes, indisposed"

I had tricked myself into thinking that Laura was *it*. It didn't work out with the others, but Laura was *different*. It felt like before Laura, my life was a metaphorical Rorschach test. Everything I looked at—relationships, people, even fucking trees—were black and white blobs without any structure or meaning left for me to decipher. Then I met Laura, and the amorphous shapes solidified, the world had color, and everything made sense.

But that had been naive. The lyrics to Slipknot's "Vermilion" played through my head over and over again: "She isn't real, I can't make her real." I had to concede that the fantasy of Laura wasn't real.

After yet another afternoon of doing nothing, I finished my seventh beer. The clock had just struck five, so I was ready to switch to liquor. I poured myself a nice glass of eight-dollar rum and opened my laptop to write another note:

There are five stages of music associated with each stage of infatuation:

1. *The Pop Rock Stage.* This is when you see a girl or guy for the first time, or you share one conversation with him or her, and you just feel that fucking *click*. It's like this single interaction is

more important than any other you've had in the past year. You drive home singing songs like "Ocean Avenue" by Yellowcard or "First Date" by Blink-182. After years of listening to these songs, you finally realize that every fun, catchy, power-chord-filled song is about him or her. You suddenly can't stop singing these great hooks, and they get stuck in your head for days on end.

2. *The Stadium Anthem Stage.* This is when your feelings become unbearable, and you can't keep them in. You realize you need to tell this person all of the crazy things going on in your head, because if you don't, you'll explode. You listen to large, profound songs like "Strange Currencies" by R.E.M. or "With or Without You" by U2 that you want to scream to hundreds of thousands of people all night long, and you won't sleep until you do just that.

3. *The Beautiful Ballad Stage.* This is when you tell your significant other how you feel, and they reciprocate your feelings. It's truly the best stage of all. Nothing beats that intoxicating feeling of *true love.* The songs you listen to in this stage can be any genre and talk about any subject. The song itself can be as endearing as "Yes it Is" by the Beatles, as trite as "Wonderwall" by Oasis, or as dumb as "The Reason" by Hoobastank. The important thing about these songs is you have found something beautiful in them that's worth bonding over with this very important person, and that's exactly what you do.

4. *The Sad Bastard Stage.* Unfortunately, all good things must end. Whether your significant other cheats on you, abuses you physically or emotion-

ally, or is an absolute perfect companion for half a century and then leaves you behind by dying of old age, true love will *end*. Whether it lasted three months or three decades, if the person was worth these feelings, it will hurt. You'll choose to listen to a multitude of songs, anything from the emotionally void Deftones, to the furiousness of Asking Alexandria, to the high tear-manufacturing Avett Brothers. You'll binge these songs nonstop for days on end, and they won't make you feel a shred better; all they'll do is keep you from feeling worse.

5. *The Reflective Stage.* The nice thing about life is, no matter how bad it gets, no matter how much you think it won't get better; it goes on. After what feels like an eternal stage four, you will start listening to reflective songs. Maybe they won't be happy right away; maybe you'll start with "Black Hole Sun" by Soundgarden, "I Would Hate You If I Could" by Turnover, or "Like a Stone" by Audioslave. These songs aren't exactly joyous, but they make you think about all you've been through, and sometimes you realize these terrible experiences were worth it. It's worth writing stupid love songs, professing your feelings in front of friends knowing they won't want to spend time with you afterward, and telling someone they're the most important thing to ever happen to you, because you learn from these things, and you'll know what to do differently next time . . . if you're lucky enough to get a next time.

DEAD ON ARRIVAL
By Fall Out Boy

September 2015

"Hope this is the last time"

I first met Kyle in 2014, when he was my coworker at Grafton for the entire summer. We hit it off almost immediately; we spent every morning talking about our favorite bands and movies, while we spent every afternoon trying to get the theater's Pandora stations to play unconventional songs over the auditorium speakers. For example, our biggest goal for the summer was to get the Michael Bublé station to play a Slipknot song. Then, hopefully, one of the student affairs managers would welcome new students for the upcoming school year, load up the theater's Pandora account for background music for their slideshow presentation, and out of nowhere, soft pop would be interrupted by wonderful, wonderful heavy metal.

We never got it to play Slipknot, but we did get the station to play Disturbed, Papa Roach, Three Days Grace, and a few other bands you tell people you totally didn't listen to in middle school.

I knew Kyle and I would forever be thick as thieves after I invited him back to my apartment for *Rock Band* one afternoon. He asked to play the drums for Avenged Sevenfold's "Beast and the Harlot" (arguably the most difficult drum song in the *Rock Band 3* catalogue) and got ninety-seven percent on expert level. We immediately became friends.

After graduation, my roommates moved back to their hometowns. I was definitely not planning on living with my parents any time after I turned eighteen, so I decided to move in with Kyle, with no job and about four hundred dollars to my name. He was working at a summer camp in Texas in July while I moved our stuff in, got blackout drunk, and moped about Laura every night. By the time September rolled around, Kyle moved in, and my friends who were still students began taking classes while I stayed home playing video games and surfing the web for most of the day. I did end up getting the job at Court Square in late August, but they paid me $8.50 an hour and could only afford to give me ten hours a week. Needless to say, I was poor.

I was finally beginning to get over Laura, and I wanted to find some way to prove to her and myself that she had messed up when she dumped me. This was very hard to do on my eighty-five-dollar weekly salary. But as if serendipity itself struck me with a bolt of lightning, the moment presented itself soon enough.

It was just a regular Tuesday night. Kyle was unpacking his extensive DVD collection, and I was browsing the internet. That's when I saw it.

"Holy shit, dude! Free *Rock Band 4*!" I jumped up out of my seat and threw my hands on my head.

"What?" Kyle said puzzled, looking up from his packaging box.

"The *Rock Band* Facebook page says if we submit a three-minute video of a huge *Rock Band* party, we could win *Rock Band 4* and brand-new instruments!"

"Holy fuck!" Kyle said, equally as excited as me. We had been anticipating *Rock Band 4* since they had announced it in January, and we had expected to pay for it like schmucks.

"We have to do this," I said. "We have to throw a HUGE *Rock Band* party. I'll get all of my UPB friends who are still around to fill the apartment, and we'll make the most bitchin' video of all time!"

"Dude, perfect. I'll use the GoPro cameras I got from camp to capture footage from the entire night!"

And just like that, the plan was in motion. I would invite several college friends who still lived here and do what I do best: play fucking *Rock Band* like my life depended on it. I took to Facebook to create an event page. This is verbatim what I wrote:

> For those of you who don't know, *Rock Band* 4 is upon us. Harmonix has issued a contest in which a few dedicated fans will receive *Rock Band 4* and brand-new instruments (a $250 value) two weeks before its release date. What do we have to do, you ask? Make and submit the most bitchin' music video Harmonix has ever seen. We will have a GoPro filming the intense, intimate, and crowd-favorite songs we have been playing all these years, and maybe, just maybe, we will get three solid minutes of footage. Show up to Hunter's Ridge 1348, Apt. L, at nine on Saturday, dressed in your best *Rock Band* attire (anything you would want to be wearing in a real music video). And for those about to rock . . . we salute you.

The post got a lot of likes and a wide range of comments; everything from Violet commenting "Yes!" to Layne commenting, "I will be singing my best rendition of 'Somebody Told Me' by the Killers after shot-gunning a Four Loko in Cade's bathtub." At one point, we had fifty-five people RSVP to play *Rock Band* in our tiny-ass apartment that, according to the fire code, only fit twenty-five people. The best year of my life was followed by the worst summer of my life, and this competition was exactly how I was gonna get back on my feet.

I was gonna throw the biggest *Rock Band* party of all time.

After a week of planning and waiting, it was showtime. My apartment was full of friends and strangers, old and new. I ended up living in that apartment for almost two years, and this was the most packed I would ever see it. People stood on the couches in front of our many movie posters on the walls; *Pulp Fiction, Interstellar,* and *Anchorman 2* were in the background of every video filmed that night. Kyle's record player with the world's shittiest speakers sat in the corner, with his massive collection of records underneath it. He usually kept the frequently-played albums— Turnover's *Peripheral Vision,* Microwave's *Stovall,* and Brand New's *Your Favorite Weapon*— prominently on display, but in an attempt to keep them safe from drunk rockers, we hid them in Kyle's room. The air smelled like stale Bud Light and the off-brand liquor I had left over from my summer of binge-drinking. We made a sign for the door that read, "Music video being filmed! Anyone who comes inside gives us consent to distribute a video that you may or may not star in." This only attracted more people from outside, who wanted to see what the hell was going on.

The apartment layout was that of a standard college town dwelling: we had the TV and instruments in the living room, which was basically the same room as the kitchen. Suspended above the TV was a staircase that led to Kyle's room, while my room and the bathroom sat at the bottom of the staircase. The living room was full of people. The kitchen was full of people. I had a bass player, a drummer, and a guitarist all ready to play, in addition to two microphones in mic stands for backup singers.

I grabbed my mic and stood at the front of the room on a piano bench. I had been playing *Rock Band* for eight years, and it all led up to this moment; the audience was ready, the band was ready, I was ready.

I towered over the crowd from my spot on the piano bench. "All right, everyone!" I shouted. "Let's get this shit started!" Everyone cheered, and I loaded up the first song of the evening: Green Day's "Boulevard of Broken Dreams." I had chosen this song for several reasons: it was easy to play, it was guaranteed to get the crowd excited because everyone knew the lyrics, and I fucking love Green Day.

The band played well. The guitarist, Cody, was the only person in Harrisonburg besides Kyle and myself who still purchased *Rock Band* games and accessories. The bassist, Lisa, was another friend from UPB the previous year, and she had developed a love for the game more than anyone else I shared it with during my time at JMU. The drummer was named Cary, another UPB kid. He played the drums in real life and had personally reached out to me asking if he could play drums in our video. The backup microphones were being passed around the audience as more and more people got into it. I sang my heart out, but the party was just getting started. People were still filing in, and I was ready to play all night long.

At the end of the song, the crowd cheered. "Jessica," I shouted from my perch above the crowd, "come up here and sing the next one with me! It's our duet."

"Already?" She said from the back. She and our mutual friend Krista were dressed up like members of KISS. They looked rad.

"Right now! Let's do it!"

Jessica was right to question the order in which I was trying to play this song; whenever she had attended other *Rock Band* parties of mine, we had closed with it every time. I cued up Good Charlotte's "The Anthem," and the crowd went wild. Everyone was jumping up and down while pushing each other. My living room had turned into a mosh pit full of nostalgic middle schoolers. Jessica stood next to me at the front of the room, her brown hair cascading under her Starchild headband. We both belted the chorus, "I don't ever wanna be you!" and the crowd lost it.

We had positioned one GoPro on the wall and put one on a handle, so Kyle and I could take turns throughout the evening getting all of the up-close shots and angles. At the moment, Kyle was standing on the staircase overlooking the living room, singing along to our pop punk.

The song ended, and Jessica did a bow and jumped back into the crowd. People were still filing into the apartment. The ratio of drunk to sober people was starting to favor the former, and I myself was slowly becoming three sheets to the wind. That's when I had a thought: What does every drunk person want to do when they're at a *Rock Band* party? *Sing along.* And what's the absolute most fun song to sing along to? "Bohemian Rhapsody."

I cued it up. As soon as the intro line, "Is this the real life?" made its debut, the entire apartment erupted in song. Every person in that room sang every lyric of Queen's masterpiece. I drunkenly stood on my piano bench, holding a beer in one hand and a mic in the other, belting the words at the top of my lungs. At one point during the song, I thought to myself, *This is what it's all about. You're peaking right now. This is the most excellent life can be at any given moment.* I looked out at the crowd singing along with me, and I finally felt better. That was the first time in months I was truly happy, and I owed it all to *Rock Band*.

Unfortunately, much like Icarus, I was flying too close to the sun. God must have noticed that my happiness meter was off the charts, and decided he had to get involved. Right as the song ended, Laura walked through the door.

I froze in place. Everyone was applauding and begging for more music, but I couldn't hear any of it. My head was suddenly filled with what she had said to me on that horrible night, the thing that had catapulted me into a summer of self-destruction and despondency: "I can't do this anymore." I stared at her. She was as beautiful as ever. She had curled her hair, and she was wearing tight jeans and a Slipknot t-shirt I had once told her drove me crazy (in a romantic way). She walked over to some of our mutual UPB friends and started to make small talk. She carried a water bottle that I was sure contained gin. My brief moment of supreme confidence was over. The crowd began to notice my silence and started to chant my name, so I snapped out of my stupor.

"All right, everyone, switch up the instruments. Give everyone a chance to play," I said. "Kyle, come down here and take the mic."

"Bitchin'," he said.

I walked over to the most crowded kitchen in the world to grab another beer. Kyle had cued up his first song choice of the evening, "Sweetness" by Jimmy Eat World. I had to push three people out of the way to open the fridge wide enough to fit my arm through. Before I could close the door, Laura appeared next to me.

"Hey," she said.

"Oh . . . hey," I said, surprised, mostly because it was so crowded it had taken me seven minutes to move ten feet across my apartment, and she somehow had found a way to teleport.

"How are you?" she asked.

I looked around me. "Living the dream, I guess."

She smiled. "I'm happy for you. Are we gonna get to sing our duet at some point?"

"Umm, yeah . . . we can do that."

Laura hesitated. "It's not weird I'm here, is it?" Kyle started up his second song of the evening, "Thrash Unreal" by Against Me.

"No, no, no, it's not weird at all," I said, in the same tone I'd use if she had asked me if it was weird she thought Ringo was the best Beatle.

"Okay, good," she replied. "I told Brianna I'd grab her a beer, so I'll catch up with you in a bit!"

"Sounds like a plan," I said, dreading the plan. Right as I began to sink into another sad bastard stupor, Kyle finished his song.

"Cade, get over here!" he shouted. "Get the camera on this one! This is it!" I grabbed the GoPro and pushed through the crowd. "This is it, we're gonna win this fucking contest!" Kyle said to a rapt audience. Everyone cheered as Kyle cued up "Dead on Arrival" by Fall Out Boy. The guitar player strummed the intro power chords, and the drummer and bassist followed along. Kyle jumped all over the room with his corded microphone as he sang the intro line, "Hope this is the last time," with incomparable enthusiasm. Our living room was bouncing from side to side as if it had turned into a trampoline park. In my many years of throwing *Rock Band* parties, I have had a few shut down by the police due to neighbors calling in a "sound disturbance"—I once even sang so loud that an officer told me the speaker volume was fine but my voice could be heard from a block away. This was not one of those parties. Whenever neighbors knocked on the door to find out what the ruckus was, we would just invite them inside to play more songs with us. Before the end of the night, I sang "Livin' on a Prayer," "Santeria," and "All the Small Things" with three completely different strangers.

Meanwhile, Kyle was taking his performance to the next level. As soon as the bridge hit, he climbed to the top of the staircase and shouted, "Bring it in, bring it in!" while he motioned a crowd of drunk college students to gather around the side of the staircase. There were gasps and shouts of joy as soon as everyone realized what he was attempting. Kyle was about to jump fifteen feet off the top of the staircase into a crowd of drunkards, and I was recording the entire thing on a GoPro. The whole crowd sang along as he sang, "Soooooooooooooo, this is side one! Flip me over! Flip me over!" And just like that, he barrel-rolled off the staircase into the loving arms of the mosh pit. Everyone cheered as he jumped out of the crowd's arms and went right back into singing the song. Some people swore in amazement, a lot of people gasped, and I was drunkenly shouting like an idiot fangirl and doing both of those things. Kyle finished the song with the words, "Here is your," as he pumped the microphone twice in synchronization with the two drum crashes at the end of the song.

The last shot we got in the video was the entire crowd shouting, "*Rock Band 4*!" and jumping on Kyle.

This was it. This was what life was all about. Why had I spent the entire summer torturing myself over a girl? I looked around the room and saw a lot of faces I didn't recognize, but almost just as many faces that I did. I saw Layne and Violet screaming in excitement, Jessica doing a victory dance, and Lisa and Cody taking celebratory shots. *I made this happen,* I reminded myself. *I threw together a killer fucking party, unlike any party that anyone in this room has ever or will ever attend.* Rock Band had always encouraged me to be anybody I wanted to be, and I didn't want to be a mopey anxiety bomb anymore. I didn't need Laura—or any girl, for that matter. I just needed some close friends and my favorite video game.

We submitted the "Dead on Arrival" footage and won the competition. I'll never forget that moment in Kyle's car several weeks later: we were stationary at a stoplight, and he was casually scrolling through his phone while we waited for the light to turn green. We hadn't heard anything from Harmonix for weeks, and had assumed that our video didn't win . . . which made it all the more surprising when Kyle said, "Oh shit. . . . I got an email from the *Rock Band* people." Ten seconds after he opened it, we were shouting and awkwardly hugging over the middle console in the front of the car while blocking traffic.

Though that was the best *Rock Band* party we ever threw, and Kyle jumping off the balcony will forever be my favorite memory of him, it actually wasn't the most unexpected thing that happened that evening.

Right around 3 a.m., most people started to leave. The party technically went on until 6 a.m., but there were only devout fans of the game left . . . and Laura.

Laura and I sat next to each other on the couch, having just sang "Linger" by the Cranberries together, which had become our song shortly after I kissed her for the first time several months ago. She clutched her water bottle full of gin in her left hand, but her right hand inched its way towards me with each passing minute. We watched the few leftover people play more songs for a while.

Still intoxicated (both from alcohol and the joy of my first day freed from depression), I turned to face Laura. She turned to me, and we locked eyes right as "Wake Me Up When September Ends" came on. We both awkwardly smiled, and then she moved her face toward mine. I thought she was going to kiss me, but instead she put her mouth next to my ear and said, "Take me to your bedroom."

And I did.

ARE YOU GONNA BE MY GIRL
By Jet

September 2015

"Well I could see you home with me."

"I was in love with you, ya know," I whispered to Laura.

"I was in love with you too," she said, lying in my bed with her head on my chest. We had drunkenly stumbled into my room as the party died down, leaving Kyle to entertain the few guests that were still around while she and I . . . well . . . you know. After a couple of hours, we lay intertwined in my bed, exhausted.

"Then why did you *leave*?" I asked her.

"I don't know. You weren't around, we were thousands of miles apart . . . but now we're not," she said through a smile as she looked up at me.

"This summer . . . was *so* shitty, Laura." I sighed, defeated.

"I'm sorry. I didn't realize how much we . . . how much I needed you. That song you wrote me for my birthday . . . I listened to it on a loop for an hour after you sent it. I showed all of my roommates. It was the nicest thing anyone has ever done for me."

"Oh, you just . . . you didn't seem really impressed when you—"

"I don't know what to say other than I'm sorry. It was hard being away from you for three months. But it doesn't have to be anymore. I'm here, you're here . . . we can give it another shot," she said with a glimmer of hope in her blue eyes.

"I just don't know if I can go through that ever again. I mean, what about Gus?"

"You won't have to ever go through that again," she promised. "I've made up my mind: it's you. It's *always* been you! Nothing else matters, nobody else matters!"

I tried to think of a response, but it was almost 5 a.m., and it was getting harder and harder to articulate my thoughts. "It's just . . . that's what I thought the first time."

Laura paused. "Remember the first night I slept over?"

"Yeah. I had a paper due the following morning, and you wouldn't let me write it." I smiled.

"We talked for hours until I fell asleep on your arm while we listened to U2."

"And I spent the entire night typing a paper on my laptop with one hand." My arm tingled just thinking about it.

"You didn't want to wake me," she said, smiling right back.

"That's a good memory."

"We can make every day just like that," she said. And then she kissed me.

GO WITH THE FLOW
By Queens of the Stone Age

September 2015

"Falling in and out of love"

My relationship with Laura wasn't as ideal as I thought it would be after I gave her a second chance. Every other night, she would get drunk and send me a text that said, "Let's have sex," or "Come over right now," which I know sounds amazing on paper, but it was far from it. After we'd hooked up, she would always leave around 3 a.m. for different reasons that she didn't always disclose. Then I'd wake up at 7 a.m. to a series of texts that told me I was a horrible person for sleeping with her while she was drunk or "distracting" her while she should have been studying for her exams. Loud arguments were becoming her favorite thing in the world, while they continued to be my absolute least favorite. After she had berated me all day over text or in person, I would break down and tell her I was a shitty person and that I was sorry for sleeping with her, or sorry for not texting her back quickly enough, or sorry for texting her back too quickly, or sorry for saying something offensive like, "I don't think Kanye West is that great." Then she would say something like, "Apology accepted," and we would repeat the cycle the following day.

It wasn't just a bad relationship. It was a literal hell. I didn't know it at the time, because it was technically my first proper relationship with a girl, and as far as I knew, that was what it felt like to be in love.

233

One September morning started like all the others. I collected my check of $82.67 from my place of infrequent employment, deposited it into my bank account (which had just reached an all-time low of four dollars), and began my two-mile walk home, because I couldn't afford a car. My phone buzzed with a text.

"Hey, my stomach feels really queasy. Could you grab me some ginger ale?" Laura asked.

"Yeah, of course. I'll be there in an hour!"

It was foolproof. If I bought her ginger ale and took care of her all day, she couldn't possibly be mad at me! She would finally come around and share the unconditional love I had for her. *Pssshhh . . . you idiot,* my brain interrupted. *Anybody can buy her ginger ale! You need to go above and beyond.* I realized that my brain had a valid point. If I was going to earn Laura's love, it wasn't going to be because I simply did something she had asked me to do. Anybody can build a theme park, but only one man can build Disneyland.

I began the two-mile walk to Laura's house and stopped at the grocery store along the way. I bought her ginger ale, saltines, cold medicine, and Pepto Bismol. Then I walked across the street to McDonald's to buy her favorite sandwich, a Big Mac. Then I walked to her house in eighty-five-degree weather carrying all of the items I had bought while contemplating how I would pay rent in two weeks.

When I arrived at her apartment, I walked in to a very nonchalant greeting from Laura on the couch. She didn't look very sick; there was an open bag of Chips Ahoy on the table next to the couch, but in her defense, there were also some empty cans of very adventurous flavors of healthy-looking soups on the kitchen counter.

"Hey!" I said. "I brought you a whole bunch of stuff so you'll feel better." I pulled out my spread of foods and medicines one at a time and showed her each one. I never got more than a shrug in response. "I also got you your favorite sandwich!" I said, holding up the McDonald's bag.

"What's my favorite sandwich?" She looked at me, puzzled.

"A Big Mac!" I pulled it out of the bag, wide-eyed, with a finesse that would make Ronald McDonald, the Hamburglar, and that weird fuck, Grimace, proud.

She raised an eyebrow. "When did I tell you that?"

"We were Facebook messaging each other while you were in Rome. You couldn't sleep, and we started talking about our favorite foods."

"Hmm. Don't remember that," she said, and turned back to the TV. "Might have been drunk." She finally sat up and looked at me. "How long is the thing you're at this weekend?"

"Nathan's wedding? It's just the weekend."

"When will you be back?" she asked, pulling me next to her on the couch.

"Sunday night at the latest."

She lay down and put her feet on my lap. "You're probably gonna meet some better girl there and sleep with her," she pouted. I tried to massage her feet, but she pulled them away and retreated to the other end of the couch.

"Laura, I would never do that to you. I couldn't. You know how I feel about you. You wouldn't go off and sleep with someone this weekend, so why would I?"

She looked at me with her brow furrowed, then wiped it from her face and looked out the window blankly. "Do you think we spend too much time together?"

"What? No. Why would I think that?"

"I mean, we're not married. We don't have to spend every day together. We're not that serious."

"I thought you wanted to be serious . . . I mean, we've been sleeping together and we've both said I love—"

She cut me off. "You should go. We already spent enough time together yesterday. Let's not rush this."

"Laura, I just got here. It's four miles—"

"Just leave!" she shouted, standing up and storming off to her room.

I tried to say more, but my mouth was dry and I became too choked up to let any words slip out. I think I was too dehydrated from the walk over and carrying twenty pounds of fucking saltines. I slowly walked out of her apartment, hoping she would change her mind, but she didn't.

As I've mentioned before, I didn't have any friends in high school. That is, I didn't have any really close friends; Nathan was the person that came the closest. We had homeroom together and once spent an entire semester playing one continuous game of *Monopoly* every day at lunch. Overall, I was only able to spend about ten percent of my high school career with him, but he really seemed to like me for some reason. Toward the end of senior year, he invited me to a huge house party and asked me to bring *Rock Band*. It was a major hit, and Nathan had me bring the game to every one of his house parties from then on, for years to come. We didn't hang out much once I went to college, but we always had a great time when we did.

I was a little surprised when he called me in late 2014 asking if I would be a groomsman at his wedding. I accepted, and before I knew it, I was borrowing my sister's car and on my way to Richmond with The Fratellis' *Costello Music* playing on full blast.

I had met Nathan's soon-to-be wife, Lilly, at a *Rock Band* party a couple years before then, but I was pretty drunk and only remembered that she had been very polite. She didn't drink or sing a single song, which I thought was odd, because Nathan could drink enough booze to kill a family of gorillas and loved singing just as much.

Their wedding weekend couldn't have come at a better time, because Laura was slowly destroying my soul piece by piece, and the only cure I could think of was getting hammered at a bachelor party. I pulled up to the rural wedding venue, got out of the car, and walked inside what looked like a renovated barn.

I was greeted by an excited Nathan and his groomsmen.

"Hey, you old son of a bitch!" Nathan said, walking toward me and smiling.

"Nathan, language!" Lilly said, pausing a conversation with a bridesmaid she was having on the other side of the barn.

"Sorry, hun," he said, right before he came in for a hug. "How was the drive?"

"Not too bad. Just ready to hang out with the boys. Bachelor party is tonight, right?" I said, grinning.

He laughed nervously. "We won't have too much, but we can certainly share a couple of beers for old times' sake." *A couple of beers? What happened to the Nathan who made moonshine in his bathtub? I'm here for that guy's wedding.*

"Ah trying to save money for your new family, I respect that. Don't worry, all of your drinks are on me," I said, accidentally promising the remaining forty dollars in my checking account to Nathan.

The rest of his groomsmen walked over to us. There was Donnie, a tall fellow who I had seen at multiple *Rock Band* parties in previous years. Facebook had notified me that he had become a chef a couple of years back. Gary was a short, scrawny, redneck-looking character very similar to the rest of Nathan's family, probably because he was Nathan's half-brother. He gave a kidney away to a cousin and as a result, couldn't drink more than one beer without getting plastered. Then there was Nathan's father Frank, who was apparently the Best Man at the wedding. Nathan's father was a very kind man, who was almost exactly like Nathan in every way. My favorite memory of Frank is when Nathan, myself, and a few other guys got drunk at his house one night and decided to shoot a gun at spray paint cans in his backyard fire pit. Frank immediately heard the gunshot, stormed outside, and shouted, "Nathan, you fucking idiot, how many times do I have to say it? No guns and alcohol!" He then returned inside while all of us started laughing uncontrollably.

"We're about to head over to the rehearsal dinner," Frank said. "You guys better get your asses over there. I didn't pay for Chipotle catering for nothing!" Frank walked past the rest of the guys to his car. We all returned to our respective vehicles and drove over to the reception hall, where the food was being prepared.

I've never considered myself a person who has a drinking problem; every instance of overindulgence can be traced back to anxiety caused by intense infatuation, almost exclusively relating to Laura. So, if anything, I have a problem with dating, not alcohol. When Laura went away to Europe right after I had fallen in love with her, I was completely lost. I drank more in the summer of 2015 than I had up to that point combined. And it was starting to seem like that fall wasn't going to be much better. I was poor as shit, most of my friends had moved away, and I was still in love with Laura, no matter how badly she treated me. I desperately needed a beer.

We arrived at the rehearsal dinner. It was a rental space next to a pool and playground. Close family and the wedding party filled the room, and, as promised, there were several tables topped with fresh trays of Chipotle ready to line our stomachs for the inevitable drink-a-thon that I was going to instigate the second we returned to Nathan's house.

Nathan stopped us before we could reach the table. "Be careful not to swear here, guys," he said. "Lilly's pastor is very old and sensitive to bad language."

Who the fuck are you, and what have you done with my friend who once coined the term "twat-waffle"?

The preacher stood up at the front of the room. "Attention, everyone. Let's take a minute before we eat to pray . . ."

UUUUUUUGGGGGGGGGGHHHHHHHHHHHHHHH

". . . and also to reflect on what Nathan and Lilly mean to each of us before they are presented as a union in front of God tomorrow. Does anyone have anything they would like to say regarding the happy couple?"

The thirty-ish people in the room went silent.

"I have something to say," I said as I stood up.

"Go ahead, Cade," Frank said.

"Nathan, I didn't have a lot of people I was close to in high school, but you befriended me almost immediately with open arms. You invited me into your house and your family on many occasions. We've had a lot of great times together, mostly including *Rock Band.*" There were some small laughs from the crowd. "We once went to see Green Day—which ended up being the best concert of my life—and they played for three hours and it was *really* hot outside. When my mom came to pick us up, she commented on how sweaty we were by saying it was the worst smell she ever had in her car." More people laughed.

That's it, I told myself. *Keep it up and before you know it, we'll be eating Chipotle and drinking enough beer to forget about Laura making you walk four miles the other day.*

"One night after a *Rock Band* party and a few beers, Nathan suggested we climb up onto the roof and look at the stars while we drank. Then he told me he had just met a girl named Lilly, and he was going to marry her one day."

A young high school girl sitting near me dropped a quiet "Aww." Everyone applauded, and I sat down, wishing in vain that a burrito would appear magically in front of me after I did this good deed. Nobody else raised their hand to speak, so Frank stood up with a typed-up speech he had prepared.

"Nathan, I couldn't have asked for a better son. You're kind, funny, and loyal, and I'm so proud of the man you have become. I will admit that when you dropped out of college and started living at home, you were frustrating sometimes. I started to get worried when you turned twenty and you still weren't close to getting married."

Well fuck me, I guess.

"Lilly, you couldn't have picked a better man to love and provide for you. I hope you're just as kind to him as he will be to you, and I hope you'll be there to comfort him whenever he cries during

Marley & Me!"

This got more laughs than anything I had said, which added to the frustration I felt from not eating a burrito.

"God bless you both as you enter this very special union. He truly is smiling down on you from Heaven."

Well, God should be watching the Haitian family that's about to get crushed by a fucking boulder, but I guess watching two twenty-two-year-olds get married in a barn is an equally good use of his time.

Everyone applauded Frank's speech, and after a five-minute prayer, we were finally able to get the much-anticipated Chipotle we had all been promised an eternity ago.

Nathan sat down next to me after we got our food. "That was a nice speech," he said, and elbowed me. "Thanks, brother."

"I'm really happy for you, man. It's fun talking about old times."

"Hell yeah it is," he laughed, biting into his burrito.

"You know what's even more fun? Drinking."

Nathan shot me a hesitant grin, but it was all I needed to get us to the next part of the evening.

★ ★ ★ ★ ★

"So, this is it," Nathan said, opening the door to his brand-new apartment. "I just started renting it yesterday. I'm gonna surprise Lilly right after the wedding. She thinks we're living with her parents for a few months, but I've already furnished and decorated our very first place. She's gonna be beside herself!"

The rest of the groomsmen and I (excluding Frank) followed Nathan into the apartment while carrying several cases of beer. It was a basement apartment with a bedroom and a combined kitchen, living room, and dining room. It was a small place, but Nathan had put a lot of effort into making it look like a home, and it showed. We all made ourselves at home on the couch.

"It looks great, man," Donnie said, putting down the case of

Gatorade we would inevitably all need in the morning. "Now, who's ready to get wasted?"

"Guys, I appreciate the enthusiasm," Nathan laughed, "but just a quick heads up: I *cannot* be hungover tomorrow. Lilly will literally kill me."

"Then you better finish your case of beer quick enough to have time to hydrate," Gary said, opening the first beer of the night.

"Fuck," Nathan said covering his face with his hands and shaking his head. I had once watched Nathan drink an entire fifth of rum while soaking in a hot tub. He truly was a changed man. Maybe life-changing love *did* exist. Maybe if I let Laura be mean to me a little bit longer, it would turn into something real.

"Cade, what are you drinking?" Donnie asked, putting the rest of the beer away in the fridge.

"Hand me an IPA," I said, wanting a quick buzz. I must have wanted it quicker than I thought, because that beer was gone in four minutes.

We played drinking games for a few hours, huddled around the hand-me-down coffee table Nathan had received from his parents. Nathan nursed only three beers over that time. Gary's single kidney wouldn't let him drink more than one IPA, so he spent the rest of the night on the bathroom floor. Meanwhile, I hit my sixth beer and began to realize I was drunk. I knew I needed to eat something fast, or this night was gonna go south.

I left the three-man party and stumbled into the kitchen, which was technically the same as the living room, so I didn't have to travel far. I opened the fridge to find the leftover Chipotle catering. *Fuck. Yeah.* I could feel my stomach starting to reject the alcohol, and I knew I was running against the clock. I tore apart the take-home boxes to reveal the only ingredients left from the rehearsal dinner: rice and tortillas. This didn't deter me. I whipped up the world's shittiest burrito and began to eat. It was incredibly bland, but I do remember finishing it.

Unfortunately, that's the last thing I remember.

I woke up at 6 a.m. to Nathan punching me in the shins.

"Ow! Goddammit! What the hell, dude?" I shrieked. I looked around the room and rubbed my eyes. Nathan was playing some Madden game on his Xbox One while sitting on the couch that I had apparently turned into a bed mere hours before. It wasn't a large couch; it barely fit just me sleeping on it, let alone a big guy like Nathan.

He glared at me. "I've been up all night and you keep fucking kicking me and you vomited all over my kitchen and my house smells like fucking vomit and Lilly is gonna smell it as soon as we get home and I'm getting married in eight hours!"

I was still too foggy to fully understand what he had said. "Why am I so hungover?"

"Maybe because you drank most of the beer in the fridge by yourself."

"Ugh," I grumbled, standing up slowly. I walked around the apartment to assess the damage. The bathroom door was still shut, so I assumed Gary had spent the night in there. Nathan's bedroom door was closed, which was odd because it appeared he had spent the night sitting wide-awake on the couch, taking up valuable real estate in my bedroom, the living room. I was about to inquire about the closed bedroom door when it opened, and Donnie walked out of it. He looked even worse than I did.

"Nathan . . . I've got some bad news. . . ." he mumbled.

Oh, thank god, I thought. *Please be worse than ruining Nathan's kitchen and the scent of the apartment forever.*

"What is it?" Nathan asked with a look of fear in his eyes.

"Your sheets," was all Donnie said.

Nathan jumped off the couch, and he and I darted down the hall to the bedroom. Donnie had spilled what appeared to be an entire bottle of red Gatorade all over Nathan's brand-new silk sheets. If Lilly didn't notice that the apartment smelled like a row of brewery urinals, she would definitely notice the fact that her bedsheets looked like Nathan had wrapped an animal corpse in them.

"Fuck, dude! Those sheets cost a hundred bucks!"

Gary heard the commotion and walked out of the bathroom looking, somehow, worse than all of us. "What's going on, fellas?" he asked, his voice gravelly.

"Let me guess!" Nathan shouted at Gary. "You threw up all over the bathroom!"

Gary scowled. "Well, in the toilet, yeah. But I flushed . . . What's wrong?"

"What's wrong," Nathan began, "is all of you got plastered even though I told you not to, and then you ruined my house right before my wedding!"

Donnie stepped toward Nathan. "Nathan, calm down," he pleaded. "We'll take the sheets to the dry cleaners and get them all cleaned up before the wedding. We'll get some cleaning spray and air fresheners too."

We all piled into Nathan's car, each of us with a hangover that could slay an elk. We ran the various errands required to fix Nathan's home/save his marriage and even had enough time to buy the groom-to-be his last meal as a single man. Obviously, we chose to go to Denny's. As we stood in the restaurant lobby waiting to be seated, I thought about how much we had gotten done before 11 a.m. I then thought about Lilly, and whether or not her bachelorette party was just as crazy, and whether or not she had a bridesmaid who also got drunk enough to eat a plain rice burrito. Then I imagined a new life with this burrito girl, a life where a girl was actually happy to see me and spend time with me. I realized this was an impossible delusion. *You've fallen in love with Laura. It's permanent. 'Til death do you part.*

"Did you hear me, dipshit?" Nathan asked, interrupting me from my trance.

"What?"

Nathan then hit me in the balls, and I fell to the ground. He and Gary laughed while Donnie helped me up; he was laughing too, but at least he was making a kind gesture.

Despite Nathan's wedding day jitters, everything went perfectly. We cleaned the house with plenty of time to spare and got to the wedding grounds an hour early. The event itself was perfect. Lilly and Nathan said their vows (during which Nathan cried), took their bride and groom pictures, and had their first dance to some terrible Garth Brooks nonsense.

After several hours of eating food, dancing, and enjoying my first party in a barn, it was time to return to my low-paying job, binge-drinking lifestyle, and girlfriend who made me hate myself. Lilly was dancing with her bridesmaids when I approached Nathan outside the barn to say goodbye.

"I gotta head out, man. It was a beautiful wedding," I said. The aroma of a gentle country breeze mixed with smoke from a bonfire several yards away.

"Thanks, man. I really appreciate you coming out. This was a good weekend." He leaned against a tree in his four-hundred-dollar suit.

"I'm . . . I'm sorry I helped destroy your new house," I said reluctantly, not able to make eye contact with my friend until the end of my sentence.

"Shit happens, man. We've all been there." Nathan gave me a soft punch in the arm and smiled.

Before I turned to walk away, I paused. "I got a question," I said, turning to look through the barn window and see Lilly dancing with her bridesmaids. "How did you know Lilly was the one?"

Nathan thought about it for a second. "When you know, you know," he said, and he shrugged.

"I've been seeing someone for a while. I think I know, but feel like I shouldn't know, you know?"

"No," he said, laughing.

I shook my head. "Sorry. I guess I'll figure it out."

"Do you love her?"

I hesitated. "Yeah, I do."

"Don't let that go, man. It's not always gonna be perfect, but when it is, it's . . . well, perfect."

After this very memorable conversation between the two most verbose wordsmiths of our time, I wished Nathan good luck and walked to my car. I plugged in my phone, which had died right around the time I had been awakened by shin-punches. My phone buzzed nonstop for several seconds. I had missed several texts from Laura.

"Hey, I'm really sorry about yesterday. I wasn't feeling well so I took it out on you, and that was wrong. I'm really sorry and just want to spend the night with you. Come to my apartment. Let's just sleep in and spend the whole day together. Text me back when you read this."

I sat there for a long time, looking down at the messages and back at the barn where the happy couple was celebrating an eternity with each other.

"I'll meet you at my apartment. I'm on my way," I texted back.

FOREPLAY/LONG TIME
By Boston

September 2015

"I'm trying to forget your name and leave it all behind me"

I spent the entire trip back from Nathan's wedding deep in thought. I was sure he had what I wanted, but I was unsure if there would ever be a day when Laura would walk down the aisle to me. As I drove, I reminisced over the highs and lows of the past six months.

March 2015

Why didn't it work with Kayleigh? Because you never talked to her. But if you did, she would have found out how great you are. Your best is enough, trust me. I thought to myself.

Laura and I had our first date at Ruby Tuesday on a Sunday night.

"How was your spring break?" Laura asked, barely finishing a third of her meal.

"It was amazing," I said. The juice from my bacon cheeseburger fell on the napkin in my lap. I wiped my mouth before I spoke again. "Arguably the best week of my life. I could tell you a lot of stories."

"I think I saw them all over Snapchat," she said, smiling.

"You're probably right. There were a lot of very filmable moments over the trip. We had to take advantage." I smiled at her, still brimming with excitement that Laura had agreed to go to dinner with me. "It was a really great week. I wish I could go back." I paused, noticing her smile was wearing off.

"I'm . . . I'm sorry about you and your boyfriend," I continued. "I'm happy to talk about it if you want."

She looked up from her food with a half-smile. "Oh, thanks. You know, it sucks right now, but I'll get over it."

"I've been there, you know. I once dated a girl who meant the world to me in high school."

"What happened?" she asked urgently, with her eyes wide open.

"It's kind of a long story, but she cheated on me."

She gasped. "I'm so sorry, Cade. That's so shitty. You don't . . . nobody deserves to be treated like that. Especially someone as great as you."

"That's nice of you to say," I tried not to smile too big as I reached for my drink.

"I would never do that in a relationship," she continued, shaking her head. "I can't imagine."

"Why didn't it work out between you and Gus, if you don't mind my asking?"

"Well, I'm about to go to Europe this summer and he's studying in D.C. this fall, so we decided to quit while we were ahead I guess. It kind of ran its course." She shrugged and looked at her plate still covered with food.

"I'm sorry to hear that."

"I guess the biggest thing was passion. I'm a really passionate person, and he isn't."

"Passion's important," I agreed. "If we don't love what we do, what's the point?"

Laura smiled. "Can I ask you something?"

"Anything."

"If you could go on a date with anyone at JMU right now, who would it be?"

"Is this not a date?" I asked.

Laura blushed. "I guess it is, isn't it?"

"I'd love to go on another. That is . . . if you'd want to."

"I'd like that a lot," she said, still blushing.

April 2015

Why didn't it work out with Penny? Because she wanted someone more experienced with relationships, someone more attractive.

Someone better.

"Hey, can we at least talk about this?" I asked.

"Oh, it's not a big deal. I just need to go home," she said, crying.

Laura and I had just had sex for the first time. Well . . . I guess it's more accurate to say I lost my virginity, and the sex stopped halfway through when Laura inexplicably burst into tears. Looking back on it now, I realize it was because she had just cheated on the boyfriend she was still in love with, but at the time it was the most confusing fucking night of my life.

"Laura, I really think we should talk about this," I begged as we walked to her car. She refused to look at me; I could have been on fire and she still would have averted her gaze.

"I don't want to. Get in the car," she said sternly, still a little choked up.

I got in the passenger side of her car. I will never forget the way it smelled; she had some shitty vanilla air freshener and forever that smell will be associated with the horrible feeling I felt almost exclusively for six months in 2015. It was a feeling composed of love, lust, anxiety, sadness, and complete disarray.

"Laura, I don't get it. I feel like we had a really fun day today, and then when we . . . I mean, that was really fun too."

Laura just kept crying for the entire drive home. All I could think about was what I did wrong. *I know it was my first time and I probably wasn't very good, but I never thought I'd make a girl cry my first time. I fucking suck. I'm a piece of shit.*

She dropped me off at my building and said goodnight through tears. I walked into my apartment, still speechless, and was greeted by a crowd of people in my living room; Gavin, Bruce, Julian, and Damon were all drunk as shit watching *Power Rangers*.

"There he is! How did the date go?" Gavin asked.

I couldn't think of anything to say, so I just said, "I need a beer," and walked to the fridge.

I opened my beer and looked in the living room to see my roommates looking at each other completely puzzled. Bruce broke the silence. "So . . . good?"

"I just want to watch *Power Rangers*," I said, and fell onto the couch next to them.

I eventually told my roommates we had sex, and it was great. I didn't know how to tell them what really happened. I was still trying to figure it out myself.

I spent the rest of the night wondering what was wrong with me.

May 2015

"Eileen, you really don't need to do this," I said. "It's almost your birthday. I should be buying *you* dinner." I sat across from Eileen at a table next to the bar in Capital Ale House. She had offered to take me out to dinner to celebrate my impending graduation.

"You're graduating college and you're done with UPB! This is the end of an era! I have to buy you dinner." She said, grinning ear to ear. Eileen will always have one of the top ten most memorable smiles.

"Thank you. That means a lot," I said and sipped my beer.

She cut into her baked potato. "So, are you excited for Germany?" she asked.

"You have no idea. This trip is gonna be so amazing. We're gonna travel a lot, and Delynn says she's taking me to a surprise country at some point, so I'm kind of hoping I get to see Laura while I'm over there."

"Oh yeah. How's that going?"

I paused. "Really well, actually. That last night she was here was just . . . perfect."

"Oh good. I'm happy for you two," she said before taking a bite of potato.

"You mentioned Drew came to visit a couple of weekends ago."

She nodded and placed her hand in front of her mouth so she could talk while chewing. "Yeah, it was really great. I hadn't seen him in a while."

"I'm glad. It sounds like you two finally worked things out." I placed my empty pint glass back on the table.

"What do you mean?"

"You're going to get back together with him, right?"

"Oh, I don't know. I mean, we've always been friends, but—"

"Where did he sleep when he stayed with you?"

"What?" she whispered as if we were speaking about something inappropriate.

"Come on, Eileen. We've been friends for two years! You can talk to me about this stuff."

"I guess it just feels weird talking about it with . . . well, we did sleep together."

"See? Good for you." I was surprised with how comfortable I was talking to a girl I was once in love with about another suitor. If this had been a year ago, I would have gone into a sad bastard stupor, but now I was in love with someone new and I wanted everyone to be as happy as I was.

"What are you gonna miss most about JMU?" she asked, poking at the remainder of her food.

"Hmmm . . . I'm not really sure," I replied, caught off-guard by the question. "I'll miss Grafton, I'll miss exec, I'll miss you and all of our other friends . . . really everything, I guess."

She finished her potato and placed her silverware on the table. "What's your favorite memory?"

"Eileen, there are too many to count. I really have no idea."

"What about when we invited the JMU Ghost Hunters to stay overnight in Grafton while they tried to find ghosts?" she asked, smiling.

"That's a good one. Or when that Christian organization on campus tried to prevent us from playing *50 Shades of Gray* at Grafton because it was inappropriate."

"We showed *American Sniper* the week before and they didn't give a shit about us playing that one."

"Well killing Iraqi children isn't nearly as bad as BDSM with a billionaire," I said, laughing.

Eileen laughed and tried not to spill her water while doing so. "What about the time you threw that Halloween party?"

"Oh yeah! I dressed up as Dexter and you dressed up as Mike Wazowski from *Monsters Inc.*! I kept trying to take a picture of you and you kept blocking your face."

"I didn't want my mom to see any drunk pictures of me on Facebook the next day!"

I paused for a second. "I'm really gonna miss you, Eileen."

"Me too. Don't worry, you're moving in with Kyle like a mile away. We'll still see plenty of each other."

"Yeah. I guess you're right. You're not wrong about it being the end of an era, though."

"I know. It feels weird," she said as she gave the waitress her credit card.

"Thanks again for dinner."

"Anytime."

We walked outside and were about to go our separate ways when she stopped. "My favorite memory is when you told me I had food on my chin."

"What?" I asked.

"When we watched *Dexter* that one night. You told me—"

"Oh no, I know what you're talking about, I'm just . . . How the hell do you remember that?"

"I don't know." She shrugged. "It's just a good memory."

"We've got a lot of those, and more to come."

"I hope so." She reached out and hugged me.

"I'll see you around, Eileen."

"See ya," she said as she walked to her car.

I stood there deep in thought for a minute, until I received a message from Laura. It was the first message I'd received from her since she left for Europe, and truth be told I already missed her even though it had only been about twenty-four hours since we last spoke.

Why didn't it work out with Eileen? Because she never reciprocated the love that you felt for her.

"Hey, would you be mad if I told you I was in love with you?" Laura texted.

Do you remember that moment? That wonderful moment when someone you're infatuated with says "I love you" for the first time? Do you remember that *feeling*? It's like the two of you can take on the entire world by yourselves. Right in that moment, I felt as if I belonged to her forever. There it was: the first time a girl had ever reciprocated affection for me. It was the most incredible feeling in the world.

"I love you too," I said, completely forgetting about all of the other people in my life except the two of us.

June 2015

Why did it never work out with Emily? Because you obsessed over her and it freaked her out. People like space, you creep.

They say it only takes twenty-one days for addiction to alter your brain chemistry to the point where your body then *needs* something it previously didn't. I needed Laura. Whenever she texted or called me to check in, I was fine, but every day I didn't hear from her, I had withdrawals. I would mostly fill the void with booze, but I'd occasionally change it up by binging other things. One day I woke up and ran for seven miles, just so I could be too exhausted to feel lonely. I tried TV and video games, but I could never get through more than twenty minutes before my thoughts spiraled me into an anxiety attack. *What if she's sleeping with other guys? What if she loves Europe so much she wants to stay there?* Whenever I felt an attack coming on, I would play Weezer's *Everything Will Be Alright in the End* from top to bottom, in an attempt to convince myself that everything would, in fact, be all right in the end. But really, anything I did was a temporary fix in a world of no permanent solutions.

One night, Laura called and broke me out of my depression.

"Hey!" I answered.

"Hey! How are you?" she asked, sounding just as excited as I was.

"I'm doing well," I lied. "Still working on booking my trip to Germany, actually."

"That's awesome! Maybe you could take a train to come see me at some point."

"I'd really like that. I'll see if I can talk Delynn into a train ride, but I can't make any promises."

"Oh. I see." She grew quiet.

"Don't get me wrong, I really want to! I'm just not sure if Delynn will—"

"No, I get it. You and Delynn can hang out and then you can meet a nice German girl and marry her instead!"

"I would never . . . I mean, I'm with you."

"Sure, whatever."

"Have you been drinking?" I asked.

"Yeah, we just got back from the bars. What? Am I not allowed to drink?"

"No, I was just—"

"You can't boss me around. Gus used to do this shit all the time."

"Laura I'm not trying to—"

"He told me you were bad news when I started seeing you."

"Yeah, well, he also hit you, so why would you listen to him?"

There was a pause on the other end of the line. When she spoke, her voice was quiet again. "Why would you bring that up?"

"I don't know, Laura. I'm sorry. I just really miss you."

Laura hung up.

July 2015

Why didn't it work out with Allison? Because she, and every other girl you've ever met, simply could not love you.

Crying was hard at first. After so many back-to-back days of binge drinking after Laura had dumped me to be with Gus, I decided it would be healthiest to let it all out with a good cry. The problem was that I was so numb from the alcohol and afraid of the pain of heartbreak that I just couldn't get the waterworks flowing. I tried everything I could think of, from listening to Bright Eyes on repeat to watching an extensive collection of sad movie clips on YouTube, but nothing came out. I cued up the final scene from *Field of Dreams* and watched it over and over again. Nothing. I watched the final scene of the first season of *Mad Men*, when Don Draper's family leaves for a trip without him, and he sits on the stairs crying and realizing what a piece of shit he is. Still nothing. Not only was I stuck in a deep pit of despair, but I couldn't properly express how awful it felt.

Fortunately for me, my drunk self had had the foresight to text Emma my Laura bombshell the day after it happened. I had told her that I needed to talk to someone as soon as I could. She was on a beach trip with her roommates at the time, but she promised to stop by my apartment the second she got back to

Harrisonburg.

A few days later, Emma finally made an appearance.

"Hey, brother," she said, walking into my apartment carrying several plastic bags.

I sat on the couch in the same Aerosmith t-shirt and pair of tan cargo shorts I had been wearing for a week. By the time Emma came to visit, they were both covered in food and beer stains.

"Hi," I said from the couch, trying to remember the last time I had spoken to a human face to face. "Did you bring beer?"

"No, you don't need beer," she said. "You need food. I brought you Qdoba." She walked into the kitchen and placed the bags on the kitchen counter. The smell of tacos filled the room.

I didn't get up. "But they sell beer there. It wouldn't have been that much of an extra step." I kicked over a few empty bottles next to the couch.

"Eat your tacos," she said, handing me a plate and opening the window to let the sunlight in and the smell of booze and sweat out.

By that time, I was almost completely moved out of this apartment and into Kyle and I's new place, but I was staying there moping for the last few days of my lease. I had one couch, a mattress on the floor of my bedroom, and a TV that had exclusively streamed sad content for the past forty-eight hours. If my sister could have pulled up the watch history on that TV, it would probably have been more worrisome than any list of porn sites imaginable. *Why the fuck did he watch just the end of* Jumanji? *Why did he only watch the first ten minutes of* Up?

"Why don't you tell me what happened," she said, sitting next to me with her own plate of tacos.

I put the plate on the floor and leaned my head back on the couch. "Laura said she loved me. Then she said she didn't love me. Then she said she didn't want to see me anymore and she wanted to be with her boyfriend who she was actually in love with the whole time we were together. I'm such an idiot."

"You're not an idiot, you're just in love."

"What the fuck is the difference?" I asked, still wishing I had a beer.

"Did you sleep together?"

"Yeah."

"Did you have sex?"

"Well, yeah, we were in love."

"*You* were in love," she repeated, pointing at me. She sat up straight. "I hate to break it to you, but if she's still dating her ex-boyfriend, then she probably didn't love you."

"Then why did she say it? I wrote her a song for her on her birthday and she told me over and over again how she was in love with me. Then the next thing I know, she says her ex-boyfriend gave her some shells from their favorite beach back home, and she went on a trip with him to Boston and posted all about it on Facebook." I slid further down into the couch.

Emma laughed, nearly choking on a taco. "Shells? He got her *shells*?"

"Better than songs, apparently."

"Do you still love her?"

"Yes. I don't know how to fucking stop. She's poison, I know that. But I can't stop being in love with her, even though I want to more than anything."

"If you love her, then you want her to be happy, right?"

"Well, yeah."

"It sounds like she's happy with her social media likes and a boyfriend who picks up the beach equivalent of a rock and passes it off as a gift," she said.

I turned and glared at her. "I'm glad this is funny for you."

"I'm sorry," she said. "I know it sucks now, but you'll meet someone better."

"No, I won't. This was love. Lightning in a bottle. This only happens once in a lifetime."

"I know it seems like that now, but it won't feel like that forever. The Bible says—"

"Don't bring up the fucking Bible right now. I need a sister, not a savior."

"Sorry, you just might feel better if—"

"I'd feel better if children didn't get cancer. I'd feel better if people spent more time caring about other people, and less time forcing their religious agendas on people. I'd feel better if I didn't have to live in a world where I hate the person I am!"

We were both quiet for a moment. Emma put her hand on my shoulder. "Cade, I love you. You're great."

"I know that. I *know* you love me. But I can't *feel* it. The only love I can feel is Laura's, and she doesn't care at all."

I waited for an argument, but Emma didn't respond. When I turned to her, she was staring at me, her eyes wet with tears. "I'm sorry you don't like God," she said quietly, "but I love you, and religion is the only way I know how to show you that."

We sat in silence for a while. Eventually I said, "I should go to bed. I have to work in the morning."

"Okay," she said. "I love you, brother." Then she got up, hugged me, and left.

I went to the kitchen to clean up the plastic bags and paper plates. I noticed that Emma had left a pile of receipts and other paper on the counter, presumably after emptying her pockets of trash when she arrived. I was about to throw the stack away when I saw a note card. The top said, "Pray for" with a list below. There were about twenty names on it, most of which I didn't recognize.

The very last name on the list was mine. *Pray for Cade.* And that's when I cried.

September 2015

"Wouldn't you want to live here someday? Maybe raise a family?" Laura asked from the passenger seat. After we had patched things up the night of the *Rock Band* party, we had decided to take a trip together to beautiful downtown Charlottesville.

"It's the perfect city," I agreed. "I think we're close to the bar Rob Sheffield used to frequent when he lived here."

"Then let's go there!" she said with her face pressed against the passenger window.

I parked the car that Emma had let me borrow for the night and looked at my phone. I had just received a text from her saying, "Hello, brother. Been hanging out with anyone terrible lately????" Apparently, Laura had posted a picture of us together, and my sister saw it. I knew Emma wouldn't have let me borrow her car if she knew Laura was coming with me on this trip.

I decided to ignore the text. I knew I wouldn't be able to explain it to her. Laura and I were in love. We had finally put everything behind us and were ready to start creating new memories. It didn't matter if other people couldn't understand that.

According to the internet, a Latin American restaurant called Mono Loco occupied the same building that once was the bar where music journalist Rob Sheffield had frequently dined with his first wife. Laura and I sat on the patio and enjoyed a sunny afternoon in the low seventies, and both ordered meals we could only eat half of, just like on our first date; two peas in an anxiety-ridden pod. I didn't have enough money to pay for the meal, but Laura read my mind and put her credit card on the table.

"I got this."

"Oh, you don't have to—"

"No, I mean it. Congratulations on the job. I . . . I'm really glad I'm back . . . and we're—"

"I'm glad too," I said, smiling. "Oh, I almost forgot! I got you something."

"What? This is your dinner. You didn't have to get me anything."

"It didn't cost much," I said, pulling out a CD.

"Awesome! What songs did you put on it?"

"Songs to commemorate the trip. We can listen to it on the way home if you want."

"Yes!"

And that's exactly what we did.

Later that night, we were still in the car, parked in the parking lot of my apartment complex. We sat awkwardly in the front seats with our arms around each other; the middle console made it uncomfortable, but neither of us wanted the night to end.

"Can we listen to it again?" Laura asked.

"We've listened to it like three times! You're going to wear out the disc."

She smiled. "Do you remember when you made that first mix CD for me after you went on spring break?"

"I wanted an excuse to get dinner with you again," I remembered.

"It was a really good CD. Remember when you made the second CD before I left for Europe?"

"Yeah, I remember that one too. They were mostly long-distance songs."

"I really liked that one too. But honestly, I think this one is my favorite."

"Wow, high praise."

"Rob Sheffield would be proud of you," she said.

"Now that's a review I can get behind."

She laughed. "So, if the first CD was generic love songs, and the second CD was long-distance songs, what's the third CD?"

"They're all songs I listened to while you were away. Some nights were harder than others, so I needed music to cope. I've listened to this album nearly a hundred times."

"And you thought *I* was going to wear out the disc." Laura's grin turned into a kiss. After a few minutes of kissing, she stopped and said, "Don't worry. I'm not going anywhere anytime soon."

The drive home from Nathan's wedding was long. I got home around 1 a.m. and parked Emma's car in my parking lot. Even after all the self-reflection on the drive, I still hadn't reached a definitive conclusion about my future with Laura. I sat there in silence with no idea what to do. Did we have our problems? Absolutely. But what couple doesn't? On the other hand, I was pretty sure Nathan and Lilly weren't secretly dating anyone else when they told each other "I love you" for the first time.

"Why is this so difficult!" I shouted as I smashed my hands against the steering wheel. I pressed my forehead against the car horn button and unintentionally set off the horn. When I pulled my head back, I saw a shadowy silhouette in my driver's side window.

"Fuck!" I yelled, completely startled. It was Laura.

She opened the car door and pulled me out of the car into a hug.

"I'm so sorry we fought," she whispered. "I don't want to fight anymore." She pulled back and looked at me. "I missed you!" she exclaimed, near tears. I looked into her blue eyes. Despite my doubts, she was still the same beautiful girl I had fallen in love with. "Let's go inside," she whispered. "I promise I'll make it up to you." She grabbed my hands and pulled me toward my apartment.

HERE IT GOES AGAIN
By OK GO

October 2015

"Just when you think you're in control"

Most sleepovers took place in my apartment, so I rarely woke up in Laura's room, but I remember the few times I did quite fondly. She had pink bedsheets with a blue comforter, and a curtain so thin that light flooded the room the second the sun came up. On her nightstand she kept pictures of her family, and one of Gus (facing down) that she had yet to get rid of.

A few weeks after Nathan's wedding, we woke up together one morning in October. The sun illuminated her messy hair on the pillow, and I took a moment to study her face. I was so infatuated with her. I went in to kiss her shoulder and then put my arms around her.

"Good morning," she yawned. "When's the last time we woke up here together?"

"Not since May," I said.

She pushed me to the other side of the bed and put her head on my chest, "Last night was pretty fun."

"Yeah. It really was." I was fully awake now, hoping for themes from last night recurring this morning. No such luck. Laura got up and put on her robe.

"I gotta get ready for class," she said. "I can drive you home if you want."

"That would be nice." Experience told me I wasn't very fond of the walk. Especially half asleep at 7:30 a.m.

"Are you excited for Gordon's wedding this weekend?"

"Oh yeah," I replied, putting my hands behind my head. "This is gonna be a big one. All the Saint John's Boys in one spot again. I can't wait."

She moved back over to the bed and leaned over me. "Can I be an honorary Saint John's Boy?"

"If you kiss me right now."

She smiled. "You're sweet," she said, then went in for the kiss.

Oh please, God, I thought. *I know I don't ask for much—maybe a job that pays more than $85 a week, or a car to get me there—but please, if you just did one thing for me, please convince Laura to do what happened last night again this morning. I would never ask for anything again.*

As though I hadn't learned by then that God hates me.

Laura walked back over to her desk and started brushing her hair. "I wonder what I'm going to do while you're out of town," she said.

I sat up and leaned against the headboard. "I'm sure you'll find something. Your roommates seem to be one season deep into a *Gilmore Girls* binge."

"You know, Gus did reach out earlier this week and asked if I wanted to see him in D.C."

I wasn't mad. I wasn't sad. I wasn't even surprised by this news. I had known this would come up at some point, so I greeted it with the most ambivalent attitude I could.

"Cool."

"Would you have a problem with that?"

"Nope."

"What? Really?"

"Go ahead, spend time with Gus." By this time, I knew she craved negative attention as much as I craved morning sex. *Looks like both of us are going to be disappointed today.*

She walked back over to the bed, looked me in the eyes, and kissed me. "Fight with me," she said.

"I'm not fighting with you, Laura."

"Do you want to walk home?"

I threw my hands up. "I've fucking done it before!"

"Come on, fight with me! Like you did last week."

"Last week you texted Lisa from my phone asking if I wanted to go on a date with her! You just want to fight for no reason."

"You told me she was cute! Why wouldn't you want to go on a date with her?"

"Because I'm with you! And she knows that! Then I had to explain how it was an elaborate joke because *you* wouldn't let me tell her it was you!"

"I didn't want her to think I was being mean to her."

"But you *were* being mean to her!" I couldn't keep from raising my voice. "If you want to be with Gus, go be with him!"

"I don't want to be with him! I just . . . I just don't want him to end up with anyone else."

"Laura, that's completely unfair. Have . . . have you even told him about us?"

"Well, no. I don't want him to feel bad by telling him that I've moved on."

"Is that really why? Or do you want him to be an option in the future if we don't work out?"

"You're being a real dick, like Ben Affleck in *Gone Girl!*"

"What?" I asked.

"Ben Affleck in *Gone Girl!* He's a total dick to his wife in that movie!"

I stared at her for a moment, stunned. "Laura, his wife is a fucking psychopath, and clearly the villain in that movie."

"He's the villain! He cheats on his wife!"

"His wife stages a kidnapping with an old friend, who she then *murders*, and gets pregnant to make Ben Affleck look like a garbage human if he leaves her loony tunes day-to-day shit."

"I'm not the only one who thinks this! You're wrong!"

"Why are we even doing this? We have fun at night and then in the morning all you do is explain to me how shitty a person I am."

"Do we even have fun at night?" she fired back.

I shook my head in disbelief. "I don't know. You show up drunk almost every time, begging for me to sleep with you, then in the morning you leave as soon as the sun comes up."

"Fuck you!" she shouted.

I got up and put on my clothes in a rush. "Laura, I'm leaving."

As I walked past her to the door, she glared at me. "You can't run from this!" she yelled. "All you do is run away from your problems!" I kept walking through the door and down the hall. "Get back here right now!" she screamed after me.

Why isn't it working out with Laura?

Because we accept the love we think we deserve, and you have had a low opinion of yourself for quite some time.

The walk home was a very sobering two miles. I thought about my future. I thought about how to get away from the girl I was in love with, the girl who was slowly killing me from the inside. But I had no idea how. I couldn't bear to part with her "love," but I also almost felt lonelier when I was with her. It was exhausting. Sitcoms had raised me to believe that the first girl I fell in love with would be the person I would spend the rest of my life with. They were wrong.

I finally realized this was the farthest from true love I had ever been.

CAN'T LET GO
By Death of the Cool

October 2015

"You picked me up and cleaned me up and taught me self-respect."

"This can't be real," Annie said.

"Oh, it's definitely real," I replied with a grin.

The Saint John's Boys and Gordon's soon-to-be wife all gathered around a small thirty-two-inch TV screen in Gordon's childhood bedroom. It was the night before their wedding, and as a last-minute jest, the groomsmen had decided to show Annie a very important video from our youth (a.k.a. four years prior).

"Why the *hell* would you throw a rock at a hornet's nest?"

"Wait, this part's amazing," Julian promised, as we watched Gordon swat away hornets from his head. Keith's iconic laugh echoed through the television speakers.

"I'm marrying this man tomorrow!" Annie said, shaking her head and staring at the screen.

It was really great having everyone together again. Even though I had lived with Bruce and Julian in college, it was a rare occurrence after 2007 to have Jimmy, Martin, and Gordon in the room with us as well. The fact that Gordon, the kindest person I've ever known, was marrying an equally incredible girl made the occasion all the better. It was surreal to think about how we used to hang out in this bedroom watching Adam Sandler movies and playing

265

Guitar Hero: Van Halen (because Gordon's taste in music video games was shit). And here we were, nearly a decade later, with one of us tying the knot in mere hours.

I guess this is growing up.

★ ★ ★ ★ ★

"Thanks for bringing the video, man. That was a lot of fun to relive old times," Gordon said as we sat in his car on the way to the wedding venue. Gordon had graciously offered to drive. Julian was in Martin's car, and Bruce rode with Jimmy (Bruce apparently made Jimmy pull over because he needed to vomit up some of his beer from the night before, but we didn't find out about that until we arrived at the venue).

"Don't mention it," I said, and patted Gordon on the shoulder. "Anything for you, buddy."

He smiled, but his smile quickly faded. "So, I have to bring this up," he said. "When we were all hanging out the other night you said something that really bugged me."

"Really? What?"

"This Laura girl, she sounds terrible. She treats you like shit, and you just put up with it."

"I know. She's kind of crazy."

"She's not the only crazy one."

His words caught me off guard. Gordon had never said anything mean or judgmental to *anyone* in the twelve years that I'd known him.

I shrugged. "I don't know what to do, man. I mean, I think I'm in love with her."

"That's not love. Love is both people feeling the same way about each other. From what you've told me, it sounds like she doesn't love you at all."

"I mean, I think she loves me . . . she just has a weird way of showing it."

"Explain how she shows it," he said, gripping the steering wheel so tightly that his knuckles were white.

I looked out the passenger window. "Well . . . I mean . . . she sleeps over a lot."

". . . Uh huh . . ."

"Okay, whenever one of our mutual friends says something mean to her, she comes over and tells me about it, and how I should hate that person. Kind of flattering that she comes to me before anyone else."

"You're not really winning me over."

I sighed. "I mean, I've tried to break up with her whenever she treats me this way, but whenever I do, she'll either take off her shirt or start crying, and I'm left completely defenseless. If I still feel like being with her after all of this, isn't that love?"

"No. It's not love. It's emotional manipulation. She knows that you're a great fucking guy and she knows how to exploit the shit out of it."

"I mean, maybe—"

"Not 'maybe'! Definitely! You don't deserve to be treated this way. I've never met her, but she sounds fucking awful. I know you can do way better."

This was the most upset I'd ever seen Gordon. Picture Kenneth Parcell from *30 Rock* mixed with Rita Bennett from *Dexter*, with a dash of Gonzo from *The Muppets*, and you'd have Gordon. If Gonzo from *The Muppets* told you to break up with your emotionally abusive girlfriend, wouldn't you?

"Thanks, man. That means a lot. I . . . It seems like I didn't have a ton of friends this summer, during all of this Laura stuff. I'm just glad we're all back together."

Gordon was quiet for a few minutes. We pulled into the venue parking lot and into a spot, and Gordon turned the car off and turned to face me. "You know, back in 2007 when we all left Saint John's and went our separate ways, I really thought that was it. I had met my best friends, and I was about to lose them forever.

I think we all thought that. But not you. You were the one who kept us together all of these years, planning cabin trips, beach trips . . . just randomly visiting whenever you were in the area. You're the reason we're still together almost ten years later. There should never be a point in your life where you don't think you have a ton of friends."

Maybe it was the slowly approaching hangover, or the lack of sleep from the night before, but Gordon's speech really got to me. "Thanks, man."

He nodded. "Anytime. Now let's go get dressed. I'm getting married in an hour."

After the ceremony, we all met in the reception hall for the usual post-wedding shenanigans. Gordon and Annie had their first dance to Styx's "Come Sail Away," and the eating and drinking commenced soon after. All of the Saint John's Boys (excluding Gordon) shared a table for dinner, excited to discuss the first marriage in our brotherhood—and especially the ceremony song. As the wedding party had walked down the aisle, the keyboard player's instrument had malfunctioned: the "strings" setting was inadvertently changed to a "slap bass" setting, which sounded like different variations of farts. The keyboardist finished the entire song, much to the amusement of the audience; all of the guests and the wedding party were laughing nonstop. It was a nice spin on the classic approach to traditional matrimony, and needless to say a huge conversation piece at dinner.

Right before we got into the meat of the discussion, Gordon's father stood up and addressed the crowd. "Hello, everyone. Thank you all for celebrating this very special occasion with us. We're so happy you could all be here to celebrate Gordon and Annie. Before we get into the Best Man and Maid of Honor speeches, would anyone like to share anything about the happy couple?"

I stood up. I felt the need to say something, not only because of Gordon's moving monologue in the car, but also because I had already written something.

"Hi, everybody. I'm Gordon's friend, Cade. I prepared a speech for the new couple." I began to read from my script: "My top ten memories of Gordon Jackson Michael Summers." (Gordon's middle name was Jackson, and he was confirmed under St. Michael the Archangel in the eighth grade. So per Catholic tradition, Gordon added the name Michael after his middle name, which made an unintentional reference to the King of Pop. His friends never let him forget it.) "Number ten: When we first met Gordon, he named the cafeteria tables after the different houses in *Harry Potter*, and we all secretly thought to ourselves, *Wow. If this guy ever gets married, we're totally not going to his wedding.*"

The crowd laughed, which gave me enough confidence to continue with the other nine things. "Number nine: The week before we all left for college, we went to my cabin and found a hornet's nest, which, to a group of eighteen-year-old boys, was like finding the sorcerer's stone. That's a *Harry Potter* reference just for you, Gordon. We all threw rocks at the hornet's nest and dared each other to run past a huge wall of hornets. After a few minutes of arguing about who would be first, someone started chanting 'Gordon,' and the rest of us quickly joined in. He said something to the effect of 'Okay, might as well.' He ran through the hornets, and we watched as he got repeatedly stung in the head by three hornets. It was more entertaining than a tri-wizard tournament."

More laughs. *Keep 'em coming, Cade.* "Number eight: In high school, Gordon was in an indie film called *Kidney Beans*, and he randomly called me one day after school, asking if I wanted to be in a scene for it. Because of you, Gordon, I have an IMDb page for playing Chris, who was known for his one line, 'My name is Chris, and I too like Rocky Road ice cream.'

"Number seven: In eighth grade, Gordon got to pick one person to go with him to Busch Gardens and he chose me. But that's not the best part of that story. Gordon thought it would be best to tell me by giving me a typed letter in a sealed envelope which read, 'Don't read until you get home.' I decided to go with him on the trip, despite the fact that I had a huge crush on Linda Karver, and she would be at the school Halloween dance that also happened to be that weekend. Linda got married a few months ago, so I can finally say I made the right decision going to Busch Gardens with you, friend." I lifted my glass to Gordon across the room, and he lifted his to me.

"Number six: In eighth grade, we performed the song 'Twist and Shout' together at the talent show. I played guitar, while Gordon stole my thunder and did the *entire* dance from *Ferris Bueller's Day Off*. Number five: We used to walk around the school sharing a pair of headphones while listening to the Police's *Greatest Hits* album. We didn't care how much people made fun of us—and by 'people,' I mean the bastards sitting next to me right now." The bastards sitting next to me chuckled.

"Number four: Gordon always says 'I love you' to every single one of his friends whenever he says goodbye. Does everyone know how difficult it is to be a guy in high school and say 'I love you' to another guy who is just your friend? Gordon doesn't." This one got a particularly high amount of laughter, probably because everyone in the room knew exactly what I was talking about.

"Number three: Gordon is the most selfless person I know. He puts everyone else before himself at all times, which isn't easy to do. Number two is about Annie, because I feel bad for leaving her out this long. Annie, none of the Saint John's Boys knew you that well before this month, but I'm happy to say we've all loved getting to know you more personally in the past weeks. Everyone thinks you're absolutely wonderful, and my favorite thing about you is that you greet us with the same warmth and enthusiasm that Gordon has all of these years. You're gonna fit right in with us."

I turned to the rest of my friends for the last topic. "Number one: They say if you learn something the wrong way, it's immensely more difficult to learn it correctly. When I was only a kid in grade school, I knew who my best friends were; I learned that once you make a friend, they're your friend for life. This has been a very difficult thing to 'unlearn,' seeing as most friendships—most *relation-ships*—are very brief in the grand scheme of things. Over the years, I've attached myself to countless people with the expectation that they will care about me as much as my first friends, even though they have no reason to. My favorite thing about Gordon, and the rest of the Saint John's Boys for that matter, is how great a friend each and every one of them is. We've been good friends, we've sometimes been bad friends, but no matter what, we've been there for each other when we needed to be. And when I look at Gordon and Annie, I know that's the exact relationship they're going to have. So, if everyone will join me in raising their glasses to the new couple."

"Cheers!" everyone shouted as they raised their beverages.

Right as I sat down, Gordon's father stood up again. "Could the Saint John's Boys stand up so everyone knows who you are?"

Martin, Julian, Jimmy, Bruce, Gordon, and myself all stood up for the whole room to see us. Everyone applauded.

After a long day of celebrating, I received a text from Laura that said, "Come over tonight," with a flirty emoji attached.

I looked at Gordon and Annie as they got into their newly decorated "Just Married" getaway vehicle, and I thought to myself, *That's what I want.*

I responded to the text: "I'm not coming over tonight. This summer was unbelievably terrible, and I thought we could try again. But you haven't changed at all. I'm done, Laura."

I hugged my friends goodbye, walked to my car, and ignored the flurry of furious texts that blew up my phone for the rest of the night.

I was finally free.

WHEN YOU WERE YOUNG
By the Killers

February 2016

"He doesn't look a thing like Jesus"

A few weeks after Gordon's wedding, my mother called to let me know G-dad had been diagnosed with cancer. I honestly didn't think much of it at the time. When you hear about a loved one receiving serious medical news, it doesn't feel dramatic like in the movies. You just think, *Huh. Everything will probably be okay though. My life isn't interesting enough to warrant such a big plot twist.* I genuinely figured he would go to the doctor, get treatment, and everything would be back to normal. This unfortunately was not the case. A couple weekly trips to the doctor eventually turned into a permanent stay at the hospital, and my denial started to wear off.

My sister and I decided to pay him a visit when we found out he wouldn't be coming home anytime soon. As I walked into the hospital, I thought about some of G-dad's legendary stories; there were a lot of greatest hits, but nothing will ever top the pie tin story. To this day, no one can say for certain how much of it is true, but it has always been and always will be an amazing legend, nonetheless.

The first time I heard it was in Ireland in 2013. G-dad had paid for the whole extended family to stay in a large house in the county where our ancestors had lived before they moved to America.

"Did I ever tell you the pie tin story?" G-dad asked.

We were sitting in wooden chairs on the patio, overlooking a lake. I was listening to Rise Against's "Appeal to Reason" on my Mp3 player and enjoying my first legal beer. "No," I said, taking my earbuds out.

He moved his chair closer to mine. "Before I tell you the story," he said, "I want you to know that I was young, and like all of us, I did some stupid, regrettable, and sometimes mean things. Hopefully you and your cousins can learn from my mistakes."

"What's the story G-dad?" I asked, now fully intrigued.

He took a sip of wine. "I went to a Catholic all-boys college, and the priests were very strict. We all ate together in a big cafeteria, and the best thing to eat was always the pie. My roommate and I stole a pie tin every night and brought it back to our room."

I laughed. "Why?" I asked.

My grandfather shrugged. "We thought it would be fun! After about a month of stealing pie tins, we had a random room inspection. When the Residential Advisor opened our closet, a stack of pie tins poured out. He told the principal, who called us into his office the next day. The principal told us we would be expelled unless we did him a favor, so naturally we told him we'd do it."

"What was it?"

"He wanted us to take his daughter and her friend to a school dance."

I shook my head. "I've already seen this episode of *Three's Company*, G-dad," I said, laughing.

G-dad powered through it. "I promise you, this story is far more notable than any sitcom you've ever seen. Anyway, we agreed to take them to their dance, and he dropped the charges. My roommate and I were actually excited—there was a chance the girls would be attractive, and we might end up having a good time. This was not the case. When we went to pick them up and saw them for the first time, I turned to my roommate and asked, 'Where do you think the coin slots on these things are?'"

"Ugh, G-dad!" I continued laughing.

"We took them to the dance and had a horrible time. They kept asking us to dance with them. Finally, we told them we had to go home because we had class early the next morning, so we got in the car and drove back. I admit we had to drink a bit in order to tolerate these girls, and it was reflected in my driving."

Now, if anyone else in the world had told me this story, I would have thought they were a horrible person. But G-dad was my undisputed hero. His word was gospel; every single one of my cousins—and even my grandmother—loved hearing him tell this story.

"We made it home safely," he continued, "but when I went to park on the street in front of the girls' house, I crashed into a parked car in front of me. Then that car caught on fire . . ."

"Holy shit," I said. I didn't care if any of it was true—this was a better story than anything C.S. Lewis ever wrote.

Apparently, my grandfather wasn't done. "There was a breeze that day," he said. "The car caught fire, and the wind blew the flames toward the neighbor's house, which then caught fire. A half-naked man ran out of it. It turns out their neighbor had a mistress he'd invite over every time his wife went away, and sure enough, this was one of those times. The fire department and the police came, and this man lost his car, half his house, and when his wife got back, his marriage. The girls' dresses even caught fire, and they rolled around in the yard to put it out."

I sat in disbelief clinging to every sentence.

"My roommate and I stood in the street and watched all of it happen. Right as the fire department arrived, the half-naked man approached me and, knowing everything he was about to lose, said, 'You might as well take my fucking keys too!' Then he threw his keys at me and stormed off."

I was in stitches. This was the most insane story I had ever heard. To this day, nobody knows if it really happened the way he said it did—even our parents and grandmother.

But I still believe every word.

I couldn't help but smile as I walked through the entrance of Inova Alexandria Hospital, but a lone tear rolled down my face.

VASOLINE
By Stone Temple Pilots

February 2016

"It isn't you, isn't me"

There is no anxiety in the mosh pit. For a brief window of time, all of the chaos, frustration, and concern is outside of your head instead of inside, crashing into your torso, legs, and face every chance it gets. Depending on the show, the window of time can be a variety of lengths, ranging from a sixty-second punk song to a ninety-minute metal set.

There are five basic types of mosh pits:

1. *Standard Mosh Pit*: This usually breaks out at punk rock/emo shows and is fairly simple to understand. In the middle of the general admission/ standing room portion of the venue, a collection of sad bastards and angry idiots collect and begin pushing each other. Contrary to popular belief, punks are generally very friendly people cast out by society just trying to fit in somewhere. If you get knocked down in the pit, they will almost always circle around you and ensure you get up safely.

2. *The Circle Pit*: Similar to number one, this type is also simple to grasp. Everyone in the middle of the venue forms a pit, this time running in a cir-

cle. This option is safer for those too scared to try out the more aggressive types of mosh pits; you will get pushed, but it will be kept to a minimum as long as you go around and around at the same pace as everyone else.

3. *The Sock Pit*: This is the best type of pit for a first-timer or a middle-schooler. Everyone takes off their shoes, then slides around and bumps into each other. This almost exclusively happens at small venues, where the band knows everyone in the audience, but it's a pleasant experience when one pops up.

4. *Hardcore/Metal Pit*: Unlike punks, metalheads are not forgiving. If you fall over in this pit, few people will try to save you. Keith and I once went to a metal festival, and, thinking I could hang with the metalheads, I jumped into the pit during a Bullet for my Valentine set. I bumped into a huge dude with a bandana wrapped around his face who looked like he was from *Mad Max*; he pushed me down with one hand as if he wasn't even trying. I fell to the ground and immediately got kicked in the ribs by another metalhead running around. I rolled to the side of the pit and caught my breath before I went to find Keith. The good news is I didn't feel any anxiety for the rest of the weekend.

5. *The Wall of Death*: This one sounds menacing, and it certainly can be, depending on the crowd. But it's more spectacle than anything else. This is when the singer tells the crowd to create a line down the middle of the venue, and then the two divided sides charge at each other like they did in the final battle of the third *Lord of the Rings* film.

What happens when the two sides collide is entirely up to the participants in the Wall of Death.

On this particular night, I was in a standard mosh pit with Kyle. We were seeing the Used play their self-titled debut album in its entirety. For the moment, I wasn't anxious. I wasn't anxious about my lack of income. I wasn't anxious about my lack of a car. I wasn't anxious about texting a girl, or the date I was going on with her tomorrow, or even whether or not we'd end up together. I was in a mosh pit.

The band finished their set, and Kyle and I waited for them to come back and perform an encore. I wasn't ready to go back to reality just yet. We'd been told the encore song would be "Choke Me," the hidden track at the end of the album. After a few minutes, the stage lit up, and we heard the introduction to the song ring through the speakers. We saw Bert McCracken take the stage with the rest of the band, as he screamed the first line: "AS OF NOW I'M DOWN, STRAIGHT UP!" Kyle and I looked at each other and nodded, and then charged into the circle of disarray without hesitation and began shoving everyone who got close to us. My anxiety was once again lifted from me as I crashed into countless sweaty strangers. The chaos was on the outside of my head, where I could deal with it.

Unfortunately, life is not a mosh pit, and I have to concede to the fact that anxiety bests me from time to time. The next day, my anxiety was back in full swing, this time because I had a date with Tara that night, and the fact that my usually dependable kid sister was doing very little to help me prepare.

"Dude, I really need to borrow your car," I pleaded.

"You can't! I need it for youth group tonight," Emma responded.

I rolled my eyes. "I really need it for a date. You're being selfish by not addressing *my* needs."

Emma laughed. "Just ask her to drive."

"This is the first date. Do you know how bad of a first impression that would make?"

"Yeah, that's definitely not a great first impression. Oh well, wish I could help you. How's your anxiety, by the way? Are you keeping down all of your meals?"

"Yeah, I'm fine. I just need a car."

"That's great! You're not even nervous talking to her?"

"Well, I'm kind of nervous texting her. After we met, we texted all day, every day, and then these past three days . . . not so much. I just don't want to scare her away by texting too much."

"You should call her."

"What?"

"Texting is a much harder form of communication to interpret. If you call her, you'll both be on the same page. Plus, girls think it's flattering."

"No, they don't."

"Yes, they do! It shows them that you're willing to take an extra step. Anybody can text her. How many people call her on a daily basis?"

"None. They all have better sense."

"All I can offer is my advice."

"Well, I wish it could drive me places."

"Love you, brother. I have to go."

"Love you too."

Tara was great. We had met a few weeks prior, through a mutual friend at her birthday party. She liked beer, her favorite band was Twenty One Pilots, and she loved *Rock Band*; needless to say, I was infatuated. We had been texting every day since we met, so I was starting to think she felt the same way. I asked her on a date to grab dinner right outside my place of infrequent employment. I still had very little money to my name; I had a potential part-time job at the Paramount Theater in Charlottesville, but still no car to drive the hour to get there. I couldn't afford a car because of my current job, and I couldn't get a job because of my lack of a car. Poverty is a vicious cycle.

Tara had stopped texting me a couple days before I called my sister. I assumed the date was still on, but she had not responded to my last message. To make things worse, I had sent a follow-up text about eighteen hours later, containing a weak joke about how she might not have received my previous text, which she also did not respond to. I couldn't text her without looking like a crazy person, so as much as I hated to admit it, it was sounding like Emma's suggestion was the only thing left to do.

What's the worst that can happen?

I picked up my phone and dialed her number. She answered after a few rings.

"Hello?"

"Hey, Tara. What's up?"

"Oh . . . not much. How are you?"

"I'm good. Still excited for tonight?"

"Um, yeah. Are you?"

"Yeah, definitely. Just wanted to call to make sure."

"Oh, cool . . . you could have just texted."

Son of a BITCH!

"Oh, yeah, I just like calling better."

There was a brief silence that felt like an eternity before she responded.

"Okay, well, see you tonight."

"Bye!"

Fuck fuck fuck fuck fuck fuck fuck.

I met Tara at the agreed-upon location later that evening. She greeted me with a smile and a hug, which was very nice of her, considering the verbal diarrhea I had just spewed over the phone to her. We walked over to Clementine's, a great restaurant/bar in downtown Harrisonburg. I told her to "get whatever" off the menu, even though I couldn't afford it. I decided I would just live off of cereal and water for the rest of the week. Fortunately for me, Tara preferred Bud Light over the thirty craft beers they had to offer, which balanced out with the undeservingly expensive salad she chose for her meal. I ordered fish tacos because I was unsure how long was "too long" to look at a menu on a date, and it was the first thing I saw. We talked while we waited on our food.

Okay, quick: why didn't it work out with Kayleigh? Because you didn't talk to her. Start talking.

"Favorite song?" I asked.

"'Migraine' by Twenty One Pilots. You?"

"'Hey Jude' by the Beatles.

Why didn't it work out with Penny? Because she was more attracted to her manager at the movie theater she worked at. This is perfect, I work at a movie theater now!

"Any siblings?"

"One sister. Younger. She goes to Virginia Tech. We're close but we're also pretty different people. Do you like your job?"

"Well, it pays the bills." There it was. The first lie in the relationship.

Why didn't it work out with Emily? Because you played a Snow Patrol song in front of an entire crowd and dedicated it to her on what turned out to not be a date. Don't do that.

"What do you want to do when you graduate?" I continued.

"I'm gonna be a nurse. I still have one more semester in the fall."

Why didn't it work out with Allison? Because she had a 4.0 GPA, and you would frequently skip studying to spend time with her. She hated that.

"Wow, that sounds hard. You must have straight A's," I said, taking a sip of my beer.

"Pssshhhh . . . yeah, I wish. I probably partied more than you during undergrad," she said, grinning.

Why didn't it work out with Laura? Because she had a male best friend she was in love with throughout your entire relationship.

"Where do you plan on going after you graduate?" I asked.

"Probably back home to Ashburn. That's where my parents and my best friend live."

"Is she your age?"

"It's a 'he,'" she said. "His name is Paul, and yeah, we grew up together."

God fucking dammit! Oh, wait . . . maybe he's gay.

"He goes to school in Florida. He's gonna have to move back though, which really sucks because his girlfriend lives there, and they'll probably break up."

Fuuuuuuuuuuuuuuuuuuuuuuuccccccccccccckkkkkkkkkkkkkk.

Our food arrived. Tara began eating her salad, and I took the first bite of my fish taco. It was literally the worst-tasting thing I have ever paid for. I didn't want to spit it out after only one bite, or do anything that would ruin the date, so I continued to sit there and smile while eating a meal that might have very well come from a trash can.

"Kyle showed me that video you guys used to win the new *Rock Band*. I'm really jealous. That looked like a lot of fun."

I didn't know how I was going to gather the appropriate amount of strength required to swallow my food fast enough to respond to the rest of the conversation. I nearly choked, but I coughed out an answer. "Yeah, it was a great party."

"I haven't played in forever, but it was my favorite game when it came out."

"I've been playing since it came out back in 2007. It was really fun to bring it back in college, because most people also hadn't played it in years. They start playing because it's such a throwback, but they keep playing because of all the new songs I've bought over the years."

"How many songs do you have?"

"About nine hundred."

"Holy shit!" she said a little too loudly for a nice restaurant. Her reaction was everything I could have ever wanted from a first date.

"Yeah, you should come over and play some time."

"I'd love to! I play guitar on expert level, so watch out."

I chuckled. "Neat."

"What's so funny?"

"I don't want to brag, but while other people were going on dates and throwing keggers in high school, I was basically playing *Rock Band* with my eyes closed."

Tara nearly spit her beer out onto her half-eaten salad. "Challenge accepted. I guess we'll have to play soon."

"I guess we will."

After I finished the worst meal I had ever eaten and had a few more beers to wash out the taste, we left the restaurant. Fortunately for me, the date seemed to have gone much better than my food order. I just had to spend the next few minutes tiptoeing around the fact that I had walked to the restaurant and didn't have a car to drive her home.

Why did it never work out with Eileen? Because you were too scared to make a move.

"I had a lot of fun tonight," I said, suddenly nervous as we stood in the dark outside Clementine's.

She paused for a little too long. "I did too," she finally said.

"Would you want to—"

"Hey, real quick—I just want to say up front I'm not looking for anything serious. I'm about to graduate and I'm not a hundred percent sure what I'm doing. Tonight was fun, but I don't really want to make it a regular thing, you know?"

"Yeah, I know."

"Oh, great. Really?"

"Yeah, I figured you mostly agreed to the date because I mentioned the other night that my grandpa was in the hospital and—"

"No, that's not it! I really wanted to come out with you. This was really great. You're great! I just . . ."

"Don't worry, I totally get it. I'm okay with just having a *Rock Band* buddy for now."

Tara smiled. "I'd really like that."

"Me too. Want to play next week?"

"Definitely! Just send me a text, and I'll be there."

"Sounds good."

We hugged goodbye, and she walked toward a parking lot, which led me to believe she had a car. Having the guilty burden of driving her home lifted from my shoulders, I enjoyed a peaceful two-mile walk back to my apartment.

NIGHTMARE
By Crooked X

July 2000

"My pillow's covered with sweat"

I was seven years old. I was awake. No matter how hard I tried to sleep, it wasn't happening. My sister was in the bed across the room from me, fast asleep. But I had a completely rational reason to be awake: I had seen a commercial for the new Jim Carrey version of *How the Grinch Stole Christmas* earlier in the day, and that shit had terrified me. It was a thirty-second trailer where that tiny girl from Whoville interacts with the titular character for the first time, and Ace Ventura himself gives a very menacing facial expression as he declares he's "the Grinch!" It was dumb, but I couldn't sleep out of the fear of being eaten by Jim Carrey; despite the fact all his character ever wanted to do was ruin Christmas for a whole bunch of people who were slightly better off than he was.

My parents were out celebrating their wedding anniversary while G-dad watched my sister and me. He had sent us to bed about twenty minutes before I walked back downstairs to share my troubles with him. I found him in the den, reading.

"G-dad?"

"What is it, pal?"

"I can't sleep. I'm scared of the Grinch."

He chuckled. "Don't be scared. That's just silly."

"I can't sleep."

"Don't worry, I'll walk you back up."

He poured me a glass of water and followed me to my room. I crawled into my bed, and he left the water on the nightstand. Then he checked for monsters in the closet and underneath the beds without waking my sister.

"Goodnight kiddo," he whispered.

"Goodnight, G-dad. I love you."

February 2016

A week had passed since my date with Tara, and all I had to show for it was another sleepless night pondering my fears: *How am I going to pay rent this month? Will I ever meet a girl whose favorite part of being with me isn't sleeping with other people?* A call from my sister finally woke me from my trance.

"Hello?"

"Hey." Her voice sounded tired. "G-dad isn't doing well. The doctor said this is probably going to be our last chance to see him. I'm gonna drive up today. Can I give you a ride?"

I tried to speak, but the words weren't coming out.

"Cade?"

When I finally spoke, my words surprised me: "But I already saw him a month ago. I don't know if I can see him like that again."

"I know it's hard. But if you don't come with me, you'll regret it forever."

"Okay," was all I could say, and I hung up the phone.

I called work to let them know that I would not, in fact, be able to work the only shift they had been able to give me that week, then texted my sister: "Ready when you are."

As I waited for her to arrive, I pulled out my guitar and played the Dispatch song "Josaphine." Before he had met my grandmother, G-dad once told me about a girl he'd had a crush on, named Josaphine. Obviously, my grandfather didn't follow through on his infatuation with this girl I only knew by name, but I couldn't stop hearing the song in my head, no matter how hard I tried. I played it over and over again until my sister arrived.

NEXT TO YOU
By the Police

February 2016

"All I want is to be next to you"

I stood next to Emma and my cousin, Tristan, in the hospital waiting room. My parents had already paid their respects earlier in the week, along with the rest of the family. My uncle Jerry, the doctor in the family, had travelled hundreds of miles to convince the doctors in this hospital to try and remove the cancer and prolong G-dad's life, but his efforts were in vain. The doctors said the cancer had spread too far, and there was nothing that could be done.

They say the first stage of grief is bargaining. My uncle took a long time to take "no" for an answer, which is why we ran into him outside of G-dad's hospital room door.

"Hey, guys," he said. "How is everyone?" He looked like he hadn't slept in days and his eyes were full of despair, but he put on a smile when he greeted us.

"We're all right," I said, knowing that nobody in the family was "all right."

"That's good to hear. Hope the drive wasn't too bad."

"Cade and Tristan forced me to listen to screamo music," Emma said, rolling her eyes. "Other than that, there wasn't a lot of traffic."

I had, in fact, "forced" my sister to listen to *The Black Parade* by My Chemical Romance, one of my top five favorite albums, and definitely *not* "screamo music." It had seemed only fitting to listen to a rock opera about death on the way to see our grandfather for the last time.

"They only want one person in the room at a time," my uncle said, nodding at me. "Why don't you go first, Cade?" He gave me a light push toward the door.

Without a word, I walked inside. I was anxious about what I would see. I honestly had no idea what to expect. Inside the room was a huge machine that took up half of the space; I had no idea what it was, but it looked as important as it was expensive. In the corner of the room were two chairs, which didn't make sense, considering they only wanted one of us in the room at a time.

In the middle of the room, hooked up to the big machine, lying on his hospital bed, was G-dad. He looked worse than I had ever seen him. There were tubes connected to several parts of his body, including the inside of his mouth. His lips were peeled back in what looked like a very uncomfortable position. He looked like he was part of an alien autopsy; I almost didn't recognize the man in front of me.

I was in that room for twenty minutes, alone with G-dad. I could completely make up what I said in this room, and everyone would have to believe me, because they would have no other way of finding out the truth. But I'm going to be completely honest about what I said to G-dad for what would be my last interaction with him forever: nothing. I said *nothing.* I stood there for twenty minutes, paralyzed by sadness, and watched my hero lie completely still in his discomfort. Every time I thought of something to say, it didn't come out. I couldn't stop thinking this was going to be the last time I saw him, and nothing I could say would measure up to that moment.

Eighteen minutes into my visit, G-dad opened his eyes very briefly—which scared the *hell* out of me. Then he spoke.

"Cade's here."

I tried to say something, but again, no words came out.

G-dad spoke again. "The *notable* doctor, was *not able* to operate, because he had *no table*."

It took me another minute to process what he'd said: the answer to the riddle he had come up with over a decade ago. I had actually figured it out when I was in high school, but I never told him because I knew how much he enjoyed holding the mystery over me whenever he got the chance.

He closed his eyes and went back to sleep. A tear rolled down my cheek. I turned around, opened the door, and as I left the room, I whispered, "Goodbye, G-dad."

(DON'T FEAR) THE REAPER
By Blue Oyster Cult

March 2016

"Together in eternity"

If you think about funerals, there's so much tradition that seems irrational. The family members are usually asked to stand at the front of the building where the service is held (in this case a Catholic church) and greet people as they come in. Friends and relatives pile in and give you their condolences with sympathetic expressions on their faces, but the truth is they have no idea how you feel in that moment. They may have lost someone of equal importance to them, but they have no idea what *you* are going through, no matter how hard they try. I guess I understood the concept of closure, and how we might feel a need to properly say goodbye to people we'll never see again. But it seemed all too odd that somebody could be in that church, on that day, and feel anywhere close to ambivalent about my grandfather.

I *loved* G-dad. Very, very, very much. And on this day, I was surrounded by family, friends, and strangers whose feelings for him all varied. Some were as sad as I was, others thought about that one time they had met him at a dinner party and thought of him fondly, and other people were wondering why this particular Catholic church didn't have padding on the kneelers. After we all took our seats, I sat contemplating how important religion was to G-dad, and how very little I felt connected to it. He was a devout Catholic, and I often wondered how an all-loving God could let people's homes get destroyed, let infants die, or give me $30,000 worth of student loans, no car, and a low-paying job. I've always believed that, in my life, everything happened for a reason, and every time I step back and look at the big picture, it's truly beautiful how the events of my life have gotten me to where I am. That being said, I don't believe this is the fairest of processes to many, and I also question why the omniscient being who created this master plan should be worshipped for it.

The reception was held at a country club our family had rented out for birthday parties many times before. We gathered in a large ballroom with a high ceiling and several set tables with eggshell white tablecloths draped over them. It was pleasant to see so many family members I hadn't seen in years . . . plus there was a great brisket. But on this particular day, it would take far more than comradery and slow-cooked meats to make me feel better.

As if God himself had heard my thoughts, he sent one of his employees to do his bidding.

An older woman with short brown hair wearing a black dress approached me. "Are you Cade? The grandson?" she asked.

"I am," I said, putting down my drink and brisket. I reached out to shake her hand.

She reached out her hand. "It's so nice to meet you. I just wanted to let you know how great a man your grandfather was," she said, nodding and clutching my hand in both of hers.

"Yeah, I know." I gave her a single nod and a forced smile, then went back to my neutral facial expression.

"I was in his Bible study group for ten years. We met once a week. He was a very dedicated member. He really loved God."

"Don't we all," I offered.

"He sure does work in mysterious ways . . . but I'm sure your grandfather told you all about that."

"He mentioned it a few times, yes." I continued to nod.

"Did he ever tell you about the nickname we gave him?"

"No, I don't think so."

She cracked a smile and leaned in before she spoke. "We called him 'the heretic.' It means someone who disagrees with the word of God."

My superficial smile disappeared as I raised an eyebrow. "I know what it means. I'm a bit confused as to why that's the name you gave to someone who really loved God."

She chuckled at my response. "He did really love God, but he questioned *everything* we read. In fact, he would say certain parts of the Bible were 'stupid' or 'wrong;' he always saw the deeper meaning in God's word and work. He questioned several things about his faith constantly, but through it all, he always believed God was real and working in mysterious ways we don't always understand. Sound like anyone you know?"

"Yeah. It does," I said, as my first genuine smile of the day came on.

"Well, it was great meeting you," she said as she walked away. I was thinking about what she'd told me as my mother approached me.

I was shocked to see that she was grinning ear to ear. "I've got some really good news for you," she said.

"What is it?" I asked.

"G-dad left you his car. You can finally get that job in Charlottesville you wanted," she said.

As if G-dad hadn't already given me enough throughout his time on Earth, he gave me the last piece of the puzzle I needed to get a real job and start my adult life. My grief now mixed with gratitude. Were it not for him, I would probably still be stuck in a part-time job in Harrisonburg, looking older and older as a new wave of college students took over the town every year.

I wouldn't be where I am today without him; I miss him every day.

ENTER SANDMAN
By Metallica

February 2016

"Exit light"

I was completely devastated when G-dad passed away. I had no real job, no real girlfriend, and now no real grandfather. I was completely lost. Fortunately for me, even when I was without all of these things, I at least had a best friend.

Two days after G-dad's funeral, Keith bought us tickets to see Wolfmother to cheer me up. He had become obsessed with Wolfmother the moment we first heard them on *Rock Band* years ago, and immediately bought all of their songs for the game and made me play them over and over again. *Cosmic Egg* is one of his favorite albums to this day.

No matter the band, I had never needed the healing power of music more in my life.

Of course, I didn't have any money, so the day of the concert, we decided to drink Keith's dad's beer before we went out. As serendipity would have it, Delynn was home from Germany visiting for the week, so she had agreed to be our designated driver that night.

We celebrated our reunion over a drunken game of *Monopoly* before the concert.

"Wait, I have immunity on this shit!" Delynn said, throwing her hands in the air.

"Oh yeah," Keith said, laughing.

"If we make deals earlier in the game, you have to honor them," Delynn scolded him. "This is why you're winning right now!"

"Delynn, he's never won the game before," I reminded her. "Let him have this one."

"He's cheating!" She pointed furiously at her brother. "It's like I'm playing with Chris!"

"You stayed in Marvin Gardens, in a *really* nice hotel. It's only logical Keith would want to charge you for it," I stated holding up the yellow card.

Delynn rolled her eyes. "I gave him Boardwalk for immunity on the yellows. I don't owe him shit!"

"Whatever, I'm getting another beer," Keith said. "You want one, Cade?"

"Pope Catholic?" I joked.

"How many have you had?" Delynn asked.

"Only six. Why?"

"Just wanted to make sure the pregame doesn't turn into the game."

I scoffed at her. "Delynn, do you know how many years we've waited to see Wolfmother?" I asked.

"Eight!" Keith shouted as he walked into the room with two new beers.

"Exactly. We're not missing this show for *anything*! No matter how drunk we get."

"There will be beer *there*," she tried to remind us.

I scoffed *again*. "Yeah, for like twelve dollars! Go to more concerts, Delynn."

"Yeah!" Keith agreed. "And pay me for landing on Marvin Gardens."

Two hours later, we were on the D.C. Metro, on our way to the concert. "I'm just saying I had a plan all along, and you two fell right into it," Keith bragged.

"Will you shut up about the game?" I whined. "It was two

hours ago! You know how many times I've kicked your ass in *Monopoly* and not brought it up?"

Keith hit me on the shoulder. "Bitch, you bring it up every time!" he shouted. We both laughed. We might have been the two drunkest people on the D.C. subway that random Wednesday afternoon, but we didn't care. We were finally seeing Wolfmother.

"God, I've never had to pee this bad," I said, putting my hands between my legs.

"You should've gone before we left."

"I did!"

"Your bladder is the *fucking* worst." Keith placed his hands over his face and shook his head.

Fifteen minutes later, we got off the subway and walked to the closest bathroom we could find, which was coincidentally a Subway restaurant.

I ran to the back of the restaurant as Keith yelled, "Hurry up! I have to go too!"

I took the most relieving piss of my life while taking in the smells of sandwich meats and cheeses. As soon as I finished, I opened the door, accidentally locked it, and pulled it closed behind me.

"Move! I really gotta go," Keith said, and pulled at the locked door handle. "What the fuck? Why is it locked?"

"My bad, bro," I said, unable to keep from laughing.

"What the hell? I have to pee so bad!"

I shushed him. "Don't worry," I said, "we're only a few blocks away. You can go in the venue."

"Son of a bitch."

We got to the venue about twenty minutes later. Both of us were shocked to discover we were two of the first fifty people in line. What we did not know ahead of time is that the first fifty people in line were allowed into the 9:30 Club's VIP bar before the show. We followed the line of people into a part of the venue I had never seen before, despite having seen countless shows in the non-VIP part. After Keith finally went to the bathroom, we sat down at the bar .

. . and with one sentence, Keith sent the entire night off the rails.

"All right, brother, drinks are on me."

My eyes widened. "Wow, I guess it would be fiscally irresponsible for me *not* to drink."

The bartender walked over to us. He was a bald man with a goatee, and he definitely looked like he belonged there.

"What'll you boys have?" he asked.

"We'll both have a rum and coke," I said confidently. As the bartender poured our drinks, the last bit of my sobriety tried to warn the rest of my brain about how drunk I was. *You idiot! Don't you remember? "Beer before liquor makes you sicker!" Oh, wait. Maybe it's "Liquor before beer and bad times are near." No, no, no. It's "Beer before wine makes you sick a long time." Which is perfect, because I'm not even drinking wine! I'm really glad we had this talk.*

We proceeded to drink ninety-dollars' worth of rum and cokes. By the end of my fifth rum and coke, I noticed a Rob Zombie concert playing live on the TV behind the bar.

"Oh shit, dude, look! It's Rob Zombie," I pointed out.

Keith nodded. "Nice. We gotta see him again. He put on a great show."

"You guys fans?" the bartender asked while wiping a glass.

"Hell yeah. We like the heavy shit," Keith said, trying to impress him.

I followed Keith's lead. "We saw him in 2013 for the *Venomous Rat Regeneration Vendor Tour*. That shit was awesome." I hoped naming a tour would make us seem like legitimate fans.

"I'm a fan too," the bartender said. "I keep this concert DVD down here. Makes the day go by faster." The bartender placed the glass he was polishing underneath the bar and started pouring a shot for a girl a few seats down from us.

Throughout this whole interaction, I was so drunk I failed to notice that the Rob Zombie DVD had no audio coming through the TV. Instead, a metal radio station was playing "Enter Sandman" through ceiling speakers. In my uninhibited state, I watched Rob

Zombie on the screen and couldn't tell that the Metallica music was coming from a different source.

"Holy shit, dude! This is the best Metallica cover I've ever heard!" I shouted.

The bartender smiled at what he thought was a funny joke, instead of a big warning sign that I should have been cut off the second I sat down at the bar. "You guys are all right," he said, pouring two shots of whiskey. "Here's some shots from one metalhead to another." He handed us the shots, and we happily drank them.

After Keith closed out his tab, we walked upstairs to the actual venue. "Holy shit, dude," Keith gasped. "There's like nobody here! We can stand in the front row!" He ran straight to the barricade in front of the stage. He didn't spill his drink on the entire run over, which I found to be the most impressive event of the day. I was personally doing much worse—I felt great, but I could feel my actions slowly falling out of my control as I inched closer toward blacking out. I got to the front as quickly as my wobbly legs would carry me and leaned on the barricade next to Keith. If I didn't have something to lean on, I would've eaten shit at several points throughout the evening.

A crowd slowly filled the room, and the opening band, Deap Valley, came on stage. It was a rock duo made up of two girls: one on guitar and vocals, and one on drums. They were really talented musicians, and I wish I had been sober enough to both enjoy their set and not make an ass of myself in front of them. I felt sicker and sicker by the second, and I also needed to pee worse than before.

The last thing I remember that evening was leaning on the railing and thinking about G-dad. He had once told me a story about a Christmas party he attended in a government building in D.C. many years ago (he told us it was the White House, but no other member of the family had been able to confirm that). Much like me, he had had to pee with the power of a thousand fire hydrants, but the bathroom line was far too long. So he had found a grandfather clock in an empty room, opened it up, and peed in it.

As I leaned on the barricade, constantly being shoved into it by the hundreds of people behind me, I had the thought, *If I peed right here, right now, nobody would know.* It was the perfect crime: the front row was watching the opening band, and everyone behind me couldn't see my front.

That was the last thought I had before I blacked out.

I woke up at five the next morning, lying on an air mattress in Keith's basement. Like many mornings in college, I immediately had the thought, *What the fuck happened last night?* I looked at my phone for pictures, but there was no evidence. I looked through texts, but nothing. The only evidence of note were two X marks on my hands, which I did not remember receiving. I quickly ran upstairs to look for my best friend, then I remembered how early it was and realized that he'd probably be sleeping. I panicked. *Fuck, I need to find out what happened! I don't even remember seeing the band! The last thing I remember is . . . oh, fuck . . . did I pee in the front row of the 9:30 Club?!*

I don't know if you've ever blacked out before, but it's a very frustrating feeling not being able to recall a couple hours' worth of your life. I decided to take a shower to pass the time and hoped somehow it would jog my memory.

I sat on the floor of the tub for what seemed like an eternity, spiraling deeper and deeper in thought. *What happened last night? Why did I drink so much? Why don't I have any money? Why can't I get a decent job that pays well? Why did Laura choose Gus over me? Why did I think it was a good idea to get back together with her? . . . Why did my G-dad have to go away forever?* Tears came to my eyes. I could feel the stress of an entire year of shit fall on me all at once. *Laura was right,* I thought. *I'm such a worthless piece of shit.*

Keith's father, Paul, was the first member of the family to stir that morning. As soon as I heard him head downstairs, I ran to the kitchen to meet him. I made sure to act casual, as to not indicate I had been awake for ninety minutes, crying in the shower.

"Good morning, Dad," I said, rubbing my eyes. Keith and I

had known each other's parents for so long we felt comfortable calling them Mom and Dad.

"You're up early," he said, pouring coffee into his mug. He was dressed in his work attire: khakis with a shirt and tie.

I had to think of a casual way to ask him what had happened the night before, so he wouldn't know how drunk I had been. "What happened last night?" *You suck, Cade.*

"You drank a lot," he said simply. He sat down at the dining room table and sipped his coffee, looking up at me.

"I gathered," I said, joining him at the table.

"Keith drank a lot too, but he seemed to remember more of the night. He told me all about it after you went to bed."

"Great. So, what the hell happened?"

"What's the last thing you remember?" he asked as he took off his glasses to wipe a lens.

I closed my eyes to remember. "Watching the opening band play. It was two girls." I placed my elbows on the table and covered my face with my hands.

Keith's dad smiled. "You apparently kept shouting, 'Marry me!' to the lead singer."

I facepalmed. "And then what?"

"They took you back to the bar and cut you off." He placed his glasses back on his face.

"Is that what these X marks on my hands are?" I showed him the back of my hands.

"I would assume so. I haven't been cut off at a venue in quite a while." He smirked and took another sip of coffee.

"What else did Keith tell you?" I asked reluctantly.

"You rushed back to the front row, pushing through hundreds of people, and made it back to the barricade."

"Okay. Wait . . . so that's it?"

"No. You asked Keith for some ice from his drink because you wanted water."

I shrugged. "Makes sense I guess."

He smiled. "Not to the security guards. They kicked both of you out because he shared his drink with you."

"Ice doesn't count," I scoffed.

"Yes, that's what Keith told security. But they didn't care."

I put my hands over my eyes and peeked through my fingers. "Did we even see the band?"

"Keith said they grabbed you both right after Wolfmother came on stage."

"Fuck." I hit my forehead on the kitchen table several times.

"At least you got to see the actual band for a few seconds."

I groaned with my face still pressed against the table. "How did we get home?"

"Keith walked you to the Metro and I came to pick you two up after you reached our stop." Paul got up and walked to the counter with his coffee mug. "He said you kept trying to hold his hand the entire time and tell him how good a friend he was."

I laughed for the first time all morning. "That does sound like me," I said, sitting up and leaning in back in my chair.

"It was a pretty entertaining story," Paul said, filling a thermos with coffee. He walked back over to pat me on the shoulder. "Sorry you don't remember it, but I promise we won't let you forget it."

"Why am I not hungover?" I asked under my breath.

"You were insistent on drinking about a gallon of water when you got home. But . . . you could possibly still be drunk."

"Guess I'll know in a couple of hours."

"Indeed. Keith blew up the air mattress and set you up downstairs. Then he came back up to drink more with me and talk about how close you two were to hooking up with the opening band."

I laughed. "I *definitely* don't remember that."

He smiled. "I don't think Keith will either. Anyway, I'm off to work. I'll see you next time you're in town." He waved goodbye and opened the front door.

"Bye, Dad," I said, waving.

I spent the next few hours stewing in anxious regret. *Keith paid two hundred for this fucking concert and I got us kicked out. I'm the absolute worst. Any friend in his right mind would be so pissed off they'd never let this go.*

Keith opened his bedroom door at around 10 a.m. and walked downstairs. I braced myself for whatever angry words he had for me.

"Hey, brother," he yawned, grabbing a cereal box.

"Hey, man," I replied. "Last night was—"

"Hilarious!" Keith said. "That's one for the fucking books."

"Wait, you're not mad?"

"Why the hell would I be mad? We got kicked out of a rock show! That's fucking awesome!"

There have been several moments throughout my life where Keith has made me realize why we were, are, and always will be best friends. When I felt as if I had hit rock bottom, Keith was there celebrating every facet of who I was. I went over to hug him.

"Woah, calm down. You did plenty of PDA last night," he said, pushing me away with one hand and pouring cereal into a bowl with the other.

Delynn walked into the kitchen holding her iPad. "Oh, wow. You're both alive," she said.

"No thanks to you," Keith mumbled with his mouth full of cereal. "You were supposed to pick us up!"

"I didn't anticipate you leaving the concert two hours before it ended."

"In our defense, neither did we," I chimed in.

"I have Chris on the phone if either of you want to talk to him. I have to go to the bathroom." Delynn placed her iPad on the counter next to us and left the room.

"Oh shit! Put it on speaker!" Keith nudged me.

After a few seconds, we heard Chris's voice through the tablet. "What's up, boys?"

"Hey, buddy," Keith said.

"Hey, Chris," I said at the same time.

"Delynn said you went to a concert last night. Who'd you see?"

"Wolfmother," Keith said with a mouth full of cereal.

"Nice!" Chris responded. "A *Rock Band* classic!"

"It would have been nicer if we actually saw them," I interjected. "We got kicked out of the venue."

Chris laughed. "You idiots. How much did you drink, Keith?"

"Less than Cade," Keith said, grinning at me.

Chris gasped. "No way. Cade got you kicked out?"

"Yep," I said.

Chris laughed some more. "Definitely didn't see that coming. Did you throw up?"

"No, this is the part that's bullshit," Keith explained. "I gave Cade ice from my drink so he could get a little hydrated, and the security guys said we were sharing drinks."

"What? Ice doesn't count!" Chris exclaimed.

"That's exactly what I said!" Keith agreed.

"Well, I guess it's only fair. Think of all of the people our bouncers had to kick out during our Krazy Unikerns shows over the years."

I laughed. "That's a good point."

"I don't even remember you drinking at our old shows, Cade, and now all of a sudden you're getting kicked out of venues? That's not fair to your bandmates."

"I think college did me in. We would play *Rock Band* and drink Rolling Rock almost every weekend. We called it *Rolling Rock Band.*"

"Damn. I should've gone to fucking college," Chris said as Delynn came back into the room.

"I'm back, lover!" she said, and grabbed the iPad from the counter.

"Later, boys," Chris said. "It was great catching up."

"Same, bro. Let's hang out soon," Keith said. We gave simultaneous goodbyes to our former bandmate as Delynn removed him from the room.

I still had to wait a month for the vehicle title for G-dad's car to transfer over to me, so I was without wheels for the next few weeks. Keith kindly offered to drive me the three hours back to Harrisonburg that day, after I ruined our two-hundred-dollar concert experience, after he bought me a hundred bucks worth of drinks, and after I locked him out of a Subway bathroom. He's a better friend than I will ever deserve.

During the drive, we spent two hours listening to the new Bring Me the Horizon record, *That's the Spirit*, which both of us loved. After it ended, I broke the silence.

"I'm sorry I ruined our night, bro."

"You didn't ruin it."

"I just feel like you should be mad. I've known Bruce, Julian, Jimmy, Martin, and Gordon for almost just as long as I've known you, and if I did this to any of them, they'd be furious. Well, maybe not Gordon."

"He *is* the nicest man alive."

"You're really not mad at all?"

"Of course not. That's gonna be a story we fucking remember forever. We can see Wolfmother next time they come to town, and it'll be just as good."

"I feel like I should buy you food to thank you for the drive, but I can't really afford it . . . unless we go to Taco Bell."

Keith smiled. "Taco Bell is just fine."

TOM SAWYER
By Rush

July 2016

"Love and life are deep"

About a month after the Wolfmother concert, the deed to G-dad's '98 Subaru Forestor was finally in my name. One of the very first things I did was drive to Charlottesville and interview for the front-of-house manager position at the historic Paramount Theater in downtown Charlottesville. I got the job and was finally making enough money to live without constant worry about paying for food and rent. The summer of 2016 was great. I had a great new job, I was free of Laura's clutches, and I had a great *Rock Band* partner to play with. Tara stopped by nearly every week. We went to concerts, played *Pokémon Go*, watched *Dexter*, and vigorously competed over our favorite video game.

One Wednesday afternoon in July, we found ourselves playing *Rock Band* as usual. "Why can't I play guitar?" she asked.

"We had an agreement: the higher score gets to play guitar, and the lower score plays bass." I pointed to our scores on the screen.

She rolled her eyes. "But you've played guitar like the past three songs."

"Guess you need to play better," I said, grinning. She smiled and flipped me the bird.

"I'll let you pick the song, how about that?"

"Hm. How about . . . Kelly Clarkson?"

"Hell no," I said, grabbing my beer off the shelf.

She glared at me. "Then why do you even have this song?" she asked.

"It came in a pack!"

"Whatever." She looked back to the screen. "How about Toto?"

"Now we're talking," I took a sip of beer and put the bottle back on the shelf.

We continued playing *Rock Band* into the evening, which led to more drinking while playing more *Rock Band* into the night, which led to a spontaneous walk through JMU's campus. I only lived two blocks away, so the quad seemed as good a place as any to have a drunken midnight stroll.

"There's no way Tyler Joseph does a better backflip than Brendon Urie." I threw my hands up in the air.

"Tyler's is way better!" she replied. "Plus, he did like three when we saw them!"

"Twenty One Pilots *might* have been a better show than Panic! at the Disco, but I won't budge on the Urie backflip. This is the hill I die on."

Tara laughed. "You're ridiculous."

"Brendon's backflip was so unexpected. He paused in the middle of "Miss Jackson," stood with his back to the audience, and then did a backflip right as he started the last chorus."

"Tyler did basically the same thing."

"Nuh uh! In fact, lemme show you what his backflip looked like." I leaned back and turned into a wet noodle, immediately collapsing on the ground. I rolled over onto my back on the grass and laughed. Tara laughed too, and lay down in the grass of the quad right next to me. It was a warm night, but the ground was wet from late evening dew, which made it much cooler.

We lay there next to each other, our faces inches apart. Up until this moment, we hadn't even kissed. If this was going somewhere, it felt good to take things slow.

"I know what we have to do," I said.

She moved her head onto my chest. "What?"

"We have to listen to our song!"

"Hell yeah," she said with a quiet laugh.

I pulled out my phone, opened YouTube, and played Car Seat Headrest's "Drunk Drivers/Killer Whales," my favorite song of 2016. Damon had showed it to Tara and me one night after a party a few weeks ago, and we had ended up replaying it over and over until it was suddenly four in the morning. We lay on the quad and talked for nearly an hour, listening to our favorite song on repeat. I wasn't worried about making a move or saying the wrong thing. I was just enjoying the perfect moment with my *Rock Band* friend.

She turned her face up to look at me. "This was pretty fun," she said.

"It really was," I said, beginning to sober up and feel the cold, wet grass.

She sat up. "Are you okay? You're shivering."

I sat up too. "I'm fine," I said. "I just have to get out of the grass."

She put her hand on my forehead. "Do you have a fever?"

"No, I'm really fine."

"I'm studying to be a nurse, Cade. This is how people catch pneumonia. Let's get you home."

"You gonna take care of me?" I said, still a little drunk and cold.

"I'll take care of you," she said with a smile.

I reached out to grab her hand, weaving my fingers together with hers. I warmed up immediately.

When we got back to my apartment, she let go of my hand and looked me in the eyes. "You'll warm up here," she said, rubbing my arms.

"I had a lot of fun tonight."

"Me too," she said.

"Well . . . I guess we should go to bed."

"I guess so."

I wasn't ready for the night to end. "Hey, would you wanna . . . I mean, we're almost done with season one of *Dexter* . . . maybe watch it in my room?"

She smiled. "Sure. I'd like that." She followed me out of the kitchen.

We both lay in my bed, under the covers, while I turned on the TV. And then we . . . watched *Dexter*. We didn't kiss. We didn't have sex. We just lay there together and fell asleep.

It was a good night.

GREEN GRASS AND HIGH TIDES
By the Outlaws

August 2016

"They helped me find myself,
amongst the music and the rhyme"

For my twenty-fourth birthday, Kyle and I opened up our apartment once again to what would be the *Rock Band* party to end all *Rock Band* parties: *Rock Band Fest 2k16*. The idea was born one evening in early August, when Kyle and I received a knock on our door. It was our neighbors, whom we had never met before. We learned three things about them pretty quickly: 1) They were in the army; 2) The army was paying to relocate them but would not pay to move their beer and liquor; 3) They had *a lot* of beer and liquor. They gave it all to us for free. Everything you can imagine: gin, rum, whiskey, vodka, really cheap peppermint schnapps (which was fucking gross), a handle of Everclear (which was illegal to sell in Virginia), and a wide variety of beers.

The day following what seemed to be the luckiest day of my life was even more strange. My boss called me to the storage closet in the theater and told me he had six "expired" cases of Budweiser he had to get rid of. Knowing that there was no way for an expiration date to ruin the taste of Budweiser, I agreed to take all six cases off his hands.

Kyle and I invited our friends to our tiny apartment and prepared for hours of nonstop rock 'n' roll. Everyone was thrilled with the idea; Martin even made a graphic design poster of all of the bands featured on the *Rock Band* soundtrack as if it was an actual music festival.

Within an hour of the party starting, the room was full; there were people standing on the couches, the stairs, the chairs, and even the counters. People were lighting shots of Everclear on fire and drinking them. So many of the friends I had made throughout the course of my life were there: Bruce, Martin, Damon, Griffin, Nicole, Eileen, Jessica, Matt, Tara, and tons more. I had duets to perform with everyone: Nicole and I sang "Nine in the Afternoon," Jessica and I sang "The Anthem," Tara and I sang "Africa," my buddy Steve and I did Evanescence's "Bring Me to Life," and I assembled the whole crowd to bring down the house with the Goo Goo Dolls' "Iris." Tara was drinking red wine straight out of the bottle—which she managed to spill all over our carpet while playing drums at one point in the evening, but I was too happy to care. I took off my *Rock Band* cap (the one Violet had found for me while we were on spring break together) and put it on Tara's head. She looked up and smiled at me, and we both chimed in with whatever song was happening at the moment.

The party went late into the night. People were wasted on Everclear shots and good times. My friend Krista got me a cake that said, "Tits out for cargo shorts!" to remind everyone of how I almost exclusively used to wear cargo shorts to UPB meetings, much to the disgust of the entire committee. Kyle got locked out of his bathroom because someone was throwing up in it, and a girl was accidentally kicked in the face by someone trying to vault over the staircase in the same vein as Kyle at the *Rock Band* party a year prior.

By 4 a.m., only the core party members remained, including Tara and myself. We wandered off to bed together and had sex for the first time. I ended my perfect birthday with a girl I was falling in love with; in this specific moment, I didn't want to change a thing.

"Fuck," she said suddenly, her head on my chest. "We forgot to play 'Stressed Out.'"

I laughed. "Shit. You're right. Wanna go back out there?"

She sighed. "Nah, I'm pretty tired," she said.

We were quiet for a few minutes. Before I drifted off, I whispered, "I had a lot of fun tonight."

"Me too," she whispered back. There was a pause, and then: "I just . . . I . . . don't want you to get the wrong idea that this is going to be a regular thing."

I opened my eyes. "Wait, what?" I said, suddenly awake.

"Don't get me wrong," she said, "you're really great, and I love hanging out with you and playing *Rock Band* and all, but I'm not ready to be in a relationship."

"Oh. . . . I just thought . . . why are you telling me this now?"

"Guys have done this to me, and it really sucks when they stopped talking to me after we hooked up. I don't want to be like them."

"Oh. Does that mean you don't want to talk anymore?"

"We can still talk. I just didn't want you to think this was going to turn into anything."

I sighed. "Yeah, I understand," I said. "Well, if you ever change your mind, I can always use a bass player for my *Rock Band* sessions."

She laughed and hit my chest. "You're such an asshole."

The conversation went on like this for a few more minutes. Neither of us was angry. I was a little sad, but I had been through worse. I would survive. And there was a part of me that hoped Tara didn't mean any of it; both of us had been drinking all night, after all. I hoped we would wake up tomorrow, go our separate ways for a few months or so, then she would send me a text about how she wanted to play *Rock Band* and be with me, or listen to "Drunk Drivers/Killer Whales" and fall asleep on the quad. I never got that text, though—she married her best friend Paul a couple years later and moved far away.

Sometimes that's all love is, I guess: a brief window in time where two people cross paths and enjoy each other's company, until one or both of them need to keep going on their merry way. I don't regret any moment I spent with Tara. I even hope we get to play *Rock Band* together again one day.

CELEBRITY SKIN
By Hole

March 2017

"Yeah, now you really made it"

I followed the footsteps of my literary hero Rob Sheffield and moved to Charlottesville, VA. All my passion for Grafton landed me in my dream job: I'm now the house manager of the Paramount Theater. I orchestrate and oversee a wide array of events, everything from classic films to internationally acclaimed musicians. I've coordinated weddings and receptions, helped make and sell over six hundred white russian cocktails for a showing of *The Big Lebowski*, and had a beer backstage with Cage the Elephant. Although several of my Paramount experiences have been unforgettable, there is one that stands out above all the others.

"Hey, Cade, can you do me a huge favor?" our stage production manager, Robert, said as he walked into my office. He seemed out of breath. The entire production team had been working since 6 a.m. to get ready for the show.

"Absolutely," I replied. "What's up?"

"Rosanne Cash's tour manager just got here and told us he was expecting the theater to provide a ride for the artist and her guitar player. I still have a lot of prep work to do for the show. Would you mind picking her up from her hotel?"

I didn't know how to respond—it would have been too odd if I shouted, "Oh my fucking god!" and jumped up and down on my computer desk for several minutes.

Instead, I responded as professionally as I could. "I'd be happy to. Where do I need to go?"

"She's staying at the Hyatt Place near Stonefield. Do you know where that is?"

"Yeah, it's five minutes from my house. I'll head right over."

"Great. Thank you so much!" Robert said, as if a burden of responsibility had been lifted off his shoulders and placed upon my head.

I walked to my car, but as I approached the garage, a wave of paranoia hit me. *What if I crash the car and kill Rosanne Cash? That would absolutely make national news.* I had never been given the responsibility of driving someone this important around before. *What if I accidentally offend her during the car ride over and she refuses to play? I'll definitely avoid bringing up the fact I like Trent Reznor's version of "Hurt" better than her father's.* The most realistic concern I had was, *What if she wants me to turn on the AC and I can't?* G-dad's old '98 Subaru Forester was a great car, but it had a severe overheating problem. I had to turn the heat on full blast year-round, just to keep the engine at a non-flammable temperature.

By the time I arrived at the hotel, I stopped thinking about all of these things—but not because I had calmed down. In fact, I was too nervous to think about anything. It was like a first date with much higher risk. After ten minutes of sitting out front, I saw a man walk out the front doors and look around. I got out of my car to greet him.

"You with the Paramount?" he asked.

"Yessir," I answered, nodding.

"Great. My name's John. Let me load my gear in. Rosanne is right behind me."

I shook his hand and introduced myself. We loaded in his gear, and sure enough, right behind him came Rosanne Cash.

"Hey, Rosanne," John said to her, "this is our ride. His name's Cade." He nodded to me.

"Hi, Cade. I'm Rosanne," the country/folk legend said with a smile.

I wanted to say, "I know who you are," with a girlish smile as I melted into the hotel parking lot pavement, but luckily I just said, "It's lovely to meet you."

We all got in my soon-to-be unbearably hot Subaru and took off. I wasn't sure if it was illegal to go fifteen miles per hour under the speed limit, but by Christ, today was the day I was gonna find out; I wasn't risking the life of Johnny Cash's most talented seed. Rosanne sat in the back seat, while John (who turned out to be her husband) sat in the passenger's seat next to me. I knew this was a once-in-a-lifetime chance, so I decided to make small talk with the guitarist and see where it went. I didn't dare talk to Rosanne.

"So where are you guys coming from?"

"We were just in New York last night. Kind of jetlagged."

"Yeah, I gotcha. How was the weather there?"

"Pretty close to this. Both places are on the east coast."

I was failing hard. I had never dreamed that the weather and travel itinerary could make such terrible talking points. I was ready to give up. I had just started to think about how I could lie to my friends later and make this story great when, out of nowhere, the god of celebrities smiled down on little ol' average me.

"Hey, John, do you mind if I leave New York a day early to go to the Bahamas?" Rosanne said, breaking what seemed like an eternity of silence.

"That's fine with me," John said. "What's in the Bahamas?"

"It's Elton John's birthday. Katy Perry's going, Billy Joel is going . . . we're all gonna sing Elton's songs and surprise him as a gift."

I could have shit my pants in amazement at that sentence alone, but they kept talking.

"That's fine with me, babe. What song were you gonna sing?"

"I was thinking of 'Goodbye Yellow Brick Road.' What do you think?"

"That's not a bad choice, but I think your voice is more suited toward 'Your Song.'"

"Really? Let me look it up."

Rosanne pulled out her phone and found a lyric video for "Your Song." In a matter of seconds, she was singing the most hauntingly beautiful rendition of Elton John's "Your Song" in the back of my car.

"How was that?" she asked when she was done singing.

"It was intimate and despairing," John said, "and I think that's what people want to hear from you."

"I think I'll try a few others."

Rosanne Cash sang Elton John covers for the remainder of the drive. It was one of the most surreal moments in my life. I tried to take plenty of mental notes so I'd be able to tell the story in perfect detail as soon as she got out of the car.

When we got to the Paramount, Robert was there to greet them and help them carry in their luggage. The performers got out, leaving me behind with my perfect moment.

Rosanne peeked her head back in the car and said, "Thanks for the ride, Cade. It was nice meeting you."

"Happy to do it," I said, smiling.

And just like that, the moment was over.

WELCOME HOME
By Coheed and Cambria

July 2017

"I'd do anything for you"

I exited the airport doors and felt the sweet kiss of sunlight for the first time in hours. A sight for sore eyes was waiting to pick me up in what appeared to be a brand new Rav4: it was Chris, wearing sunglasses and a polo shirt, grinning just as much as the last time I had seen him.

"Hey, brother," he said, walking over to give me a hug. He opened my car door for me. "Let's hit the road. Are you hungry?"

"Yeah, I could eat. The Auntie Anne's at the airport was being renovated."

"Nobody should have to suffer through airport fast food," he said. "We'll get you *real* fast food here in Missouri."

I laughed. "How accommodating. Again, I really appreciate you driving two hours to come and pick me up."

"It's actually four, if you count the drive back," he joked. He grabbed a tin of chewing tobacco and put some in his lip. "I hope you don't mind. Delynn won't let me dip at home."

"I've literally shared a bed with Keith while he dipped, so this is very doable."

Chris chuckled. "Some things don't change."

"So how is living here in the 'Show Me' State?"

"Well, let me tell you, Cade. Delynn and I lived in Germany

for three years, during which we got to visit every European country, drink amazing beer and wine, and see every landmark or historic site you've ever read about in a history book. Missouri fucking sucks."

I laughed. "It can't be all bad. There's TV over here."

"All we watch is Netflix and HBO, which we had over there. There's a winery fifteen minutes away and a brewery forty minutes away. I hope you're prepared to be bored."

"I really didn't come here to be entertained. I haven't seen you in five years. I just wanna relive old times," I said.

"That I can do," Chris said, spitting into a water bottle. "Hope you're caught up on *Game of Thrones*; otherwise, you're gonna need to find something else to do tonight while we watch the new episode."

"I'm caught up. How great was that premiere?"

"The absolute best cold open of a show I have ever seen. Cannot wait for the rest of this season."

"What music have you been listening to? Anything new?"

"Nah, pretty much the same stuff as before. We finally got to see Muse live in London after Delynn dragged me through all of fucking Harry Potter world."

"Muse was incredible when I saw them on the *Drones* tour. You a fan of their most recent album?"

"Honestly, I haven't listened to any new stuff since we saw them," he said, spitting into his water bottle again.

"I think *Drones* is their best album as a whole. The individual songs don't rival 'Hysteria' or 'Knights of Cydonia'—"

"But the album as a whole is better than the others. I gotcha," he said, completing my thought after a near five-year dearth of practice. "Delynn told me you won *Rock Band 4*? How the hell did that happen?"

"It's a long story, but I'll tell you at some point during my stay. It mostly involved me getting drunk while my roommate and I filmed a huge party."

"Damn, I should've fucking gone to college. They ever add any more Muse to *Rock Band*?"

"Nope. Just 'Hysteria.'"

"I mean, that's a good one to have, but come on, Harmonix! Get your shit together and give us more."

After two hours and a much-deserved detour to Carl's Junior, we arrived at Chris and Delynn's new home. Their house in Germany had three floors, two bathrooms, a backyard, a basement, and countless other accoutrements; their new apartment was basically a much cleaner version of the overpriced dwelling I'd had at JMU. Not that I cared at all; I didn't take a four-hundred-dollar plane ride to see a building.

I walked into the living room to find Delynn folding laundry on the couch. She stood up with a smile on her face.

"Welcome!" she said with open arms.

I went in for a hug but stopped short and turned to the floor, for the main reason of my visit: sprawled out on the floor, squirming on his playmat, was baby Arie, the newest addition to the family. "Holy shit, Delynn. You're a mom," I said, staring at Arie.

"I know," she whispered. "It's kind of crazy. You wanna hold him?"

"Of course," I said. She picked him up and handed him to me. "He looks just like baby Keith."

"He's not as fat," Delynn said, smiling.

Chris walked over to Delynn and put his arms around her. "So, Arie, what do you think of Uncle Cade?"

Arie didn't say anything, despite having had three months to learn the native tongue, so I said something instead. "This kid is gonna be really great at *Rock Band* one day. I promise."

"Hope you like IPAs," Chris said, handing me a beer.

"Good news for both of us," I said.

A couple days into my stay, we had settled into a routine. Chris would go to work, Delynn and I would take Arie to the park, Chris would come home with beer, Delynn would make dinner while Chris and I played video games, then we'd eat our meal and stay up reliving old times. Arie would play around in his bouncy seat until he fell asleep. On the third day of my visit, we had finally reached the dinner portion of the evening.

"Come get food, guys," she said, putting it on the table.

"Thanks sweetie," Chris said, sitting down next to his infant son's bouncy seat.

"I could get used to free food and free beer every night," I said, sipping my beer.

Chris took a huge bite of his nachos. "You're welcome anytime, brother," he said.

"Or you could just get your own wife," Delynn joked. "How's your love life?"

"Um . . . nobody really at the moment," I said, realizing that I had never had a proper answer to this question. "Still waiting for the right person who will pick a good first dance song at our wedding."

"That's definitely not the most important part of the wedding," Delynn said. "There are so many more memorable things."

"I remember your first dance song: 'Sea of Love' by Cat Power. Plus, I remember the father-daughter dance was 'All My Lovin' by the Beatles, and the mother-son dance was 'Dream On' by Aerosmith."

They both stared at me. "How the hell do you remember that?" Chris asked.

"He's a savant, dear," Delynn said, sipping the half-glass of wine she was permitted to drink during her nursing months.

"I remember your vows too."

"If that's the case, do you remember how Delynn and I met?" Chris asked.

Truth be told, I did not. All I remembered was Chris magically showing up during that first time we played *Rock Band*, and that he'd been a part of the group ever since.

"It was an overnight stay in a church auditorium. We each had friends who had invited us," Delynn said.

"Delynn had that leg brace on from when she broke her ankle, so she couldn't run away from me," Chris joked.

"Chris kept finding excuses to talk to me all night long, even though the youth group kept coming up with activities that continually moved us to different places around the room."

"There was one point when we both ended up under a table for some reason, and this other guy kept trying to talk to Delynn, so I told him to scram," Chris said. "We were both so tired when this thing ended at around 8 a.m., I didn't even have enough wits about me to be nervous about asking for her number. So I did, and I texted her the following day."

"One week later we agreed to meet at a park, and that's where we first kissed."

"On the first date? Chris, you animal!" I said, shocked.

Chris looked across the table at Delynn. "When you know, you know."

Delynn laughed. "After the date ended, he kept talking about how he had parked really far away because he was too embarrassed to let me know he didn't have his driver's license."

"I hid my bike in some bushes."

"I kept trying to offer him a ride to his car, but he wouldn't let me. I thought it was really weird at the time, but here we are ten years later."

"Time flies," Chris said, finishing his beer and looking at Arie.

I had never heard that story.

Chris concluded with, "What do you say we break out the instruments for old time's sake?"

Delynn did the dishes and put Arie to bed while Chris and I went to grab the plastic instruments from their storage room and set up the game. After scrolling through a few songs, Chris landed on a Krazy Unikerns classic, and we both looked at each other grinning. Delynn joined us, and three-fourths of the Krazy Unikerns took the stage once again.

OUTSIDE
By Tribe

September 2017

"I've been there, don't remind me"

As much as I love the Beatles with unparalleled emotion, I partially blame them for my brain's "hopeless romantic" tendencies. I grew up absorbing *all* of their songs, and consequently the messages each song had to offer: ideas like "all you need is love," "and in the end the love you take is equal to the love you make," "just to dance with you, is everything I need," "I wanna hold your hand," etc. These songs painted a simplistic picture of love and made love seem all but ubiquitous. Take one of my favorite songs for example: "Ob-La-Di, Ob-La-Da." The lyrics state, "Desmond has a barrow in the marketplace/Molly is the singer in a band/Desmond says to Molly, 'Girl, I like your face'/ And Molly says this as she takes him by the hand." That's it. Desmond and Molly get married and have a fucking family! All Desmond had to say was "Girl, I like your face." That's *fucking* it! It took me longer than it should have to realize this is not how every love story goes. Sometimes love is immediate. Sometimes it takes a long time. Sometimes it doesn't make *any* sense.

Sometimes it just makes you sad.

I thought about this while trying to break a *Rock Band* record on the song "Fly Like an Eagle." I didn't particularly care for the song, or most of the Steve Miller Band's offerings, but

I was particularly frustrated with the fact that I had played it eighteen times and still hadn't achieved a gold stars rating. Just when I finally had a gold star in my sights, Emma called and ruined my chances.

"Hello?" I growled.

"Hey, brother! What are you up to?"

"Work, mostly," I said, holding a guitar without any pants on.

"You haven't been returning my texts. I just wanted to check in."

"Yeah, sorry. Like I said, work has been super busy." I took a sip of my beer.

"You can tell me the truth you know. It's Diane, isn't it?"

My sister knew me very well. I had met Diane at the Paramount a few weeks prior. She was a sales rep for a local fiber optic internet company. After three days of helping her set up her table in the lobby, I asked for her phone number. She gave it to me, and I immediately drove home and drank three rum and cokes out of sheer nervousness. We ended up hanging out a few times, and things seemed to be going really well. I was quickly approaching the stadium rock stage of infatuation: I couldn't eat, I couldn't sleep, and a crippling nervousness came over me whenever we were about to spend time together; so I just played *Rock Band* as much as I could to get my mind off of her.

"Yeah, it's Diane."

"So . . . how are things?"

"We hang out like two or three times a week. We make dinner together, we watch TV, we play guitar and sing songs—"

"It sounds like it's going really well!" she said with so much enthusiasm that I felt as if she could jump through the phone at any minute.

"That's the worst part," I continued. "I'm happy. This is the point where everything always goes to shit."

"Don't be such a pessimist! It sounds like she really likes you.

She's not dating anyone else, right?"

"No. I actually don't know if she's ever been in a real relationship. We haven't really talked about that stuff."

"So, she hangs out with you multiple times a week, you talk about everything, and she seems to enjoy it?"

"Yeah. She also sends me recordings of her playing songs on the guitar and singing," I said.

"What kind of songs?"

"She sent me a hauntingly beautiful rendition of 'Build Me Up Buttercup' last night."

"That's a love song, you know," Emma said, sounding giddy.

"I mean, not really. Maybe a Cade-and-Laura type of love song."

"I would never send a recording of me singing to a boy I didn't like."

"You don't sing or play guitar."

"It really sounds like she's into you," she insisted.

"Well, yeah, it sounds like it. When all of my friends came up for my birthday brewery crawl last week, she offered to be the designated driver."

"Oh my god, Cade!" Emma shouted. "Are you dumb? This girl likes you!"

"Oh . . . I don't know."

"She's giving you every signal in the book! She offered to drive not only *your* drunk ass around for a whole day, but all of your friends as well?"

"Well, yeah. I think she was just being friendly."

"Nobody is *that* friendly! Make a move! She'll say yes!"

"I just really—"

"Do you want to date her?"

"Well, yeah. I think she's really cool."

"And you authentically like her as a person and like spending time with her?"

I sighed. "Yeah, I definitely have feelings for her," I admitted.

"Then don't be an idiot. Make a move."

That night, Diane invited me to a small café in town to see a local hardcore metal band that attracted a total of fourteen audience members to the venue. After the show, I invited her to get drinks with me at a bar downtown; I had decided I was going to make a move that night. I knew if I didn't get drunk enough, I would be a coward and decide not to go through with it at the last second. So, naturally, I drank the whole night. Diane offered to drive me home afterward, since we lived close to each other. She sat behind the steering wheel, looking cute as ever with her straight brown hair and UVA hoodie. We had almost listened to all of Fall Out Boy's *From Under the Cork Tree* by the time she pulled up in my driveway. We had sung all the songs together. I didn't want the night to end.

Quick, why didn't it work out with Kayleigh? Because I could never talk to her. Check. Why didn't it work out with Emily? Because she was disgusted by me when I publicly embarrassed her. Shit, that's not helpful. Why didn't it work out with Allison? Because she said there was no way she could ever fall in love with me. Goddammit, brain! Why didn't it work out with Laura? Because she found her other boyfriend infinitely more desirable than you. Okay, we're getting a fucking lobotomy when we get home. Shut the fuck up.

"Thanks for the ride," I said. Remembering my failures all at once had left me a bit stunned and confused. I held out my hand.

"Anytime," she said, and put her hand in mine. I looked her in the eyes as she smiled back, and just like that, I went for it. My brain went blank, and I leaned in for the kiss without any prior inclination or mention of doing so.

Now, I've mentioned that the night I serenaded Emily on stage was bar-none the most embarrassing moment of my life. No matter how many times I've woken up hungover or still drunk, regretting the poor decisions I had made the previous night, I would always think, *At least it wasn't as bad as when I told Emily I had feelings for her over a fucking Snow Patrol song.*

That being said, if a bottomless pit had magically opened up in my front yard that night, I would have jumped into it. The second that Diane saw I was going in for the kiss, she quickly turned her head and leaned her body back against her side of her car as best she could. I ended up kissing mostly hair, and a little bit of her ear. The one positive of this horrible experience was that I was hammered, which provided me with a large portion of drunk swagger ready to be dispensed at any moment. As soon as I opened my eyes to see her looking at me with a look of pure confusion and disgust, I opened the car door and confidently said, "Welp, goodnight!"

I've often tried to imagine what was going through Diane's head that night, but I never properly asked.

I do, however, remember exactly what was going through my head.

You're a fucking idiot. You're a fucking idiot. You're a fucking idiot. You're a fucking idiot. You're a fucking idiot. You're a fucking idiot. You're a fucking idiot. You're a fucking idiot. Why the hell did you think that would work!? What girl has ever been excited to kiss you without the sweet, sweet high she gets from infidelity?! GOD, YOU FUCKING SUCK!

I went to bed that night still confident that I would be able to fix this somehow, and also aware that the reality of what I had just done would hit me like a brick wall the following morning. I fell asleep to Brand New's "Batter Up" and dreamed about that bottomless pit in my front yard.

When I awoke the following morning, my prediction was correct; I immediately regretted my decisions of the night prior. The worst part was when I decided to make my move, I had forgotten that Diane and I had made plans together for the entire next day. I was supposed to go over to her house to try her special recipe for vegan pancakes, then we'd watch *Buffy the Vampire Slayer*, then go to see a My Chemical Romance tribute band (I'm aware this is the most emo-middle-schooler day anyone has ever planned). I was originally excited because I loved My Chemical Romance, I liked

Buffy, and I tolerated the idea of fake pancakes because they were free. I mostly made the plans because I really liked Diane, and I really liked spending time with her. I had no idea how this day was going to go after what happened.

I figured it would be best if I pretended nothing had happened at all.

"Do I need to bring anything to breakfast?" I texted her.

Diane immediately responded with, "Nope, I've got everything!"

Maybe I'm in the clear, maybe I'm overreacting, maybe she has amnesia. Or maybe I still have a shot at this. . . .

I'm not sure if you've ever had vegan pancakes, but they're not very good. Instead of flour, most people use oatmeal. It basically tasted like a soggy rice cake. Luckily, I was able to smother it in syrup, because apparently stealing the sap produced by a tree doesn't count as harming nature or some shit. I scarfed them down, told Diane she was a great cook (which wasn't a lie—she did an amazing job making pancakes without any of the ingredients used to make pancakes), and then we turned on the TV. Diane's favorite show was *Buffy the Vampire Slayer*, and after making her watch all of the Marvel Netflix shows with me, I had agreed to partake in one of her passions.

So, there we were, on a couch together—two people in our mid-twenties who had shared an extremely awkward moment the night before—watching TV instead of talking about our problems.

"Wait," I said, "so there are two vampire slayers?"

"Yeah, Faith and Buffy."

"I thought there could only be one slayer?"

"Originally, yes, but then Buffy died temporarily, and Faith took over. Then when Buffy came back to life, Faith remained a slayer. So now they fight crime together."

"It doesn't look like they're getting along."

"That's because Faith accidentally killed a human instead of a vampire, and Buffy wants to turn her in to the police, but Faith thinks that collateral damage is okay, because if she doesn't get turned in, she'll kill a lot of vampires and save a lot of lives."

"Sounds like two of my close friends, Tony Stark and Steve Rogers."

Diane never broke her line of sight with the TV. "Shhhh."

"Wait, do you think Faith shouldn't get turned into the police?"

"No, I think she'll save a lot more lives as opposed to if she went to jail. Plus, most of the police are vampires."

"Well, I mean, Buffy should at least tell the mayor about Faith."

"The mayor is also a vampire."

"How many people in this show are vampires?!"

"Shhhhh!"

We watched this very confusing show for five hours. I won't lie, once I got past my initial problems with *Buffy*, it was quite enjoyable—although I think Spike is a piece of shit.

The awkward kiss attempt between Diane and I the night before never came up; not during *Buffy*, not during the hour drive to the show, and not during the incredibly stellar performance of Dead!, the world's greatest My Chemical Romance tribute band. I kept trying to get close to Diane during the show, hoping she'd see that I wasn't weirded out by the events of the night before, but every time I tried, she moved away. After about thirty minutes of this, I got the message and focused solely on the nine people on stage perfectly recreating *The Black Parade* in its entirety. At the end of the evening, we got back in the car and drove home.

"That was such a good show," I said.

"It was all right," Diane said. She had been awfully quiet throughout the evening, and it seemed like the drive home wouldn't be any different. After a few minutes of silence, I couldn't stand the tension anymore.

"Hey, my sister is coming into town tomorrow if you want

to get dinner with us. I'm sure she'd like to meet you, if you're interested."

She didn't say anything for about thirty seconds, and then she said, "Hey, Cade?"

I turned to look at her. "Yeah?"

"I don't like you."

I turned back to look at the road ahead. "Oh, that's—"

"Sorry, I didn't mean it like that. I do like you as a person, I just don't *like* you, you know?"

"Oh, yeah, I understand." I continued to stare at the road.

"Sorry, I wanted to tell you last night, but you didn't really give me a chance," she said.

"Oh yeah, I'm sorry about last night," I said quickly. "I really thought you felt the same way about me. I mean, we've spent a lot of time together this past month."

"I just moved here. You're my only fucking friend in town."

"Yeah, but we text at like 1 a.m. sometimes."

"Sometimes I get home late and I forget to respond to you until then."

"You played me a sad version of 'Build Me Up Buttercup.' It just seemed kind of—"

"We both play music. I thought it would be nice to get your opinion about a song I'd been working on."

I leaned forward, shook my head, and turned to look at her. "You drove me and my drunk friends around last weekend and put up with our bullshit for twelve hours . . . just to be nice?"

"Well, yeah."

Emma, you lying bitch.

I sat back in my seat and stared at the road ahead again. "Wow," I said. "I'm sorry, Diane. I just think you're one of the absolute coolest people I know. I guess I just got swept up in all that and really misread the situation."

"Is this why you've been holding every fucking door in town open for me?"

"Well, yeah. I was raised to believe it's chivalrous."

"I know how to open doors, I'm not an idiot. I can handle it."

"Sorry, Diane," was all I could think to say.

She paused for a moment. "I'm sorry too," she said.

"Sometimes I just . . . I just freak out when I spend time with girls I like."

"How do you mean?" she asked.

"I kind of think of it like alcoholism sometimes; many people can drink a lot without any severe consequences. Other people drink the same amount and make terrible mistakes they never would have made if they were sober. It's like something else takes control when they're under the influence. And those same people who can drink or date without consequences tell you stuff like, 'It's fine! If I can do it, so can you!' But it's not fine. Those people go on dates and fall in love and tell great stories about it, but whenever I'm interested in somebody, I get really anxious and do things I wouldn't normally do. Like try to kiss them unexpectedly," I glanced at Diane, "or tell them how much they mean to me at an open mic night in front of a live audience."

"What?"

"Sorry, it's a long story."

She smiled a half-smile. "I'm sorry you feel that way," she said. "I didn't mean to lead you on."

"Don't worry about it. It's totally my fault."

We didn't say much for the rest of the ride home. I didn't really speak to Diane after that; she moved out west shortly afterward, and I haven't seen her since. I decided to take a few months off dating so I could figure some things out. But I did watch more *Buffy the Vampire Slayer* over the next few weeks, hoping that it would all start to make sense.

FLIRTIN' WITH DISASTER
By Molly Hatchet

December 2009

"We choose our destiny"

Over our first year with the game, Keith, Chris, Delynn, and I got good at *Rock Band*. We got *really* good at *Rock Band*. By 2009, *Rock Band 2*, *Beatles: Rock Band*, and *Lego: Rock Band* had all come out, and you better believe I had all of them—as well as a large majority of the hundreds of bonus downloadable songs. We bought a second guitar so there was an instrument for everyone: I took guitar, Keith took bass, Delynn was our drummer, and Chris held down the lead vocals as the frontman of the Krazy Unikerns. We would switch it up every now and then; for instance, every time there was a song that had rapping in it, Delynn would take over vocals—Chris has said time and time again, "There is nothing better in the world than watching Delynn rap."

We eventually all started playing at the expert level of difficulty. Keith knew he was a professional the second he finished "Hysteria" by Muse on expert without failing; he told everyone we knew for a week straight. We each had a go-to song we would always choose when we got to make our own setlist or choose something for quickplay. Mine was "Livin' on a Prayer" by Bon Jovi, Keith's was "Best of You" by Foo Fighters, Chris's was "Detroit Rock City" by KISS, and Delynn always chose "Maps" by the Yeah Yeah Yeahs. For that one, Delynn would play drums and sing the chorus, Chris would get down on his knees and look at Delynn while he sang, and Delynn would try to not to let her smile distract her from the notes on the screen.

Every now and then, we had to hang up the plastic instruments. Whether it was all of us taking a break to go to the movies, Delynn and Chris selfishly not inviting Keith and I to date night, or a variety of family vacations, there were a handful of times we had to find different ways to spend time together.

In one particular instance in 2009, Chris and I were left to our own devices while Keith and Delynn went on a quick visit to see their grandmother. We watched TV and played foosball, but eventually we got bored enough to try playing *Rock Band* by ourselves. It was still fun, but it wasn't the same without the full band. It was kind of like Tom Delonge leaving Blink-182 to focus on Angels & Airwaves; we were still making music, but at what cost?

"No. Absolutely not," Chris said, looking at my song choice on the TV screen.

"We can't do 'Timmy and the Lords of the Underworld' *or* 'Chinese Democracy'?" I whined.

"That whole album is trash! Guns N' Roses used to be good."

"I will argue that this album is good overall, but bad for a Guns N' Roses record."

"That's a bad argument," Chris said, scrolling through the song list for better options.

"I don't know what it is," I continued, ignoring him. "Keith and I just really like it."

Chris scoffed. "Keith used to like the Black Eyed Peas and thinks Bam Margera is a musician! You're both wrong."

"How about some Bon Jovi?" I compromised.

He shrugged. "Can't go wrong there. Which one?"

"How about 'Livin' on a Prayer'?"

"Let's do it," he agreed, prepping the drum kit.

"You know, I listened to this song every day on the bus ride to school this past semester."

"Really? I mean, it's a great song, but I don't know about every day. Maybe if it was 'Wanted Dead or Alive.'"

"I mean, it wasn't so much about the song itself. Every time I listen to it, I think about us playing it. I would literally count down the days until I could visit you guys for winter break."

"That's some intense dedication to the band," Chris said.

"I mean, I don't really like high school. I'm sure I've said it before. I know I still have a year and a half left, but I'd be willing to bet that the Krazy Unikerns will be my favorite part of all four years. I . . . I really don't want to go back next Monday," I said quietly.

Chris looked at me for a moment. "Well, fortunately for you," he said with a smirk, "that's a lot of time to play *Rock Band.*"

I smiled. "How long do you think we'll be able to . . . keep the band together?"

"The Unikerns?"

"Yeah. I mean, how long will the four of us be able to meet up a few times a year and play *Rock Band* in this basement?"

"Well, when I graduate, the army can send me anywhere in the world. Might be hard to stick together after that."

"Yeah. I figured as much," I said, looking down at my shoes.

Chris put his hand on my shoulder. "A band isn't great because it lasts," he said. "The best part of every band is the song list they leave behind; the band may not live forever, but the songs do. Plus, all of the memories associated with these songs, they'll be with you and me and Keith and Delynn for the rest of our lives."

"Huh. I never thought of it that way."

"It's true. 'Say It Ain't So,' 'In Bloom,' and hundreds of others are going to follow you around forever. Life sucks sometimes, but the good thing is that no matter what, it goes on. Even when the Krazy Unikerns break up, your show will go on. And you'll always have the songs."

He had a point. I could already think of several life stories inspired by or related to *Rock Band* songs, and there were many more songs and stories to go.

I smiled. "Thanks, man. That's really good to hear," I said. We both heard the upstairs door open, signaling the return of Keith and Delynn.

"Anytime, brother. Now, enough of the sentimental shit. Let's get our band together and play some rock 'n' roll."

I GET BY
By Honest Bob and the Factory-to-Dealer Incentives

December 2018

"I've been in my head too long"

"You're giving up? Like, forever?" Keith asked from behind the steering wheel of his souped-up Infiniti G37. The interior of his car always smelt like leather with a hint of exhaust.

I rolled my eyes. "I'm not giving up forever. I'm just taking a break from dating to figure some stuff out." It was a really bright December day, and I cracked the passenger window to let a little more air in the car.

"How long has it been?"

"Since Diane? Like sixteen months."

"Jesus, fuck! Why?!"

"I just . . . I just want to figure out why I'm wired the way I am. Why do I do dumb shit, and why does it haunt me forever?"

"You don't have a monopoly on doing dumb shit when you fall in love. Everyone does that."

"I just feel like it's worse for me. A lot of people can do it and it's great, but when I fall in love, I do terrible, socially unacceptable things." I looked at Keith and smiled. "Like when I poured 151 in your mouth for the sole purpose of waking you up to impress a girl."

Keith laughed. "Yeah, that may be the maddest I've ever been at you."

"Case in point. So I'm taking some time off."

Keith shook his head. "You don't have a problem, you just haven't met the right person yet."

"I don't know man, I just want to figure some stuff out."

Keith has always liked fast cars. He and his marine buddies were big fans of revving their engines and going from zero to forty in three seconds. I have never been a fan of it, mostly because I hate roller coasters and love driving the speed limit, but I never really worried when Keith drove me anywhere, because I knew my best friend would never do anything to endanger me.

What happened next was a blur because it happened so quickly, and I did not have enough time to completely process what was occurring. As soon as the traffic light turned green, Keith revved the engine, shifted gears, and went from zero to forty miles an hour in about two seconds. During that time, the tires lost traction, and Keith's car began to drift. The car rotated 180 degrees until it faced the wrong direction on a crowded Northern Virginia highway. We continued to drift, hopped over the median, and found ourselves on the other side of the highway, now facing the correct direction. My brain finally caught up with what was going on, and I braced myself for the impact of the oncoming traffic from behind . . . but it never came. Traffic had halted at a red light a little way up the road. Serendipitously saved by a traffic light.

Keith immediately regained his composure after our own personal Kings Dominion ride, as if he had paused time. He quickly moved his car into the right lane and pulled into the closest parking lot. Once we parked, he got out to inspect any damage the median might have done to his tires. I got out so I could walk off the shock of what had just transpired. I thought about what to say to Keith, and immediately remembered my best friend's reaction to me being frightened of drinking for the first time. *You worry too much.* I realized how true that was; we very easily could have died in a car crash two minutes ago, but we didn't. I took this into consideration while I figured out what to say to break the silence.

I landed on, "I take it you didn't mean to do that."

He stood up from checking his tires and shook his head. "I'm a goddamn idiot."

"Well, it could have been much worse. It looks like all of the cars were stopped by a red light."

"I meant my car!" he yelled. "This is probably gonna be crazy expensive to fix."

"Oh. I thought you were worried about . . . you know, dying."

"Nah, didn't really cross my mind," he said as we got back in the car. After he started the car there were a few seconds of silence before he said, "Honestly, if I were to die, there's no way I'd rather go."

"Than driving your car into oncoming traffic?"

"No. With my brother."

Keith has never been one for words, but every so often he says something brief that sticks with me longer than any well-thought-out speech.

"I love you, man," I said.

"I love you too buddy," he said as we drove home.

RUN TO THE HILLS
By Iron Maiden

February 2012

"Pain and misery"

A week after I had made my big romantic gesture to Emily, I still felt like dogshit. I would go to class, come home, eat anything and everything because I finally had my appetite back, then lie in my bed and mope until the next day. After about a week of hating everything, I got a package in the mail: a metal tin of cookies from Delynn. I opened the container, and a note fell out. *So sorry,* it said. *College girls are literally the worst kind of people in the world. I promise they get smarter. Hope you like triple chocolate chip. Krazy Unikerns for life. - Delynn*

I texted Delynn my thanks, ate all of the cookies, and continued to mope and hate everything for two more months.

While writing this book, I found an old journal entry from the week after Emily turned me down. Here it is, in all of its short, naïve, and angsty glory: *I really thought Emily was the one. Wrong again. Listen up, future me: if you ever find someone half as good as Emily, treat her like fucking royalty. You are absolutely nothing without her.*

That kid was sick. He barely even knew Emily, but he was in love with her. Her room was directly above his, and sometimes he would touch his hand to the ceiling, hoping she was doing the same thing to the floor of her room at the exact same time. If

I could go back in time and tell past-Cade one thing, I'd remind him of the advice Chris had already given him years before: "Life goes on."

That wasn't the first time I thought the world was over because of a girl, and it wasn't going to be the last. I still don't know the answers to most of life's questions, and I still get anxious from time to time (even though I've been vomit-free since 2015).

If I had realized the world wasn't going to end every time a relationship failed, maybe I would have learned to appreciate other people laughing at my jokes, or enjoying my company, or liking me for who I was. Maybe I wouldn't have been bummed out that Allison and I weren't a good fit; I could've just been happy that she taught me how to love the incredible music of the Kooks and Coldplay. Maybe instead of peeing on my friend's bed out of jealousy, I would have been thankful he loved me way more than the girl I was blindly following around, hoping she would one day prefer my company over anyone else's. Maybe I would have realized that Laura didn't love me as the nerdy *Rock Band* enthusiast that I was, but rather the anxious wreck who was too scared to leave her.

I eventually learned I didn't need a girl who, as Weezer once said, "laughs for no one else," because I had been surrounded by people who liked me for who I was the whole time. I didn't need to fall in love to be happy, I had people who loved me and made me happy all along.

And *Rock Band.*

WON'T GET FOOLED AGAIN
By the Who

December 2018

"Pick up my guitar and play, just like yesterday"

All of the time and money I have invested in *Rock Band* has paid off over the years: I've hosted countless parties that people still talk about; I won an actual *Rock Band* competition with a fellow enthusiast; and finally, after eleven years of playing the game and buying new songs, I got to host my very own *Rock Band* party at Reason Brewery in Charlottesville, VA.

I had lived next to the brewery for several years and had been a loyal customer for many months before I had the guts to ask if I could set up my plastic instruments and share my passion with the entire city. The manager, Devon, loved the idea, and let my coworker, Rylie, and I set up speakers, bass amps, and a 110-inch projector screen inside the brewery. We invited all of our friends we had played with over the years and prepared them for the biggest *Rock Band* party of their lives.

When the day finally rolled around, it was crazy to see all of the friends I had made over the years assembled in one place, from the Saint John's Boys, to exec friends, to my Paramount coworkers. They showed up with several Charlottesville citizens to play a game they had most likely bought and thrown away at some point in their lives. What had started as a way to escape my sorrows in high school had turned into an eleven-year passion I could share with the world, and that felt pretty incredible.

My only wish was that I could share this moment with the rest of the Krazy Unikerns.

"Dude, send me tons of videos!" Keith texted.

"Of course, brother. I'll send them to the whole band. I wish you were all here right now."

"Chris and Delynn live in Korea, so it might be a bit hard, but you bet your ass I'll be there if you ever do it again."

"I'll let you know how it goes."

As "Bohemian Rhapsody" rang throughout the room, I walked over to Julian and Damon, who were playing *Bananagrams* at the bar. "Hey, you two better be ready to sing," I told them.

"Only if you and I sing *Dookie* in its entirety, like in college," Julian said, grinning.

"Done. I'll add it to the list."

Devon approached me. "Dude, this is the busiest I've ever seen it on a Sunday! Can we make this a monthly thing? We'll give you and Rylie all the free beer you want!"

I had waited my whole life to hear that sentence. "Sounds good," I replied. "We'd love to." I shook his hand and walked past him to greet Nicole at the end of the bar.

"Hey, bud," I said, putting my arm around her.

"Hey," she said, sipping her beer. "This is kind of nuts, Cade. I can't believe you guys did this."

"Reminds you of the Big Sean concert, doesn't it?"

She smiled. "Almost. I can drink here, so that's a plus."

"I miss those days."

"What do you mean?"

"Exec. I miss being around you guys every day."

"What the hell are you talking about? Griffin, Layne, Violet, and Lindsey are all over there playing your favorite game, *and* we all live in Charlottesville."

"Huh. I guess you're right. We're living the dream, aren't we?"

"A little bit, yeah."

"Ready to do our duet?"

"'Nine in the Afternoon'? One hundred percent here we come."

"Excellent. I'll go add it to the list."

"Put me down for 'Heart of Glass' by Blondie after that," she said. "I gotta beat my old high score."

"For sure," I agreed.

"Dude, killer party, man," Layne said, punching my shoulder and trying not to spill his beer. "Come sing the next song with us!"

"What's next?"

"'Say It Ain't So' by Weezer."

I smirked. "I think I know that one. Hand me the guitar."

A stranger was on the drums; he clicked the sticks together four times to count us in, and that's when I started that iconic intro riff. I didn't miss a single note as I looked around to see nearly a hundred people drinking beer and watching us play. Friends and strangers alike gathered around to watch the first song the Krazy Unikerns had ever played together. Even though they weren't physically here in this moment, the Krazy Unikerns were alive in every song we played that day. Chris was right: bands aren't great because they last. They're great because of the things they do and the memories they make while they're a band.

I finally realized I was surrounded by people who had been there for me all along, during all of my highs and all of my lows, and any of them would be there for me whenever I needed them— just like how I had felt in Keith's basement, eleven years before. I thought about what I might do next with my life, and for the first time ever, I felt okay not knowing.

After all, thanks to *Rock Band*, I can be whoever the hell I want to be.

The Krazy Unikerns playing Rock Band *together for the first time*
Painting by Joan Wiberg

"Don't waste your life looking for a perfect person when you have three perfect people playing Rock Band with you in your basement."

ABOUT THE AUTHOR

Born and raised in northern Virginia, Cade Wiberg has written creative non-fiction for over a decade. He is a JMU graduate with a passion for film, music, and television. In his spare time, Cade enjoys playing guitar, songwriting, and hosting Rock Band/Karaoke nights at local breweries in his hometown of Charlottesville, VA.

CPSIA information can be obtained
at www.ICGtesting.com
Printed in the USA
LVHW021107210622
721764LV00002B/74